Congress in Its Wisdom

The Bureau of Reclamation and the Public Interest

Studies in Water Policy and Management

Charles W. Howe, General Editor

Irrigation Management in Developing Countries: Current Issues and Approaches, edited by K. C. Nobe and R. K. Sampath

Irrigation Investment, Technology, and Management Strategies for Development, edited by K. William Easter

Improving International Irrigation Management with Farmer Participation: Getting the Process Right, Norman Uphoff

Water Markets in Theory and Practice: Market Transfers, Water Values, and Public Policy, Bonnie Colby Saliba and David B. Bush

Congress in Its Wisdom: The Bureau of Reclamation and the Public Interest, Doris Ostrander Dawdy

Irrigation Development in Africa: Lessons of Experience, Jon R. Moris and Derrick J. Thom (forthcoming)

Social, Economic, and Institutional Issues in Third World Irrigation Management, edited by R. K. Sampath and Robert A. Young (forthcoming)

Congress in Its Wisdom

The Bureau of Reclamation and the Public Interest

Doris Ostrander Dawdy

Studies in Water Policy and Management, No. 13

Westview Press
Boulder, San Francisco, & London

Studies in Water Policy and Management

This Westview softcover edition is printed on acid-free paper and bound in library-quality, coated covers that carry the highest rating of the National Association of State Textbook Administrators, in consultation with the Association of American Publishers and the Book Manufacturers' Institute.

Published in 1989 in the United States of America by Westview Press, Inc., 5500 Central Avenue, Boulder, Colorado 80301, and in the United Kingdom by Westview Press, Inc., 13 Brunswick Centre, London WC1N 1AF, England

Library of Congress Cataloging-in-Publication Data
Dawdy, Doris Ostrander.
Congress in its wisdom : the Bureau of Reclamation and the public interest / Doris Ostrander Dawdy.
p. cm.—(Studies in water policy and management ; no. 13)
Includes index.
ISBN 0-8133-7822-2
1. United States. Bureau of Reclamation. 2. Irrigation—Government policy—West (U.S.) 3. Reclamations of land—Government policy—West (U.S.) I. Title. II. Series.
HD1736 1989
353.0082'32—dc20 89-9116
CIP

Printed and bound in the United States of America

∞ The paper used in this publication meets the requirements of the American National Standard for Permanence of Paper for Printed Library Materials Z39.48-1984.

10 9 8 7 6 5 4 3 2 1

Contents

Acknowledgments

This note of thanks and appreciation extends to all persons, named and unnamed, for assistance in getting this book written and published. Foremost are the readers who took time from their own professional lives to read rough drafts which must at various times have caused them to have doubts about this book. Informative these drafts were, but well-written they were not. Harrison C. Dunning, University of California (Davis), L. Douglas James, Utah State University, and my daughter Barbara Dahl, a librarian, read early drafts; Charles W. Howe, University of Colorado, Boulder, read two later drafts. My husband David R. Dawdy, now a consulting hydrologist, who spent many years with the Geological Survey and several in consulting firms, accounts for my interest in water resources management and the years of research that culminated in this book. Without this shared interest and his determination to overcome my resistance to putting the book through word processor and printer in place of the previously acceptable typewritten manuscript, it might not have found a publisher. The hours he spent turning out a professional-looking camera-ready manuscript deserve a special word of thanks.

The Geological Survey, also, deserves more than passing mention; the dedication its scientists have shown in their eternal search for reliable information concerning our natural resources is one with which I am familiar, having become acquainted with many of them as early as the 1950s. More recently I have found a comparable degree of dedication among Fish and Wildlife Service scientists. What then can I say about a troubled reclamation bureau that has good scientists but responds mainly to political dictation? Given the Interior Department's dual role of serving natural resources development in addition to conserving those resources in the public interest, it tends to favor the former when the administration in power renders that more expedient. Nevertheless, scientists and administrators in the Bureau, the Fish and Wildlife Service, the Geological Survey, the regional Office of the Solicitor and the Inspector General's Office graciously assisted in the factfinding that built this book.

Other government personnel such as in the San Francisco branch of the General Accounting Office supplied reports that were particularly timely and Congressman Sam Gejdenson sent me the report on water subsidies he had the Congressional Budget Office prepare when the Secretary's office failed to produce all the data he had requested. John C. Peters, once the Bureau's expert on environmental mitigation when it was responding to the National Environmental Policy Act of 1969, supplied at my request his PhD dissertation, "Effects of Sediment Control on Fish Populations," which points the way to the kinds of projects the Bureau could initiate under its new mandate, "Water quality - environmental restoration and enhancement"; Gilbert Stamm, a former Bureau commissioner, discussed with me the Bureau's difficulties in California.

Others who made significant contributions through their willingness to discuss their researches and upon whose published works I relied are Kenneth W. Bruland, University of California (Santa Cruz) and his assistant Terrence D. Cooke; Peter B. Moyle, University of California (Davis); Helen M. Ingram, University of Arizona; Pierre R. Crossen, Resources for the Future; Alice Q. Howard, editor of the Selenium and Agricultural Drainage symposium proceedings cited in the text; and Don Villarejo, California Institute for Rural Studies (Davis). Janette Freitas, an avid reader of books and journals dealing with water quality and agricultural problems, sent pertinent articles from newspapers and journals; Gerald R. Ogden, historian for the Department of Agriculture for many years and now a private consultant, supplied unpublished material from his files; Jerald Butchert, manager of Westlands Water District, had his staff put together a packet of pertinent data dealing with Westlands Water District; and Catherine Vandemoer, hydrologist, supplied recent publications on Indian water rights.

So many librarians contributed to the book by being helpful in one way or another that naming just one must suffice: Gerald Giefer, archivist at the Water Resources Center Archives at UC Berkeley, who early in my research called attention to the library's recent acquisition of the Ralph Brody files.

Doris Ostrander Dawdy

Introduction

A beleaguered Bureau of Reclamation faces an uncertain future. Since passage of the Reclamation Act in 1902 the best damsites have been developed for irrigation-water impoundments and flood control. Furthermore, Bureau projects have become so expensive, the risk of developing poor damsites so great, the environmental concerns so pervasive that Congress is refusing to fund previously authorized projects.

The Interior secretary's move in September 1987 to relieve the Bureau of its engineering role in irrigation water-supply projects is perceived by many as a move to get rid of it. In 1950 the Bureau had over 19,000 employees; now it has about 8,000. Under the secretary's plan it will be cut to about 4,000, mainly by attrition.

Presumably the Bureau of Reclamation is no more equal in the eyes of Interior secretaries than other bureaus within the Department such as the Fish and Wildlife Service with which it frequently is in conflict. This book highlights the economic power and political pressures that have built the Bureau and contributed to the conflicts and it examines the impacts of Bureau projects on fish and wildlife habitats in the West. It also explores the water management role the Bureau may undertake in "Water quality - environmental restoration and enhancement," if future Interior secretaries decide to implement this priority among the several announced by former Secretary Donald Hodel in "Assessment '87" and "Implementation Plan."

Years before the Reclamation Act was passed in 1902, various reasons were put forth by pro-irrigationists for federal assistance in building irrigation systems that could provide cheap water to farm the arid and semiarid lands of the West. That subsidized irrigation systems could facilitate settlement of public lands by the urban poor and private lands by experienced farmers were perhaps the most persuasive. Inasmuch as there were among the proponents owners of large landholdings as well as small farms, it would be naive to believe the former intended to abide by the 160-acre limitation in the Act. There the trouble began.

An early proponent of subsidized irrigation was General Nelson Miles of the U. S. Army who favored populating Western farms with the urban poor. Miles was followed half a decade later by Captain Hiram Chittenden of the Army Corps of Engineers who saw federally-subsidized irrigation as a means to agricultural progress such as he had seen in the privately irrigated areas of California. Less prominent though equally persuasive were the members of the National Irrigation Congresses and the newly founded National Irrigation Association who got behind the bill of Representative Francis Newlands of Nevada, passed in 1902 and better known for some time as the Newlands Act. Other irrigation bills before the Congress there were, but President Theodore Roosevelt wanted the Newlands bill and aggressively orchestrated its passage.

Much of the language in the Reclamation Act was not Newlands' but Frederick Newell's (then a hydrographer in the Geological Survey) and George Maxwell's (leader of the National Irrigation Association). Ignoring key language in the law and catering to the most powerful and persuasive elements in the West, Newell was to compromise the integrity of the Geological Survey over who should have the water in California's Owens Valley and Maxwell was to assist his Arizona colleagues in obtaining subsidized water for their farming enterprises in the Salt River Valley. Perhaps Maxwell had them in mind when he helped to write the Act.

Not surprisingly, strategy of one sort or another gave owners of private lands an advantage over farmers and urban dwellers who moved West to farm the public lands that could be had for a nominal price. Fashioned after the Homestead Act it was not the price of public land that often did new arrivals in; it was poor soil or reclamation project mismanagement, or both. Chapter 1, after briefly reviewing former acts passed by Congress to encourage settlement of the public lands, probes the Bureau's leaders, their difficulties and failures in implementing the new Act. Known as the Reclamation Service from 1902 until 1923, its first director was Charles Walcott who also headed the Geological Survey. Frederick Newell served as Walcott's engineer-in-charge. In 1907 the Service was removed from the control of the Survey and placed directly under the Secretary of the Interior.

The Reclamation Act--in fact any act regulating water in the West--is subject to the abuse of selfish interests. Candidates seeking election, congressmen seeking reelection, Interior secretaries seeking the goodwill of private developers of natural resources, irrigation district chieftains seeking cheap water, and other special interest groups have made unreasonable demands on the Bureau of Reclamation. Few indeed were the Bureau's commissioners who had the strength of character to resist them, for it was safer to align themselves with the politically powerful. And so the Reclamation Act has more often been beneficial to the haves than to the havenots.

The manipulations to obtain projects and the heavy deficits those projects generated so distressed Congress by the 1920s that it considered phasing out the reclamation program. What saved the Bureau was the depression of the 1930s which made it expedient to provide jobs for unemployed workers. Chapter 2 discusses the Bureau's rise to power during this period and Chapter 3 the Bureau's involvement in California's Central Valley Project. Chapter 4 discusses the Bureau's Missouri Basin projects and Chapter 5 the legislative tactics and benefit-cost manipulations so characteristic of Bureau projects.

By the early 1970s, project opportunities were diminishing and past transgressions were coming to light. Former assistant commissioner of reclamation William Warne commented on the decline of the Bureau's engineering role in his book published in 1973: its work was about done; its reluctance to abide by the National Environmental Policy Act of 1969 had not gone unnoticed by a rapidly growing environmental movement; its future had been reduced to speculation. Speculation was intensified by the failure of Idaho's Teton Dam in 1976 and in 1983 by the almost total destruction of fish and waterfowl at California's Kesterson National Wildlife Refuge where the Bureau had constructed 12 evaporation ponds for agricultural wastewater from Westlands Water District, the beneficiary of the San Luis Unit of the Central Valley Project. Chapter 6 tells the Westlands story.

In 1983 the Bureau's failure to construct irrigation projects in areas where soils are suitable was called to public attention when high concentrations of selenium in irrigation drainwater, known to the Bureau since 1981, explained the loss of fish and much of the wildlife at Kesterson. Selenium is prevalent throughout the United States. In states with adequate rainfall it seldom is a problem; in arid states it is. The chemical reaction of selenium in alkaline waters is apparent at numerous refuges receiving agricultural drainwater from Bureau projects. Poorly sited federal projects, often dictated by political pressure, have caused various problems but none as environmentally damaging as those responsible for mobilizing the selenium in rocks and soils, thus making it available to the food chain through the process of bioaccumulation. Farmers are aware of its dangers to livestock and crops and to themselves wherever selenium is present in high concentrations. Chapter 7 explains the mobilization of selenium under geologic and climatic conditions, the impact of selenium on wildlife and domestic animals, the precautions taken by the Fish and Wildlife Service to protect its employees working at Kesterson National Wildlife Refuge, and the shocking absence of precautions to protect the health and welfare of ranchers dwelling on adjacent lands.

Scientists in the Geological Survey and the Fish and Wildlife Service were not authorized to investigate refuges in other Western regions until after the Sacramento Bee publicized the findings of its staff reporters Tom Harris and Jim Morris in September 1985. The reports of these government scientists began appearing in 1987. In addition to selenium they include boron and other toxic elements in Western waters. Some of these toxic elements were found in domestic water supplies as well as in the various wildlife refuges. The effects of boron on agricultural production are well known but its effects on aquatic life are confined to laboratory investigations. Excessive amounts in drain water samples have been shown to have deleterious effects.

The data in the belatedly authorized reconnaissance

investigations by Interior Department scientists in the Geological Survey and the Fish and Wildlife Service provide an overview of some very serious problems. Chapter 8 pinpoints the irrigation-induced water quality problems and Chapter 9 the regions and refuges where serious mistakes have been made that require immediate remedial action.

Chapter 10 discusses wherein the Bureau has failed to abide by congressional legislation designed to protect the public interest whether that interest be protection of fish and wildlife, public safety, or taxpayers' pocketbooks. It includes details of the authorization and faulty construction of Teton Dam, a dam desired by a small segment of the population that failed while filling and has since cost the public an astronomical sum in reparations.

Chapter 11 covers the current scene: Indian water rights to which Indians are entitled by law and who wish to put that water to beneficial use; reclamation reform as intended by the Reclamation Reform Act of 1982, but which has been misconstrued by agribusiness attorneys in the interest of their clients; and the anticipated change in the Bureau's mission to that of resources management and what that may mean in reallocating water to other uses. Urban dwellers are inclined to believe they are the principal consumers of water, little realizing how much of that commodity in streams and in the ground is consumed by the farming industry. In the arid and semiarid West between 80 and 90 percent is diverted for agriculture. Conservation is not practiced to any considerable extent, mainly because water obtained from the Bureau is exceedingly cheap. If the Bureau's new role in water resources management materializes it will have an opportunity to terminate wasteful irrigation practices on the approximately 10 million acres for which its projects supply irrigation water in 17 Western states. Water marketing for domestic consumption, combined with water conservation, can be incorporated in the Bureau's program without harming agriculture.

Irrigated agriculture is essential to adequate food production but it requires a scientific base if it is to conserve water and restore environmentally-damaged resources, whether or not the water is supplied by the Bureau. The technology is there but not the institutional framework to accomplish a balanced allocation and pricing of water by institutions capable also of enforcing water quality standards. Updating our federal, state, and regional water resources institutions to meet these needs will require more wisdom than Congress has demonstrated in the past. Perhaps no one has more concisely put the problem in a historical as well as a contemporary context than Dr. L. Douglas James in 1986 when he addressed the Philadelphia Society for Promoting Agriculture:

> Irrigation began with civilization. It built the economic base of the ancient world. It was central to the development of the American West and is being increasingly used for drought insurance in the East. However, irrigated agriculture has always been plagued with problems. The hydrologic, salinity, and institutional failures that destroyed ancient civilizations still threaten modern agriculture. Overcoming them will require a concentrated effort to identify problems, understand their causes, and develop and implement a strategy to protect the future.

1
Origins: The 1902 Act and the Bureau of Reclamation

During the years 1862 through 1872, about fifty bills to facilitate the diversion of streams to farms and mines--mainly drafted by land speculators--were introduced by Western congressmen. They were looked at in committee, but seldom voted out for congressional action. One, a grant of a right-of-way over federal lands, was passed.[1]

The policy of Congress prior to passage of the Reclamation Act in 1902 was noninterference with private enterprise. Nor did Western speculators seek federal interference. They wanted outright grants of land which they promised to develop for new settlers. Congress complied in 1875 with the Lassen County Desert Land Act, specifically for California, and in 1877 with the Desert Land Act which applied westwide. The latter provided for 640-acre parcels in the aggregate: twenty-five cents per acre to be paid at time of filing; one dollar per acre in three years upon presenting evidence (often flimsy) of compliance with conditions set forth in the Act. Its implementation left much to be desired for the intent of the entrepreneurs was to enlarge their landholdings.[2]

The Carey Act which followed in 1894 was the work of Wyoming congressmen who favored state participation. The Act was inadequate mainly because federal grants of one million acres to each arid state did not stimulate enough capital for constructing large scale projects to open land some distance from water. By 1900 the private sector had built the facilities that irrigated well over seven million acres, but seldom could build and finance large reservoirs and dams.[3]

John Wesley Powell was the foremost expert on arid lands during the last quarter of the 19th century. Like most government officials of his time, Powell did not advocate federal construction of irrigation projects. He saw the federal role as limited to damsite selection by Geological Survey engineers and geologists; streamflow data by hydrographers; geological and topographical maps by cartographers trained in contour mapping. In 1878 Congress published his definitive report on arid lands.[4]

In 1881 Powell became the second director of the Geological Survey, following Clarence King who had retired after two years. Until 1886 Powell was extraordinarily successful in obtaining congressional funding for the Survey. Then he slipped from favor, partly because he had not limited his program to the data-collection function spelled out in the Organic Act of 1879 which had merged the Western surveys into one agency;[5] partly because politicians were more interested in catering to land speculators than in preparing arid and semiarid land for settlement. In 1888 Senator William Morris Stewart of Nevada pushed through Congress an irrigation survey to hasten settlement. Instead of recognizing what Stewart was up to, Powell's opponents in Congress thought that Powell had originated the legislation. Their emotional state at the very thought of Powell being the logical person to conduct the survey was such that one senatorial opponent turned on Stewart in anger and said: "You didn't think of it, Powell did, twelve years ago. It originated in the scheming brain of the head of the Geological Survey. He expects some day to be incorporated into the Constitution of the United States as an amendment."[6] Notwithstanding Powell's aversion to settling the public lands before he had completed what he considered the requisite maps, he ordered his geologists into the field to search for damsites and irrigable land. Before Congress abandoned Stewart's irrigation survey some nine months later, the Geological Survey had identified "about 150 reservoir sites and approximately 30 million acres of irrigable land."[7]

Going much farther than Powell on the subject of federal involvement in irrigation was General Nelson Appleton Miles of the U. S. Army. Miles had been stationed at various Western posts where his job was to subdue Indians, thereby making public lands safe for settlement. He deduced that unless those lands were irrigated they were not safe from financial disaster to farmers who settled on them. An advocate of Powell's arid land studies, Miles proved to be an influential government spokesman on behalf of their settlement. In an article for North American Review in 1890 he argued that a federal program to finance irrigation projects was needed but he did not specifically address government construction, operation, and maintenance of the projects.[8] That concept was promoted by General Hiram Chittenden.

The River and Harbor Act of June 3, 1896, authorized the Corps of Engineers to identify suitable damsites in the Rocky Mountain West for water retention and irrigation. Hiram Chittenden, then a captain in the Corps who achieved wide recognition in his department before taking up private consulting and the writing of books, undertook the assignment. He did not restrict his tour of duty to locating damsites but traveled widely in states where irrigated agriculture was showing considerable promise. His report to Congress in 1897 created quite a stir for it proposed that the projects be built, owned, maintained, and operated by the government.[9] For several years thereafter the Corps held the upper hand with Congress in the search for a solution to the problem of Western settlement of arid lands but unlike the Corps of today--aggressively demanding its share of Western projects --it did not aggressively back the one person whose report had the attention of Congress.

Chittenden's interest in irrigating Western lands and his considerable expertise made him valuable to the group seeking a reclamation act to subsidize irrigation in the West led by Frederick Newell of the Geological Survey, Congressman Francis Newlands of Nevada, and George Maxwell of the National Irrigation Association. However, the bill they drafted had nothing in it for the Corps or any other agency other than the Department of the Interior despite Chittenden's able assistance and the supportive position taken by the Department of Agriculture. Had the authors of the Reclamation (or Newlands) Act Congress passed in 1902 utilized the expertise available in the Corps and in the Department of Agriculture, the Reclamation Service as it was then called might well have prepared the way for a less trouble-prone Bureau of Reclamation.

Newlands, elected to the House of Representatives in 1893,

had once favored state participation in irrigation projects. Like many other Western entrepreneurs, he believed the projects could be developed without federal intervention. By 1891, after spending a quarter of a million dollars on a Nevada project that failed for lack of state support, he decided a career in politics was a better bet.[10] Upon his arrival in Washington he shunned the group of state project advocates led by Senator Francis Warren of Wyoming. Toward the end of the decade, Warren-type bills began attracting serious congressional attention. Perhaps feeling it was now or never, Newlands, with the writings and public pronouncements of Chittenden, General Miles, the Secretary of Agriculture, and other public figures, began promoting the reclamation legislation that failed in 1901 and succeeded in 1902.[11] Some historians credit President Theodore Roosevelt's machinations with passage of Newlands' reclamation bill.[12] If Roosevelt, but recently thrust into the presidency by McKinley's assassination, had been more knowledgeable about the extent of land speculation in the West, he might have been less susceptible to the influence of Newell and Gifford Pinchot and more in tune with the implications of an Act to subsidize irrigated agriculture. Instead of leaving implementation of the Reclamation Act entirely to Ethan Allen Hitchcock, his able Interior secretary, Roosevelt asked Hitchcock to delegate that function to Geological Survey director Charles Walcott and Walcott's chief assistant, Newell. They "have been tested and tried," said Roosevelt, "and we know how well they will do the work."[13]

Isolated for years in a bureau of scientists who, like themselves, were capable of producing commendable work with a minimum of direction, Walcott and Newell were ill-prepared for their new roles: Walcott to direct the Reclamation Service as well as the Geological Survey; Newell to direct the reclamation program and serve as engineer-in-charge. By 1904, while Hitchcock was clearing Interior of the taint of past public lands frauds,[14] Californians residing in the Owens Valley were defrauded of their water rights by Reclamation's J. B. Lippincott, aided by Newell and condoned by Walcott.

Walcott had joined the Geological Survey in 1879 as an assistant geologist. Soon after Powell became director in 1881, Walcott began serving as Powell's chief assistant. When Powell retired in 1894, Walcott took his place. Walcott proved to be an able administrator as director of the Survey during which he restored it to a position of good standing in Congress. Furthermore he managed for awhile to work within the limits of the Organic Act of 1879. The Act provided for the classification by the Geological Survey of lands as "arable, irrigable, timber, pasturage, swamp, coal, mineral lands and other classes as deemed proper, having due regard to humidity of climate, supply of water for irrigation, and other physical characteristics."[15]

The Geological Survey was made to order for an intrinsic part of the action in the reclamation movement. So was the Department of Agriculture. Unfortunately both were improperly used in reclaiming the West, and the Corps of Engineers was not used at all. Roosevelt can be faulted for getting the Reclamation Service off to a bad start, but only Congress had the power to weld all three agencies into a workable relationship.

Newell, a recent engineering graduate of Massachusetts Institute of Technology when Powell undertook Senator Stewart's irrigation study in 1888, had a consuming interest in irrigation and reclamation. Powell put him in charge of a stream-gaging station in New Mexico, the first of its kind designed by the Geological Survey, to assist in training Survey employees to measure stream flow--an indispensable corollary to the planning of irrigation projects. When Congress abandoned the irrigation study in 1890, Newell was kept on as a topographer. In 1895, Director Walcott assigned him the position of hydrographer.

Walcott and Newell went much further than Powell in exceeding their authority under the Organic Act after they attained positions of power in the Reclamation Service. They ignored Hitchcock's guidelines for implementing the Organic and Reclamation Acts. They permitted Lippincott to continue as a private consultant despite his sensitive position as engineer-in-charge of California reclamation projects. And they let Los Angeles obtain a domestic water supply to which it was not entitled under the Reclamation Act. In their subsequent efforts to justify their actions to President Roosevelt they convinced him they had acted in the best interests of the greatest number.[16] Hitchcock shared the same conservation and reclamation goals as Newell and Walcott and Pinchot, but unlike them, he could not be deterred by the persuasiveness of speculators and politicians.[17]

At the turn of the century much of the water in Western streams was monopolized by large landowners who had obtained the water rights with the land.[18] With no interest in settlement beyond the availability of hired help to maintain their ranches, they did not fit into the scheme of farms 160 acres or less.

Under the Reclamation Act, funding for the federal facilities was to come from the sale of public lands to be repaid by the beneficiaries in ten years' time with a view to keeping the fund viable and free from political pressure, said the authors. To preempt speculators from grabbing what had just been made valuable by the promise of irrigation water, the Act authorized the Secretary of the Interior to withdraw public lands from private entry. Landowners adjacent to federal irrigation canals were not excluded from the benefits of the Act but they were not entitled to water for more than 160 acres. All recipients of irrigation water were required to live on or "in the neighborhood" of the land and to put it to beneficial use. The right to the water is beneficial use, said the Act.[19]

During January 1902, five months before the Act was passed, Senator Henry C. Hansbrough requested from the director of the Geological Survey answers to all manner of questions concerning federal reclamation of arid lands. Walcott responded the same day, addressing each question with a view to impressing the Senator. Relative to engineering expertise he said that the Survey had a "well-organized corps of active, experienced engineers" who had "served from time to time as experts for various municipalities and corporations."[20] These experts had been "connected with the building of important hydraulic works," he said. Although municipalities, industries, and state as well as local governments have customarily looked to the Survey for scientific expertise, such engineers as it had at its disposal then were largely from the private sector. As Newlands put it, the Survey had "in its consulting department many of the most skillful hydraulic engineers of the West."[21] Such outside consultants do not appear to have misused the Survey; a Survey employee who moonlighted as a Los Angeles consultant did.

J. B. Lippincott was a product of his time, picking up engineering experience here and there and then hanging out his shingle in full view of his Survey office. Lippincott's academic background was not impressive, but he was calculating and shrewd and he had access to the scientific expertise of the Geological Survey. From 1888 to 1892 he served intermittently in the Survey's topographic section. In 1895 Walcott put him in charge of the Survey's hydrographic investigations in California. Concurrently Lippincott opened his own private consulting firm which he knew was forbidden by the terms of his employment.

Lippincott's business address at times was the same as the Survey's.[22] Walcott was aware of the circumstances but lacked the will to discharge Lippincott, which says something about Walcott as well. Furthermore, when Walcott needed someone to supervise the reclamation program in California he promoted Lippincott to that position, apparently hoping the increase in salary would prompt him to observe government employment restrictions.

A comparison of Geological Survey and Lippincott listings in Los Angeles city directories shows Lippincott's position with the Survey as "hydrographer" and in his private listing as "engineer, Antelope Valley Water Company."[23] While Lippincott was reclamation supervisor from 1903 to 1905 he was also in partnership with Orlando K. Parker, doing business as Lippincott and Parker. In 1906 he left the Reclamation Service to become assistant chief engineer to William Mulholland and to participate in the construction of the Los Angeles Aqueduct. It had been predicted months before that a position in the Los Angeles Water Department would be waiting for Lippincott in return for his assistance in obtaining Owens Valley's water.[24] Coincidentally his consulting business disappeared from city directories at that time.

There is proof of Lippincott's chicanery in William Kahrl's thoroughly documented Water and Power,[25] and in Lippincott's personal correspondence. An example of the latter is a letter dated July 16, 1902 showing that Lippincott manipulated Geological Survey studies to his personal advantage. To a Los Angeles law firm, perhaps with a view to becoming an expert witness, he referred to a study "being done for the United States Government" at his request. He cautioned the firm that he did not "care to publicly enlarge on the fact" that he had been "instrumental in detailing these government investigations." However, the nature of the studies had given him a "particular advantage" in serving his clients.[26] What could be more advantageous to a trial attorney than a witness privy to official information possessed by a select few? What bigger boon to land speculators than a consultant in possession of water-supply data prior to publication in Geological Survey Water-Supply papers?

Government employment at that time offered little in the way of salaries and job security but it could open doors to advancement in the private sector for those with several years of technical and scientific experience in federal agencies. To gain prestige as a private consultant Lippincott needed that experience, for his formal education was limited to a bachelor of science degree from the University of Kansas.

Initially Lippincott saw the Owens Valley project as feasible. His assistants were well along with the work of streamgaging and planning the necessary structures when he was invited to participate in a scheme to make the Owens River water available to Los Angeles. Whether the invitation preceded April 30, 1904, when Lippincott called a halt to the project, cannot be determined with certainty. He gave as his excuse that it was essential to examine further the geology at the Long Valley damsite and that he needed certain equipment, then unavailable, to do so.[27] Simultaneously he assigned his assistants to another project, perhaps so he could pursue in private the prospects of a supplemental water supply for Los Angeles. Upon Lippincott's return to Los Angeles, the city's agents surreptitiously proceeded to obtain options on lands in key locations in the valley.[28] By late July 1905, the Reclamation Service's most cost effective project had not the slightest chance of materializing, for the Los Angeles Water Department held options on all the land and water it needed, including the Long Valley damsite discovered by reclamation engineer J. C. Clausen.[29]

Residents of the valley who had been bilked out of their land and water took their complaints to the local office of Interior's register of public lands where Stafford Austin, husband of Mary Austin, was in charge. Austin substantiated their complaints and forwarded them to secretary Hitchcock who immediately ordered an investigation. A lengthy report by Hitchcock's investigator recommended that Lippincott be dismissed.[30] It is said that Hitchcock would have liked to dismiss all the principals--Walcott, Newell, Lippincott, and probably supervising engineer Arthur Powell

Davis who had unwittingly followed Newell into the fray.

Hitchcock was in a dilemma; Congress had placed in his department a bureau better suited by its congressional mandate for a place in the Department of Agriculture or the Corps of Engineers. Furthermore, Roosevelt had saddled him with Walcott and Newell whom he could not replace with administrators of his choice.[31] Because they had let Los Angeles obtain options on lands crucial to the success of the Owens Valley reclamation project, he could not reactivate it. Because Roosevelt had persuaded Congress to grant all the previously withdrawn lands to Los Angeles, Hitchcock could not comply with section three of the Reclamation Act obligating him to "restore to public entry" lands not being used specifically for the project.[32] Roosevelt was the first to modify reclamation law in favor of special interests--not because he had the right to do so, but because as president he had the power.

Prior to retirement in 1907 Hitchcock found himself in an uncharacteristic position. Previously he had implemented laws to rid his department of corruption accumulated during previous administrations. Now he had to implement two acts passed by Congress to legalize what had not been legal under the reclamation act. The Act of June 30, 1906, authorized and directed "the Secretary of the Interior to sell to the city of Los Angeles" previously withdrawn parcels of public lands in Owens Valley, and to grant to the city easements through the public lands of Inyo, Kern, and Los Angeles counties.[33] Especially onerous to Hitchcock was implementing a law that invited speculation and land frauds when Los Angeles got Owens Valley water. There was no way to prevent it from being sold by the city to San Fernando Valley land speculators.

The other Act, passed June 27, 1906, took care of the second infringement. With that addition to reclamation law it no longer was improper for the Reclamation Service to furnish water for municipal use but water for federal irrigation projects was to have a higher priority.[34]

Had Davis, the next chief engineer, and director Newell been less friendly with Los Angeles city engineer Bill Mulholland, a scaled-down reclamation project for the Valley could have materialized later. Owens Valley settlers did not object to sharing their water with Los Angeles; they objected to the drying up of their valley and the destruction of their way of life. It was this once beautiful valley that inspired Mary Austin to write Land of Little Rain.[35]

In 1903 Newell had advised Hitchcock that there was "little if any, possibility of speculation, since the individual who takes up the land must live on it five years and can acquire complete title only after all payments for water are made."[36] Greedy speculators were everywhere there was a project in view despite the law's section 3 providing for early withdrawals of public lands. Newell blamed their presence for his failures, not his own lack of administrative ability and his inability to say "no" to his closest associates. In Arizona where co-author of the Reclamation Act, George Maxwell, was catering to irrigators in their pursuit of cheap water, Newell permitted the Service to take on the private and poorly maintained Salt River project where there was not one acre of public land.[37] Perhaps he was carried away by the prospect of building a show-case dam which, of course, Roosevelt Dam became.

The Reclamation Service had 30 projects underway in 1910, more of them located on private than publicly-owned lands: 1,063,111 acres owned by the government; 1,402,702 privately owned; 136,815 owned by the Western states.[38] The shortcomings of reclamation law appear to be insignificant alongside the shortcomings of Reclamation Service administrators during those formative years. The intent of the law, said Newell and the other authors, was to open the West to settlement on public lands. Newell's 1903 denial that speculation could become a problem in implementing reclamation law demonstrated the extent of his naivete. By 1914, having failed as an administrator, he was looking for a position outside the Interior Department--departing under much the same circumstances as Walcott had seven years earlier. Until Elwood Mead came along in 1923 with qualifications based on actual experience, the Bureau lacked the kind of leadership implementation of the law required. Although federal aid to irrigated agriculture was a new concept, the distribution of government lands for settlement was not. Entrepreneurs who engaged in speculation and fraud at public expense had been a part of the American scene long enough for Newell to have been fully aware of their tactics.

As early as 1802 Congress was beseeched by members representing the early West--the region between the Appalachian range and the Mississippi --for special legislation, the year it passed the Enabling Act for the administration of Ohio.[39] Then it obliged members representing the lands west of the Mississippi with a series of acts, including the Homestead Act in 1862. This and subsequent acts kept things humming in General Land Offices in the new West. Fraud was rampant. Even with the best intentions it was "impossible for the General Land Office, with its inadequate staff, to investigate the thousands of entries being made under homestead, timber culture, preemption, and desert land laws."[40]

In 1890, when the Desert Land Act was being manipulated to the point that Congress amended it on August 30 (26 Stat. 391), 80,000 entries were made in 108 land offices.[41] The GLO's annual report for that year carried a quote from Arizona's surveyor general that the "woods" were full of speculators resorting to "all manner of schemes." It was his opinion that more perjury had been committed under the Desert Land Act "than at any previous time in the history of the territory."[42] In evaluating the Bureau's reclamation program, it is essential to understand what kind of people it has had to work with.

The Bureau also has another kind of people problem. By the time Mead, who became commissioner in 1924, entered Interior's employ, it was evident that "bureaucratic control from Washington had produced in the settlers a growing inclination to look upon themselves as wards of the government entitled to generous and continuing aid."[43] Beneficiaries past and present did not and do not see themselves in that light; it is not a flattering one. But this attitude continues to contribute to the Bureau's difficulties and, with the exception of the 1906 act to legalize irrigation water for municipal use, is largely responsible for many of the 1902 Act's subsequent amendments.

NOTES

1. Gerald R. Ogden, "Reclamation Politics: Early Arid Land Laws," a paper read September 19, 1984, at a conference of the San Francisco Bay and Estuarine Association. Ogden is associated with the Economic Research Service in the Department of Agriculture and the Agriculture History Center, University of California, Davis.

2. Paul W. Gates. <u>History of Public Land Law Development</u>

(Washington, D.C.: USGPO, 1968) 637-643.

3. Barbara T. Andrews and Marie Sansone. Who Runs the Rivers? Dams and Decisions in the New West. (Stanford: Stanford Environmental Law Society, 1983) 170-171.

4. John Wesley Powell. Report on the Lands of the Arid Region of the United States, With a More Detailed Account of the Lands of Utah. U. S. Congress, 45th Cong., 2d sess., House Executive Document 73 [Serial 1805].

5. Mary C. Rabbitt. Minerals, Lands, and Geology for the Common Defense and General Wel fare, Vol. II (Washington, D.C.: U. S. Geological Survey, 1980) 116-118.

6. Congressional Record, 1888. 50th Cong., 1st sess., 7031.

7. U. S. Geological Survey. A Brief History of the U. S. Geological Survey, Pamphlet series No. INF-74-26, at page 10. (Pamphlets in this series are available without charge where Geological Survey publications are sold as well as in Geological Survey libraries.)

8. Brig. Gen. Nelson A. Miles, "Our Unwatered Empire," North American Review (March 1890). Reprinted in Appendix to the Congressional Record, 57th Cong., 1st sess. (May 14, 1902), 260-62.

9. Captain Hiram Chittenden. Examination of Reservoir Sites in Wyoming and Colorado, a report prepared under the provisions of Act of Congress of June 3, 1896. 55th Cong., 2d sess., House of Representatives Document No. 141, 1-64, Serial 3666. The report covers Chittenden's observations of irrigation practices in other Western states. Chittenden also wrote various articles on flood control, storage reservoirs, and the relationship of forests to stream flow.

10. William Lilley III and Lewis Gould, "The Western Irrigation Movement, 1878-1902: A Reappraisal," in The American West: A Reorientation, edited by Gene Gressley (Laramie: University of Wyoming Publications, 1966) 62.

11. Congressional Record (May 14, 1902). 57th Cong., 1st sess. Appendix, 253-265.

12. Lilley and Gould, supra, 73-74.

13. Rabbitt, supra, 326.

14. Dictionary of American Biography (New York: Charles Scribner's, 1927-1964) 74-75.

15. Organic Act of March 3, 1879, 20 Stat. 394.

16. Inasmuch as Roosevelt's reasons for favoring Los Angeles were not necessarily what he said in a letter to Congress dated June 23, 1906, authors of books and articles about the Owens Valley controversy are not in agreement. This author thinks that Walcott and Newell found the philosophy of utilitarianism convenient when confronted with their misdeeds by Secretary Hitchcock, and thereafter used it with Roosevelt. The philosophy was then very much in vogue, and calculated to be a convincing one with Roosevelt who shared it. In allowing Los Angeles to obtain the water, Roosevelt was also influenced by Senator Frank Flint of that city and by Gifford Pinchot. It is of course possible that Roosevelt was persuaded by the votes Los Angeles could deliver in the next election. For another view see William L. Kahrl, Water and Power (Berkeley: University of California Press, 1982), 141-44.

17. Dictionary of American Biography, supra.

18. Congressional Record, supra, App. 256.

19. 32 Stat. 388; 43 U.S.C. Sec. 391.

20. U. S. Congress, 1902. Senate Report No. 254, 57th Cong., 1st sess., 2, 6, [Serial 4257].

21. Congressional Record, supra, Appendix, 257.

22. Los Angeles city directories, 1895- 1905.

23. Los Angeles City Directory, 1899.

24. Kahrl, supra, 109, 143. Who's Who in Engineering gives Lippincott's termination with the Reclamation Service as 1904. Perhaps Lippincott (1864-1942) wished to suppress such conclusions as could be drawn from the correct year of his termination.

25. Kahrl, supra, 109-110, 143, et passim.

26. Lippincott to Messrs. Kendrick & Knott, Temple Block, Los Angeles, letter of July 16, 1902, Lippincott papers, Water Resources Center Archives, University of California, Berkeley, LIPP 23.

27. Kahrl, supra, 48-49.

28. Richard Coke Wood. The Owens Valley and the Los Angeles Water Controversy: Owens Valley As I Knew It (Stockton, California: Pacific Center for Western Historical Studies, University of the Pacific, 1973) 19.

29. Remi A. Nadeau. The Water Seekers (Garden City, New York: Doubleday & Company, Inc., 1950) 28.

30. Kahrl, supra, 119-26. Newell, in his September 1903 warning to reclamation engineers to stay clear of outside employment, said: "There are...men who desire a position on the reclamation service for the advertising it may bring them and with the hope of obtaining through it occasional outside employment as specialists," Water-Supply and Irrigation Paper No. 93 (Washington, D.C.: Government Printing Office, 1904), p. 25; Hitchcock, citing the Organic Act of 1879 as applicable to the Reclamation Service, also stressed that private employment was forbidden, Water-Supply and Irrigation Paper No. 146 (Washington, D.C.: GPO, 1905), p. 235.

31. Rabbitt, supra, 326.

32. 32 Stat. 388; 43 U.S.C. 416, 432, 434.

33. U. S. Statutes at Large 801, June 30, 1906; Kahrl, supra, 136-37.

34. Kahrl, supra, 144, citing 34 Stat. 519, Ch. 3559 (June 27, 1906).

35. Mary Austin. Land of Little Rain (Boston: Houghton Mifflin, 1903).

36. F. H. Newell, "Proceedings of First Conference of Engineers of the Reclamation Service," Water-Supply and Irrigation Papers No. 93 (Washington: Government Printing Office, 1904) 22.

37. Gates, supra, 665.

38. Ibid.

39. Ibid., 637.

40. Ibid., 641.

41. Ibid.

42. Ibid., 640.

43. Ibid., 675.

2
The Arthur Powell Davis and Elwood Mead Years

When Newell and Lippincott met with Los Angeles City water officials on November 28, 1904, and agreed to suspend the Owens Valley project while the City completed its investigation,[1] A. Powell Davis was not unaware of the implications of their actions. Devoted to Newell, whom he would succeed in 1907, he somewhat reluctantly accepted the course of events and in time became a party to them, first as chief engineer from 1907 to 1914 and then as director of the Reclamation Service until President Coolidge named Hubert Work to be Secretary of the Interior in 1923. In addition to Secretary Hitchcock, Davis served under Interior secretaries James R. Garfield (1907-1909), Richard A. Ballinger (1909-1911), Walter L. Fisher (1911- 1913), Franklin K. Lane (1913-1920), John B. Payne (1920-1921), and Albert B. Fall (1921- 1923).

Under Hitchcock Davis served as supervising engineer of projects proposed for the lower Colorado River and the Owens River valleys. When the Long Valley damsite was preempted in 1905 by Los Angeles, the settlers looked about for another. Early in 1906, having formed the Owens Valley Water Protective Association with newspaper publisher W. A. Chalfant as president, they engaged San Francisco engineer J. D. Galloway to develop plans for a reservoir on a tributary of Owens River known as Fish Slough. To bypass Newell, Chalfant sent Galloway's report to Secretary Hitchcock with a persuasive letter about the project's feasibility. In view of commitments made by Newell to Los Angeles, Hitchcock could do nothing. In keeping with office protocol he passed the report to Newell who let Lippincott decide whether the Fish Slough project was feasible from the standpoint of the City's interests. It was not.[2] The Valley did not immediately dry up after completion of the Los Angeles Aqueduct in 1913. The yield, variety, and quality of produce from existing farms continued to be impressive until the drought of 1919 when the settlers, through their leaders, again pressed for the Fish Slough reservoir. A. P. Davis, who for some time had been chummy with Bill Mulholland, turned the project down.[3]

The years preceding 1919 had been fairly prosperous for Owens Valley settlers, but the prevalence of the City's agents and their penchant for purchasing privately-owned lands caused friction between those who wanted to fight it out and those who preferred to sell out. By 1916 the City had acquired about 125,000[4] acres of privately owned lands. By 1966 it virtually owned the Valley, having acquired from the federal government and from private parties 242,000 acres in Inyo County and 59,000 acres in Mono County.[5] Since the 1920s, the City has been extending its domain into Mono Basin where rights to waters needed to preserve Mono Lake became a public trust issue in the courts in the early 1980s and culminated in the City's first setback.

In 1920 Mulholland asked Davis to have the Reclamation Service prepare cost estimates, surveys, and plans to move water from Mono Basin to the Los Angeles Aqueduct via a tunnel the City proposed to push through the ridge of land separating Mono Basin from Long Valley.[6] Davis complied, and he further obliged Mulholland by having the Interior secretary make extensive withdrawals of public lands. As time passed and no use of the withdrawn lands was being made by Los Angeles, the settlers demanded their release. In 1922 California officials sent water expert Sidney Harding to Mono Basin to investigate. In a strongly worded report, Harding chastised the Service for its subservience to Los Angeles.[7]

Franklin K. Lane, Interior secretary from 1913 to 1920, hoped to improve the image of the Reclamation Service by getting rid of Newell and replacing him with Davis. Upon taking office Lane was overwhelmed by complaints from hard-pressed farmers on federal projects. Part of the problem was political pressure to which Newell had succumbed; persons with power to influence the location of projects had done so. Some were located where the soil was so poor that farmers abandoned them when starvation became imminent. Farmers who stuck it out complained as bitterly to congressmen and Interior secretaries as those who moved out.

From Montana where the Milk River project on the forbidding northern plains had been in progress since about 1904 came a letter to which Lane responded on May 26, 1913: "As to the Reclamation Service..., there really was a very bad showing made by the Montana projects. It was disheartening to feel that we had spent so many million dollars and that the Government was looked upon as a bunko sharp who had brought people into Montana where they were slowly starving to death."[8]

Part of Montana's problem was section nine of the Reclamation Act, a section that was not repealed until 1910. To get broad acceptance of the Act by Western states and territories, the authors promised that each state was entitled to projects in proportion to the sales of public lands that financed the reclamation fund. The proportion arrived at by the administrators of the Act was 51 per cent. Montana's public land sales had contributed significantly to the fund, but its climate and the quality of its soils were far from ideal for growing food crops. (Presently the projects on the Milk River are irrigating small grain crops and pastureland, and, one might add, contributing to the selenium problem at Bowdoin National Wildlife Refuge.)[9]

Lane installed Davis as the Reclamation Service's director in 1914. Interior secretaries Payne and Fall kept him on despite reservations about his handling of the Mono Basin affair shortly after Lane departed early in 1920. In 1923 Hubert Work became secretary. To get rid of Davis, Work abolished the position of director and told Davis he could remain as a consultant on a per diem basis. At first Davis agreed to the offer; then changed his mind and demanded a hearing. Work explained to him that since the position of director no longer existed the Civil Service Commission no longer had jurisdiction.[10]

The dismissal of Davis caused a furor in the American Society of Civil Engineers where Davis had many friends. The ASCE secretary promptly wrote Secretary Work for an explanation, and furthermore, he beseeched Congress for an investigation. Congress, also dissatisfied with the reclamation program as it was being run, did not respond. The Society had to be satisfied with a lengthy letter from Work spelling out his plan for reorganizing the Service which he renamed the Bureau of Reclamation. Work said nothing disparaging about Davis, but news reporters queried Interior staff members and learned that Davis "was in many cases arbitrary and frequently insisted on having his way," and that at times "he insisted on following his judgement rather than that of Secretary of the Interior."[11]

Davis had for years run the Reclamation Service much as he pleased. Although he championed the Reclamation Act as social legislation designed to help farmers settle the West, his alliances with Mulholland and other prominent Californians bespoke personal ambition. Like Newell he initiated more projects than could be completed within a reasonable period of time, succumbed to political pressure in site selection, failed to provide drainage facilities where they were needed, and made expensive engineering errors which the beneficiaries of the projects were expected to pay in addition to what they had contracted to pay.

Such shortcomings of the Reclamation Service were expanded upon in 1923 by H. H. Brook, the president of an irrigation district in New Mexico. "Generally speaking," said Brook, Service personnel had "no farm experience and no sympathetic understanding of the farmer's problems."[12] When problems arose and farmers sought explanations, Service personnel became secretive. The principal problem was the difference in the price they agreed to pay when the project was under consideration and the price they were required to pay because construction costs had greatly exceeded the estimates upon which their contractual obligations were based. When private firms underbid they lost money; when the Service underestimated, the farmers lost money, so said these farmers. As to engineering and accounting errors, Brook thought a candid admission by Service personnel would better serve its purpose in dealing with farmers than silence. "The theory that silence reduces the amount of trouble stirred up is a fallacy," said Brook. "The farmer is an extremely suspicious individual but a staunch friend when once his confidence is won."[13] In general Brook found Service personnel capable, and the reclamation program commendable.

Davis was far more capable as an engineer than he was as an administrator, but he was also capable of doctoring the data to fit the circumstances. When he was with the Geological Survey during the early years of his career he was assigned to streamgaging the Colorado River and working up streamflow measurements. He therefore possessed considerable knowledge of the River when he began promoting publicly in 1920 the multiple-purpose Boulder Dam, now officially designated the Hoover Dam. While Albert Fall was Interior secretary, Davis wrote a report justifying Boulder Dam which became known as the Fall-Davis Report. In the report Davis overestimated the Colorado River's potential for satisfying the needs of all the river-basin states and Mexico.[14]

Known to Davis since 1916 was a report by E. C. LaRue of the Geological Survey that disputed data in Reclamation Service reports promoting Boulder Dam, including the Fall-Davis Report. LaRue's report which contained pertinent data on the river's flow, "sediment load, irrigable areas, and reservoir sites" said that the Colorado did not "furnish enough water to irrigate all available acreage." LaRue estimated a 3.8 million acre-foot shortage and urged "the adoption of a policy or plan of development" to prevent waste of water due to "evaporation and other causes."[15]

River-basin planning made sense to LaRue, but not to Davis and his water-grasping friends in Southern California. It was not accuracy of reports but action that Davis, Mulholland, and others desired. Davis wanted a dam that would be the envy of the world and Mulholland wanted more water and power for Los Angeles; the landed barons of Imperial Valley wanted a dependable flow of water uninterrupted by periodic flooding.[16] Mexico's rights to some water in the Colorado were conveniently ignored.

LaRue found himself persona non grata in Southern California from the time Davis launched his public relations pitch for Boulder Dam, but hoped for vindication when the matter came before Congress. Hearings dragged on for several years with little interest in LaRue's carefully compiled data. Finally, in 1925, LaRue told a Senate committee that in 1920 an effort had been made to silence him on the Colorado River issue. "I was informed at that time" that "I would be fired out of the [government] Service if I did not keep still or if I opened my mouth."[17]

LaRue, who had begun his definitive study of the Colorado River in 1912 has since been vindicated with the passage of time and the relevance and reliability of his reports of 1916 and 1925.[18] But his defeat was also a defeat for the Geological Survey which thereafter became little more than a data-collection agency for the next 30 years.[19] LaRue resigned from the Survey in 1927.

Davis retained his hold on the segment of Congress interested in serving its Southern California constituency long after he was dismissed in 1923, partly through his former associate Frank Weymouth, chief engineer of the Bureau of Reclamation. Weymouth, like Davis, had written a report justifying Boulder Canyon dam and had contested LaRue's testimony at congressional hearings. Weymouth also was of assistance in steering the Boulder Dam bill through House and Senate committees.[20] After its passage on December 31, 1928, he had a second career waiting for him in Los Angeles just as Lippincott had before him. It was Weymouth who engineered the aqueduct to carry Colorado River water to Southern California.[21]

After Davis was dismissed, Engineering News-Record[22] published a series of articles by leading irrigation engineers, including Newell who had become quite introspective after leaving the Service. Newell wrote that the Reclamation Act was ideal in many ways, "but to be successfully operated it must have ideal men and ideal communities." Congress, he said, had patched up the Act "to fit the needs of the inexperienced landowner, the 'town farmer' or speculator."[23] Through numerous amendments Congress has catered to the desires of irrigators, especially those with large landholdings, but in other respects it has not interfered with the prerogatives of Interior secretaries and Reclamation Service and/or Bureau of Reclamation administrators to enforce the intent of reclamation law.

By 1923, Newell could report construction of "100 storage and diversion dams, reservoirs with a capacity of 10,000,000 acre-feet of storage, 4,000 miles of main line canals, and 8,000 miles of laterals or distributaries, 28 miles of tunnels, 140 miles of flumes, 9,100 bridges, and thousands of smaller structures."[24] Though they added up to a fraction of the irrigation facilities privately constructed, especially noteworthy were those that exceeded in size the dams built by private capital. Only one federal project failed during the first 20 years--the Hondo dam and reservoir in New Mexico. The reservoir did not fill, underlain as it was by limestone and gypsum.[25]

Brook's pointed criticism of Reclamation Service operations appears to have been based on actual experience as an irrigator as well as president of Elephant Butte Irrigation District when he wrote of his concerns for publication in Engineering News-Record,[26] but he failed to give a rounded view of irrigation problems per se such as the damage to land caused by the profligate use of water by the irrigators as well as from poor drainage. Government engineers were well aware that much land had been waterlogged before they came on the scene; yet they also supported the Bureau's policy of giving the irrigators all the water they wanted. The placing of irrigation projects on marginal lands was another frequent mistake. During 1923 Engineering News-Record's associate editor visited Reclamation Service projects in various parts of the West. He wrote a jaundiced account of what he saw. "Disappointments and financial losses without number have proved that irrigation is a very dubious field for money-making," he said. Much of the so-called reclaimed land was too poor to farm and many of the settlers did not know how to farm. They were hopelessly in debt, he said, and in many instances they were living in the most primitive of conditions. He was especially concerned that the Service was "said to have no authority to use the reclamation fund" to investigate the quality of the soils and he questioned the circumstances of a situation in which the Department of Agriculture was playing no part.[27]

Reclamation's engineers were (and still are) construction oriented. Very few were concerned about the quality of the soils and the need for drainage. Most were not even concerned about the deplorable condition of the settlers. Newell, chief spokesman for federal reclamation, was safely ensconced on a university campus where he had been since he was removed from the Service in 1914. He did not see, or perhaps preferred not to see, what mitigation measures were needed to make reclamation a success.

Secretary of Interior Hubert Work, appointed by President Coolidge in March 1923, was determined to change circumstances for the better. His first effort--the dismissal of A. P. Davis and the appointment of a commission headed by David W. Davis of

Idaho--was viewed as a disaster. And so it would have been had Work not realized the limitations of D. W. Davis. Moving him into a less demanding position, Work obtained in 1924 the appointment of Elwood Mead as reclamation commissioner.

Although Work had previously had little government experience--he was a physician--he had a yen for politics. In 1923 he had invited Mead to serve on a six-man committee charged with reviewing federal reclamation projects and devising ways to make them more successful. Mead, having had experience with successful and not so successful irrigation colonies in Australia and California, knew more than most what it took to make successful farmers.

Mead also realized that the federal government's reclamation program was doomed if farmers continued to default on their payments. As a member of Work's Fact Finders Committee, Mead was influential in developing qualifications to weed out project settlers who lacked the necessary funds and experience to become self-sufficient and solvent.[28] Another hurdle to overcome was unfinished projects upon which settlers were unable to do much more than wait out their completion. Largely due to A. P. Davis' ambitious construction program, first as chief engineer and then as director, projects were being done piecemeal over a period of many years. In Reclamation in the United States, the Bureau's Alfred Golze discussed the problem without attributing the blame.[29]

The time for proper planning had come. With the Second Deficiency Appropriations Act of 1924, Congress utilized the findings of the Fact Finders Committee. No part of appropriated sums were to be used for the "commencement of construction work on any reclamation project" not recommended by the commissioner and the Interior secretary, and approved by the president as to its "agricultural and engineering feasibility and the reasonableness of its estimated construction cost.[30] Although it was said that Mead and Work held to that goal and took the brunt of Western displeasure for doing so,[31] Mead was as anxious to expand the Bureau's domain as others before and after his administration. Despite the hard times for farmers throughout the nation and the failures of a number of projects Mead had urged Congress to write off, he proposed six new projects estimated to cost $50 million.[32]

Secretary Work's contribution to the reclamation program has received little attention and appreciation in the literature. Yet Work knew far better than the engineers who rushed to Davis' defense after his dismissal what was wrong with reclamation projects. In a letter to the ASCE secretary, Work explained the state of affairs in the West. He said that unless improvement in conditions could be brought about, many projects would be abandoned entirely by the settlers; that some settlers already had left; that the Government would "lose millions of dollars invested," and that the settlers would "lose time, labor, and money already placed by them on their farms."[33]

Work explained that in order for the government to obtain a return on its investment of millions of dollars, it was necessary to integrate farming with the marketing of finished products. There were then but 53,000 farms on reclamation projects. Nevertheless there was the potential for "creameries, sugar factories and other industrial enterprises." With more intensive farming and "diversification of crops" the owners and tenants on those farms could cooperate with trained personnel in "packing, handling and marketing their products."[34] What was also needed was the subdivision of large land holdings to make room for more settlers, Work told the secretary of ASCE.

Several months after the Engineering News- Record published Work's letter, the editor belittled Work's ideas in an article entitled "A Policy for Reclamation."[35] Although the editor made some suggestions that had merit, he mainly defended an engineering approach that clearly had failed to create an environment in which farmers, except for the rapacious few, could succeed.

The farmers also were at fault, for many of them had made a practice of defaulting on their interest-free government contracts in order to put money aside to meet obligations that were not interest-free. Some who could pay saw no reason to when settlers without money were getting by without paying. Some with money told others not to pay; by not paying perhaps the government would forgive their debts. In 1922 only 9.5 per cent of the $135 million spent by the government in the first twenty years of the Reclamation Act's existence had been repaid.[36] From 1910 to 1939 Congress made the following concessions to the reclamation program:

1. The Act of June 25, 1910, provided $20 million for the completion of projects. In so doing Congress acquired authority at the

same time it took authority away from the Secretary of the Interior. Under the Act the Secretary could not initiate projects as provided in the Reclamation Act of 1902; he could recommend them. Proposed projects were subject to the scrutiny of the President after they had been examined and reported upon by a board of engineer officers of the Army designated by the President. Loans to the projects were to be repaid, one-half to the Treasury and one-half to the reclamation fund, the first payment to be due five years after each advance.[37]

2. The Act of August 13, 1914, known as the Reclamation Extension Act, extended the settlers' payment period from ten to twenty years.[38] Section 2 of the Act specified a sliding scale for repayments with a view to lightening the annual payments in the early years when other farming expenditures were likely to be high. However, there was a slump in farm prices in the early 1920s just when the installments on the high end of the sliding scale were due.

3. A joint resolution of Congress which was passed May 17, 1921, authorized the Secretary of Interior to furnish water during the 1921 season to applicants or entrymen in arrears more than one calendar year.[39]

4. The Act of March 31, 1922, extended the time for payment to two years from December 31, 1922, in cases of inability to pay on schedule.[40] Section 2 authorized the Secretary, "in his discretion, after due investigation, to furnish irrigation water on Federal irrigation projects during the irrigation seasons of 1922 and 1923 to landowners or entry-men who are in arrears for more than one calendar year...."[41]

5. The Act of February 28, 1923, further extended relief to settlers, including those on the Boise, Idaho, project.[42]

6. The Act of May 9, 1924, extended the deadline for deferrals to March 1, 1927.[43]

During the years of these concessions, Congress also was reimbursing the reclamation fund:

1. The Act of October 2, 1917, Section 18, provided that all moneys received from potassium deposit royalties and rentals under the Act's provisions, except those from Alaska, were to go to the fund for use in construction, after which 50 percent would go to the states of origin to finance public schools and/or public roads.[44]

2. The Mineral Leasing Act of February 25, 1920, Section 35,

provided that 52.5 percent, exclusive of Alaska, of money received from "sales, bonuses, royalties and rentals of public lands" would be "paid into, reserved and appropriated, as part of the reclamation fund...."[45]

3. The Federal Water Power Act of June 10, 1920, Section 17, provided that 50 percent of the charges arising from licenses thereunder "for the occupancy and use of public lands and national forests" would be "paid into, reserved, and appropriated as a part of the reclamation fund...."[46]

Repayments by settlers began to look promising in 1929. The Bureau reported a $1,009,165 increase over the previous year.[47] A failing economy, world-wide in scope, was largely responsible for the Bureau's next crisis in 1931. An advance to the fund of $5 million was needed or construction would have to cease, said Commissioner Mead to the Senate Committee on Irrigation and Reclamation.[48] From 1931 until the end of the decade Congress was called upon to give and to forgive. Public works projects kept the Bureau in business; annual leniency acts to suspend payments and/or construction charges made it possible for Mead to carry out his program under the Omnibus Adjustment Act of 1926 which Congress had passed at Mead's request.[49]

By the 1940s revenues and royalties from the mineral and power acts previously mentioned were becoming a significant addition to the Reclamation Fund. Although it could be argued that they might better be used for other purposes such as enhancing the value of public lands administered by the Park Service and the Bureau of Land Management,[50] the impetus to construct multiple- purpose projects on the grand plan of Boulder (now Hoover) Dam pushed the Bureau into the limelight with Commissioner Mead's successor playing a leading role. As will be seen, Mead's commitment to the intent of reclamation law came to a close with his death in January 1936 and with it the initial emphasis on single-purpose projects. Although Mead supported Boulder Dam and the concept of multiple-purpose projects he was not around to influence the changing face of the Bureau.

NOTES

1. Kahrl, supra, 97; full cit., 1, note 16.

2. Kahrl, supra, 204-09. For a personalized story of the Valley's troubles from 1904, see W. A. Chalfant, Story of Inyo, 2d ed. (Bishop, California, 1933).

3. Kahrl, supra, 238.

4. S.T. Harding. Water in California (Palo Alto, California: National Press, 1960) 121.

5. Los Angeles Department of Water & Power. Report on Water Supply Management in Inyo and Mono Counties, Prepared pursuant to Senate Resolution No. 184, California Legislature, 1966 First Extraordinary Session, Sept. 1966, 6, 9.

6. Kahrl, supra, 330; Harold Conkling, "Owens Valley Project Preliminary Report," U. S. Bureau of Reclamation, Washington, D. C., September 1920; "Report on Owens Valley Project, California," USBR, Washington, D. C., September 1921. Conkling's assessment favored the City of Los Angeles.

7. Kahrl, supra, 330-40; Sidney T. Harding, "Supplemental Report and Notes on Mono Basin Investigation" and "Report on Development of Water Resources in Mono Basin Based on Investigations Made for the Division of Engineering and Irrigation," Department of Public Works, October 17, 1922, and December 1922, respectively. Harding, an authority on water law in the United States, has written extensively on California water and power projects. During his career he compiled detailed information on Bureau of Reclamation projects that is now at the Water Resources Center Archives, University of California, Berkeley.

8. Anne Wintermute Lane and Louise Herrick Wall (eds.). The Letters of Franklin K. Lane (Boston and New York: Houghton Mifflin Company, 1922) 137.

9. U. S. Department of the Interior Task Group on Irrigation Drainage, "Preliminary Evaluation of Selenium Concentrations in Ground and Surface Water, Soils, Sediment, and Biota from Selected Areas in the Western United States," Draft, December 6, 1985, 56-60.

10. Anon., "Davis Removal Part of General Upheaval," Engineering News-Record, June 28, 1923, 1139.

11. Ibid.

12. H.H. Brook, "Difficulties and Complaints of the Farmer," Engineering News-Record, November 29, 1923, 892.

13. Ibid., 891.

14. U. S. Congress, 1922, Senate Document 142, 67th Cong., 2d sess.

15. Walter B. Langbein, "L'Affaire LaRue," WRD [Water Resources Division] Bulletin, April- June 1975, 8.

16. Nadeau, supra, Chap. 9, "Runaway River," 172, ff. Full citation, 1, note 29.

17. Langbein, supra, 12. For developments in Southern California, see Kahrl, supra, 263-69.

18. E. C. LaRue. Colorado River and Its Utilization, Geological Survey Water-Supply Paper 395 (Washington, D.C.: Government Printing Office, 1916; Water Power and Flood Control of Colorado River Below Green River, Utah, Geological Survey Water-Supply Paper 556 (Washington, D.C.: Goverment Printing Office, 1925).

19. Langbein, supra, 13.

20. Nadeau, supra, 230.

21. Ibid.

22. Engineering News-Record, "Federal Land Reclamation: A National Problem," October 25, 1923-December 13, 1923.

23. Newell, F. H., "Origins, Problems and Achievements of Federal Land Reclamation," Engineering News-Record, October 25, 1923, 666-73, at 673.

24. Newell, supra, 672.

25. Thomas H. Means, "Faults of Reclamation Law and Practice, and Their Remedies," Engineering News-Record, December 13, 1923, 977-81, 979.

26. Brook, supra, 890-92, 891.

27. F. E. Schmitt, "Through the Reclamation Country," Engineering News-Record, November 15, 1923, 798-800, 799.

28. For text of report see U. S. Congress, Senate Document No. 92, Federal Reclamation by Irrigation, 68th Cong., 1st sess. Also see: R. R. Rucker and P. V. Fishback, "The Federal Reclamation Program," in Terry L. Anderson (ed.), Water Rights (San Francisco: Pacific Institute for Public Policy Research, 1983) 55, 58, 67-68.

29. Alfred R. Golze. Reclamation in the United States (New York: McGraw-Hill, 1952) 38. Golze was director of programs and finance, Bureau of Reclamation.

30. 43 Stat. 685.

31. Donald C. Swain. Federal Conservation Policy, 1921-1933 (Berkeley: University of California Press, 1963, 82-84. (This is not the Donald Swain associated with the Kesterson disaster during his years with the Bureau of Reclamation, Sacramento office.)

32. Gates, supra, 678-81. Full citation, 1, note 2.

33. "Secretary Work Explains Davis Removal/ Answering Am. Soc. C. E., He Says Time Has Now Come for Business Administration," Engineering News-Record, Aug. 23, 1923.

34. Ibid.

35. Editor, "A Policy for Reclamation," Engineering News-Record, February 14, 1924, 268-69.

36. Swain, supra, 79.

37. 36 Stat. 835; 43 U.S.C. Sec. 397.

38. 38 Stat. 686; 43 U.S.C. Sec. 471, 472.

39. 42 Stat. 4.

40. 42 Stat. 489.

41. 42 Stat. 490.

42. 42 Stat. 1324, 1325.

43. 43 Stat. 116; 43 U.S.C. Sec. 384.

44. 40 Stat. 300.

45. 41 Stat. 813.

46. 41 Stat. 1072.

47. Swain, supra, 85.

48. Ibid., and fn. 64, 195.

49. The Act of February 6, 1931, Ch. 111, 46 Stat. 1064, relieved the Bureau of making payments from the reclamation fund to Treasury for two consecutive years; the Act of March 3, 1931, Ch. 435, 46 Stat. 1507, advanced to the reclamation fund the sum of five million dollars at the rate of $1 million annually; the Act of April 1, 1932, Ch. 95, 47 Stat. 75, relieved water users on federal reclamation projects of construction charges for 1931 and 1932; (Mead and Secretary Work thought up ways to avoid a moratorium on payments in the lean days of the mid-twenties, but in 1932 Mead had to accept the inevitable); the Act of March 3, 1933, Ch. 200, 47 Stat. 1427,

extended the moratorium to 1936; the Act of April 14, 1936, Ch. 215, 49 Stat. 1206, further extended relief to water users; the Act of May 31, 1939, Ch. 156, 53 Stat. 792, again extended relief to water users. Other acts during 1931-1939 granted relief for specific projects.

50. Marion Clawson and Burnell Held. The Federal Lands: Their Use and Management (Lincoln: University of Nebraska Press, n.d., a reprint of a book published in 1957 by Resources for the Future) 343-45. Oil royalties from submerged lands account for much of the increase since the 1953 legislation and according to the authors they will continue to. Projections for 1980 are given.

3
California: A Worst Case Scenario

John C. Page, groomed for the commissioner's post by Elwood Mead, served as acting commissioner of the Bureau of Reclamation during 1936 and as commissioner from 1937 to 1943. As Mead's understudy one might have expected him to lead the Bureau along the same lines as his predecessor. Mead kept the Bureau viable with his admonitions to beneficiaries that they must meet repayment obligations and otherwise comply with reclamation law. It was in their best interest to do so, he said: otherwise they would find themselves without public support for federally subsidized irrigation water.

Page kept the Bureau viable by developing a public relations program that sold Bureau projects to Congress and the general public. His principal interest was in multiple purpose projects for the generation of hydro-electric power. The sale of that power made it possible for the Bureau to subsidize even more generously the beneficiaries of its increasingly ambitious engineering structures.

The multiple-purpose Central Valley Project in California was made to order for Page: it provided a prototype for other projects he had in mind. In the interim he proved a capable administrator of the project and also took a firm stand on the Bureau's commitment to salinity control in the Sacramento-San Joaquin Delta. Each year he appeared before Congress and specifically committed the CVP to this purpose in accordance with the Bureau's agreement with the state.[1]

Not as laudable was Page's attitude toward the acreage

limitation in reclamation law wherein he aided and abetted the beneficiaries of the Colorado-Big Thompson and other projects in their efforts to get their projects exempted. (See Appendix A for congressional acts dealing with acreage exemptions, modifications, and waivers.) Less committed to family-size farms than Mead, Page reasoned that with advances in farming technology the Interior secretary should be able to use his discretion in determining the acreage limitation if circumstances seemed to call for modification of reclamation law.[2] In line with his philosophy he displayed little interest in the law's enforcement.

Before becoming commissioner Page had followed California's efforts to finance its own Central Valley Project from his position in Nevada as office engineer for the Bureau's Boulder Canyon Project. Embodied in California's CVP Act were the same components that later justified the federal CVP but the depression years of the early 1930s precluded the state from finding a market for the sale of $170 million in revenue bonds to finance the project. Aware that federal legislation was by then giving a boost to the economy with low-interest loans, the state dispatched its engineer to Washington where the project looked so appealing that the government rejected the plea for a loan and displayed only an eagerness to take it on. In quick succession Congress handed it over to the Corps of Engineers and then to the Bureau. The transactions dovetailed with Mead's death and Page's appointment as acting commissioner in 1936 and commissioner in 1937.

In taking on the CVP the Bureau agreed to the state's provision for releases of enough fresh water to prevent further saltwater intrusion and seawater incursion into Sacramento-San Joaquin Delta farm lands. The minimum daily flow set by the state was 3300 cubic feet per second "past Antioch into Suisun Bay."[3] (A daily flow of 3300 c.f.s adds up to a foot of water on an area slightly over 10 square miles.)

Apparently the Bureau also agreed that construction of Friant Dam should have a priority status.[4] This is not reflected in the Bureau's periodical Reclamation Era wherein it is stated: "The effectiveness of the San Joaquin Valley phase is dependent upon concurrent construction of the Sacramento River storage dam."[5] Throughout the period of the project's construction, Interior Secretary

Harold Ickes was prevailed upon by state officials representing San Joaquin Valley landowners to make concessions of one kind or another. The Delta region where private reclamation had begun 75 years earlier and where the reclaimed land had proved to be the richest in the state[6] was all but ignored in the frenzy to bring water to the relatively few improved and productive acres in the San Joaquin Valley. The priorities of the Bureau noted in Reclamation Era are therefore of considerable interest:

> The two primary purposes of redistributing the waters of the Central Valley are to prevent encroachment of salt water from San Francisco Bay upon the very rich lands of the Sacramento-San Joaquin Delta and to provide a supplementary water supply to lands in southern San Joaquin Valley. In addition a freshwater supply will be provided [to] the industrial cities on Suisun Bay where encroachment of salt water presents a serious threat to large developments, and hydroelectric power will be generated for the northern California market. Regulation of the Sacramento River also will assist in controlling the floods of that stream and improve navigation on the rivers.[7]

The Bureau's words reflect the state's initial plan for the Central Valley.[8] Later the Bureau increased the size of certain facilities[9] and added the San Luis Unit, the latter at the behest of San Joaquin Valley landowners. Passage of the San Luis Act materialized in June 1960.

With the San Luis Unit close to reality in 1957 the Bureau reversed its position on salinity control in the Delta.[10] The water it had committed to salinity control in the mid-thirties would soon be needed to serve irrigators on the west side of the Valley. The state, with no more compunction about robbing the Delta than the Bureau, built its own project to serve another area of the Valley following passage of a bond issue in November 1960. The latter was desired by Valley landowners who wanted to avoid the federal acreage limitation and by the burgeoning cities of Southern California that wanted more water.

Although the Bureau can and does propose irrigation projects and solicits public interest to get them authorized, in this instance the

West Side Land Owners Association came to the Bureau during the early 1940s and put up $40,000 for a feasibility study to bring federal irrigation water to the lands lying west of the San Joaquin River.[11] Subsequently the association reorganized with Westlands Water District forming its own district on September 8, 1952. Thereafter Westlands dominated the deals made with the Bureau for water from the San Luis Unit of the Central Valley Project. Westlands' liaison with the Bureau when most large landowners in San Joaquin Valley were agitating for a state water project to avoid the acreage limitation was an anomaly to those who did not know that it expected to get cheaper water by going to the feds. With passage of the San Luis Act[12] Westlands anticipated irrigation water paid for mainly by the nation's taxpayers.

Prior to passage of the Act one of the House Committee on Interior and Insular Affairs' subcommittee witnesses volunteered his own opinion of why the president of Westlands had promoted the San Luis Project. Said Harry Horton at the 1958 hearing:

> I will give you my own opinion of Jack O'Neill's willingness to sign the 160-acre limitation. He thinks if he gets water for 10 years on there without having to sell, he can make enough money out of it so he can afford to sell at any old price.[13]

Horton referred to a 1945 opinion by a regional solicitor in the Bureau's Sacramento office which extended the time to dispose of excess lands to up to 10 years. Mead had not meant for that provision in the Omnibus Adjustment Act of 1926 to be misused in that fashion; he had recommended the provision to prevent land speculation. Nor had Mead anticipated that the Bureau would condone the use of paper farmers, each with 160-acre holdings, to get excess land owners out of their dilemma to sell within a reasonable period of time as provided in the Act. He had mainly tried to retard speculation. Mead's 1926 legislation was also intended to do away with the crop-income method of repayment which during the Page years was reinstituted in the Reclamation Project Act in 1939 to charge farmers on the basis of what they could afford to pay.[14] True the depression years were harsh but they were over when Westlands got the best of all possible worlds.[15]

Little excess land at Westlands has been sold to outsiders.

Whether bona fide sales will increase under the Reclamation Reform Act of 1982[16] is doubtful in irrigated regions dominated by powerful landowners, especially in California. As in the past, sales of excess lands probably will be manipulated in favor of insiders; corporate farmers are not accustomed to complying with the intent of reclamation law.

Mead's 1926 Omnibus Adjustment Act specifically states that beneficiaries of federal water are to execute contracts for payment of costs "of constructing, operating, and maintaining the [irrigation] works during the time they are in control of the United States" before water is delivered. After receiving water they are to sell their excess lands within a reasonable period at a reasonable price determined by government appraisal. If they refuse to sell, no further water deliveries are to be made.[17] However, Westlands did not strike the first blow to Mead's recordable contract provision; other large landowner beneficiaries of the Central Valley Project did. With the assistance of Regional Solicitor Graham in the Sacramento office they got Mead's "reasonable period" extended. Said Graham on August 1, 1945, "...a ten-year period, if found to be appropriate [by the Interior secretary], is legally permissible."[18]

The regional solicitor's opinion on recordable contracts can, of course, be challenged in court, but in a region of large landholdings the court may well decide in favor of the irrigators. Most of the talk from Bureau commissioners about reclamation law enforcement is mostly talk. To enforce the law would jeopardize their careers.

Commissioner Harry Bashore who followed Commissioner Page in 1943 with a two-year stint of duty did not rock any boats, but he was more forthright than most in explaining the vagaries of reclamation law. Apropos the opinions of Interior solicitors he said in 1945:

> I will admit that the reclamation laws are a little difficult to understand because they have been developed over a period of 43 years; and it is a little difficult at times to really find out what has been changed or amended. In order to do that you must look at the decisions of the Department of Interior which have been made, say, since 1914 as they relate to the public lands and lands in reclamation projects. You cannot just pick up the

> Reclamation Manual and say, "This is the law" unless you look up the departmental interpretation of it. <u>And the departmental interpretation of the law is the law until the courts say otherwise; whether it makes the right interpretation or not, that is the law.</u>[19] [Emphasis added.]

A fourth volume of the Reclamation Manual referred to by Bashore has yet to be published. As of 1972 the set contained 2040 pages of text, much of it in small print supplied by the annotators of the opinions and memoranda of solicitors, attorneys general, comptrollers general, and courts. Without going to the original documents one can get the import of the excerpts and obtain a fair understanding of how various sections of reclamation law have been interpreted. The regional solicitor's opinion extending the period to ten years in which to sell excess lands appears to have weakened reclamation law in a way not intended by Congress.[20]

Congress has demonstrated that it can be quite subservient to the Executive and Judicial departments. For example, the power of the Executive was apparent in 1906 when Congress was prevailed upon to make legal the acquisition by Los Angeles of water intended for a reclamation project in Owens Valley. The Bureau of Reclamation, seeking to prevent litigations with its clients, has frequently prevailed upon Congress to legislate on its behalf. The opinions of solicitors in the Interior Department also carry considerable weight with Congress, permitting the Secretary to negotiate through the courts settlements favorable to the Bureau's clients.[21]

Interior secretaries have the final say in administrative enforcement, but they have been as remiss as the Bureau in implementing reclamation law. During the mid-fifties California Congressman Clair Engle stated to a special subcommittee: "since the recordable contract provisions have been in the reclamation law, not in one single instance has the Secretary of the Interior ever set a price on land and sold the land under a recordable contract." Apropos abuses of the law by the large land owners he said: "They set up corporations and partnerships and every adult or child has 160 acres and if there are not enough of those they bring in the uncles and aunts and, as a consequence, they spread it around so that the pro forma title at least is within the limitation."[22] And that is all the Bureau requires of them, though it is in a position to prevent the abuse.

In 1947, years after the Bureau should have begun executing contracts with its Central Valley Project beneficiaries, it had processed but one long-term repayment contract.[23] Its excuse was that it was more important to get construction of the project underway. Michael W. Straus who was appointed commissioner in December 1945 did not find the Bureau's excuse acceptable. Under his administration the Bureau shaped up for the better.

Heated controversy as well as significant progress characterized the Straus years. But in California the large landholders continued to agitate for a state takeover of the Central Valley Project to escape potential enforcement of the acreage limitation. Interior Secretary Ickes helped Straus with that problem in his own inimmitable way. California could take over the project only if it bore the entire cost.[24]

Commissioner Straus, whose illustrious career began as managing editor of Chicago and New York newspapers, came into the Interior Department in 1933 when Ickes made him chief of information. They worked well together. Ickes had been converted to reclamation by former commissioner Elwood Mead. Straus was a proponent of large river-basin developments for hydroelectric power as well as irrigated agriculture.[25] In California, Straus had to fight Pacific Gas & Electric over power from Shasta Dam at the same time that he was trying to force large landowners to comply with reclamation law. So influential were his adversaries that the 80th Congress was persuaded to cut off his salary and that of Richard Boke, the Bureau's Region II director in Sacramento. Undeterred, Straus continued to fight while awaiting restoration of his salary by a more responsible Congress.[26]

Although Straus was not successful in forcing California's recalcitrant irrigators to comply with reclamation law, his efforts seem to have prompted large landholders to look for another source of water than that offered by the Bureau. In Governor Pat Brown they found a strong proponent of a state interbasin water project and, as noted above, California voters approved the State Water Plan the same year Congress approved the San Luis Unit of the Central Valley Project.

In pricing water for State Water Project beneficiaries the

burden of payment fell most heavily on Southern California urban dwellers, in part because of delivery cost; in part because the state subsidized the irrigators with the surplus water the Metropolitan Water District of Southern California was required to contract for but did not then have use for. That surplus water was sold to SWP irrigators at rates comparable to those the Bureau charges its clients.[27] In recent years SWP irrigation districts have signed contracts more nearly reflecting the actual cost of delivery.[28] That they now pay substantially more than their near neighbor, Westlands, is apparent.[29]

Passage of the San Luis Act implied that the large landholder-beneficiaries were ready to comply with the federal acreage limitation. But the 6100 new and separate land ownerships promised by Congressman Bernie Sisk did not materialize.[30] Commissioner Floyd Dominy (1959-1969) who liked to talk about being a friend of the small farmer was not dedicated to reclamation law enforcement, preferring to serve the people who could do him more good.[31] Preceded by Commissioner Wilbur Dexheimer (1953-1959), Dominy was followed in 1969 by Commissioner Ellis Armstrong. Not until Cecil Andrus became commissioner under President Carter was there much evidence of intent to enforce reclamation law such as was evident under Commissioner Straus after he replaced Commissioner Bashore in 1943.

Andrus set about reforming the Reclamation Act with San Joaquin Valley landowners in mind, but when he testified in support of his proposed legislation before the House Subcommittee on Water and Power Resources he met with rudeness and resistance from various committee members.[32] His proposed legislation did not go unheeded by others on the committee who participated in framing the Reclamation Reform Act that finally passed in 1982. However, the large landowners in California again found ways to get around the intent of the new law just as they had the old law after the federal government presented California with the Central Valley Project half a century ago.

NOTES

1. John MacLeod Mac Diarmid. The Central Valley Project, State Water Project and Salinity Control in the Sacramento-San Joaquin Delta, California State Water Resources Control Board, January 1976; second printing, June 1976, 145.

2. Donald C. Swain, "The Bureau of Reclamation and the New Deal, 1933-1940," Pacific Northwest Quarterly, July 1970, 137, 143, 145.

3. University of California (Davis) Law Review. Legal Control of Water Pollution (Frank B. Baldwin, III, Faculty Editor). (Regents of the University of California, 1969) 226.

4. Mary Montgomery and Marion Clawson. History of Legislation and Policy Formation of the Central Valley Project (Berkeley, California: U. S. Department of Agriculture, Bureau of Agricultural Economics, March 1946), 84, 88.

5. Anon., "Work to Start on Several Phases of Central Valley Project," The Reclamation Era, January 1936, 11.

6. Ibid.

7. Ibid.

8. Mac Diarmid, supra, citing Cal. Stats. 1933, Ch. 1042.

9. Ibid., 112-13.

10. Ibid., 402-03, and list of appearances before Congress, references to publications, and speeches dealing with salinity, 145-49.

11. Joe S. Bain, Richard E.Caves, and Julius Margolis, Northern California's Water Industry (Published for Resources for the Future, Inc., by the Johns Hopkins Press, Baltimore, 1966) 404.

12. Public Law 86-488; 74 Stat. 156.

13. U.S. Congress, Senate Committee on Interior and Insular Affairs, Subcommittee hearings on S.1887, 85th Cong., 2d. sess., 1958, 87; Bain, supra, 405, fn. 99.

14. Barbara T. Andrews and Marie Sansone. Who Runs the Rivers? Dams and Decisions in the New West (Stanford Environmental Law Society, Stanford University, 1983) 182.

15. Ch. 832, 50 Stat. 844, Note 16, Memorandum of Regional Solicitor Graham, August 1, 1945, reprinted in Central Valley Project Documents, Part 2, H.R. Doc. No. 246, 85th Cong., 1st sess., 1957, 642.

16. Law 97-293, title II, 96 Stat. 1263.

17. Ch. 383, 44 Stat. 636, Act of May 25, 1926, Section 46.

18. Ibid; see annotation 43, "Recordable contracts."

19. Robert William DeRoos. The Thirsty Land: the Story of the Central Valley Project (Stanford University Press, 1948) 77-78.

20. Ch. 383, 44 Stat. 636, supra, Note 43.

21. A recent example is the opinion of Solicitor Ralph Tarr dated June 17,1986, and upheld by a federal court in Fresno, California, on December 30. See Anderson (ed.), supra, 73-79. Full citation, 2, note 28.

22. U. S. Congress, House Committee on Interior and Insular Affairs, Special Subcommittee, Federal Assistance for Small Reclamation Projects, 84th Congress, 1st sess., 1955, 93. See also, Bain, et al, supra, 405, fn. 99.

23. De Roos, supra, 96.

24. Ibid., Chapter XII, "Throw the Rascals Out." Also see letter of Oscar L. Chapman (Secretary of the Interior) to Hon. Samuel Wm. Yorty, dated July 10, 1952.

25. Swain, supra, 143.

26. William E. Warne. The Bureau of Reclamation (New York: Praeger Publishers, 1973) 18-19. Warne was assistant commissioner of the Bureau of Reclamation, 1943-1947, becoming an assistant secretary of the Department of the Interior in 1947. After leaving the federal government he became director of the California Department of Water Resources. In 1985 Westview Press (Boulder, Colorado) reprinted this book with a new preface by Warne.

27. Michael Storper and Richard A. Walker. The Price of Water: Surplus and Subsidy in the State Water Project (Berkeley: Institute of Governmental Studies, U. C. Berkeley, 1984); Patrick Porgans, "The Great Drought Hoax," San Francisco Bay Guardian, September 7, 1988, 7-9, 12.

28. California Department of Water Resources Bulletin 132-84. Management of the California State Water Project, State of California, September 1984, 1. This 271-page report lists in Appendix B the amounts of water delivered to each contractor, the amounts paid by each, and estimates of future deliveries and payments. Pages 141-143 contain information about the Kern County Water Agency and its customers. Forty percent of irrigated land is in cotton; 28

percent in "other field crops"; 22 percent is in orchards and vineyards; 10 percent is in truck crops; DWR Bulletin 132-86, Chapter III, 52; Marc Reisner. Cadillac Desert (New York: Viking Penguin, Inc., 1986), 357-70.

29. E. Phillip LeVeen and Laura B. King. Turning off the Tap on Federal Water Subsidies, Vol. I: "The Central Valley Project: The $3.5 Billion Giveaway" (San Francisco: Natural Resources Defense Council, Inc. and California Rural Legal Assistance Foundation, August 1985), Appendix B, Table 2. Compare rate structure with that in Appendix B of Bulletin 132-84, cited in note 28, supra.

30. Roger F. Ellingson, "Luis Water Assures West Side Prosperity," Fresno Bee, June 5, 1960; Letter of Jerald R. Butchert, Manager, Westlands Water District, dated September 20, 1984, to Mr. Max McCrohon, Managing Editor, United Press International, castigating the media. Gregory Gordon and Lloyd Carter. "Big money buys big clout for West Side's polluting growers." San Francisco Examiner, August 13, 1984, A6-A7. Anon., UPI Washington. "How 'paper farmers' got around water law." San Francisco Examiner, August 13, 1984, A7.

31. Reisner, supra, 143-44; for Dominy's career see 224-63.

32. U. S. Congress, House Committee on Interior and Insular Affairs, Subcommittee on Water and Power Resources. Hearing in Consideration of Legislation to Reform the Acreage Limitation Provisions of the Reclamation Law, November 13, 1979, page 13 and ff. of unrevised and unedited reporter's copy.

4 The Missouri River Basin Projects

The Missouri Basin Projects Act came into existence with Section 9 of the Flood Control Act of 1944. Its beneficiaries would, under the Reclamation Project Act of 1939, have more latitude in paying for the projects and Interior secretaries could exercise more authority in making reclamation law more workable, at least from their viewpoint.

Little understood in the 1939 Act are two sections dealing with contracts. Irrigation works such as storage reservoirs and main canals come under Section 9(e) contracts. Irrigation distribution systems--the pipes and small canals that deliver water to the farms--come under Section 9(d) contracts. The provisions of the latter minimize the financial burden on the irrigators by giving them up to 10 years before their interest-free payments for construction begin.[1] Section 9(e) contracts are written for 40 years or less and are renewable, but the facilities do not revert to the irrigators after they are paid for.[2] However, 9(e) contracts also minimize the financial burden on the irrigators. (As stated in the previous chapter, the Act was passed during the depths of the depression, ostensibly to recover reimburseable costs based on the irrigators' ability to pay.) The wording of Section 9(e) seems to have also anticipated an extended role for the Bureau as manager of operations and maintenance of facilities owned in perpetuity by the federal government but this has not come to pass.[3]

Extension of the repayment period with a 9(d) contract has been a boon to water users, but an additional burden upon taxpayers. Essentially it is a 50-year repayment contract.[4] Also, the Bureau's original contracts to deliver water did not include adjustments for inflation. (California's Central Valley Project presents a good example of water users paying the same cheap prices for water deliveries now that they paid during the depression of the 1930s.[5]) Water service contracts in general follow a common form that is standard throughout the 17 contiguous Western states. Although they will be renegotiated prior to expiration and the water-delivery charges increased, these contracts have a number of years to run. At present the delivery charges are so low they are not even covering operation and maintenance costs. Persons involved in assessing the economic impact of the Missouri Basin projects--past, present, and future--will need to examine all pertinent sections of the 1939 Act, as well as those referred to here.

The Flood Control Act of December 22, 1944, deals with another aspect of Bureau operations. It safeguards the states in developing their watersheds by preventing the Bureau from proceeding with projects without coordinating them with state desires. Section 1 declares it to be "the policy of the Congress to recognize the interests and rights of the States in determining the development of the watersheds within their borders and likewise their interests and rights in water utilization and control...."[6]

Although later reduced to six regions and just recently to five, the Bureau had expanded to seven regions by 1944 and was given the following designations in 1972: Region I, Pacific Northwest, Boise, Idaho; Region II, Mid-Pacific, Sacramento, California; Region III, Lower Colorado, Boulder City, Nevada; Region IV, Upper Colorado, Salt Lake City, Utah; Region V, Southwest, Amarillo, Texas (to be merged in 1989); Region VI, Upper Missouri, Billings, Montana; Region VII, Lower Missouri, which has headquarters in the Bureau's 14-story building in the Denver Federal Center.

The directors of these regions have leading roles in program and budget planning, in administering projects, in contracting with water and power users, and in maintaining relationships with state and local agencies.[7] The Bureau refers to the water users, usually known as water contractors, as "clients." Regional directors report to the

Bureau's Commissioner. Bureau personnel include various disciplines with engineers predominating, but private construction firms build the Bureau's projects.[8]

It was not the Region VI director in Billings who assumed a leading role in administering the Missouri Basin projects, but an assistant regional director named William Glenn Sloan. Several months before the Flood Control Act of 1944 was passed Sloan's plan to extend irrigation to virtually all parts of the upper Missouri Basin acquired a following in Congress and in the states to be benefitted. Although Sloan knew at the time that flood-control measures were under discussion in Congress, he made no effort to modify his plan to utilize the surplus water and power the projected projects of the Corps of Engineers could supply.

Sloan's counterpart in the Corps, Colonel Lewis A. Pick, who had little experience in water projects, having served mainly in constructing military installations, was equally rigid in adhering to his own plan.[9] Pick, however, was an expert publicist who gained what he thought was sufficient support to get his plan adopted without modifications. He did not succeed, but he later redeemed himself in Burma. After the War he became Chief of Engineers of the Corps.[10] Sloan had to be satisfied with the dubious honor of being part of the Pick-Sloan Plan.

Pick's plan projecting more and higher levees, flood-protection dams, and improved navigation by deepening an existing channel may have been in progress before the floods of 1943 caused death and devastation in the lower Missouri basin. Sloan's grandiose and voluminous plan had been in progress somewhat longer.[11] It was Pick's proposal to deepen the six-foot channel to nine that especially worried Sloan: to keep it full would deprive Sloan of the water he needed to impound for his irrigation projects in the upper basin.[12] A third plan under consideration was a Missouri Valley Authority to which President Franklin Roosevelt was committed.

Each plan had its supporters in the public sector, in Congress, and in the news media. An MVA along the lines of the Tennessee Valley Authority may have been the best answer to the Missouri basin's multiple problems, of which more agricultural development was not the most pressing. Its diverse resources were better suited to industrial development than farming. Also, a wedding of the Bureau and the Corps of Engineers--agencies extremely jealous of each others' prerogatives--was unrealistic. Among other considerations, Roosevelt had that in mind when he signed the Flood Control Act on December 22, 1944, with the admonition that it was not to rule out passage of legislation creating a Missouri Valley Authority.[13]

Initially the Flood Control Act was intended only for flood control wherever it was needed on the country's problem rivers. Congressmen looked to Pick, not Sloan, for advice in formulating House Bill No. 4485, introduced March 27, 1944, by the chairman of the House Flood Control Committee.[14] Sloan's detailed plan was submitted to Congress in May, followed in June by irrigation amendments drafted principally by Senator O'Mahoney of Wyoming and Senator Millikin of Colorado. With those amendments in hand an irrigation conference was quietly arranged at a Midwestern city hotel, September 7 and 8. Commissioner Bashore and his chief counsel were said to be in their rooms when the Bureau's friends and supporters added to the amendments a new section authorizing Bureau participation in Missouri Basin development under section 9 of the Reclamation Project Act of 1939.[15] The Corps had just been upstaged by an adversary grown surprisingly powerful in previous years.

Pending a vote on the proposed legislation, the Corps and the Bureau were given to understand that a Missouri Valley Authority was in the offing if they didn't consolidate and coordinate the respective plans of Colonel Pick and Mr. Sloan. They did so in Omaha in October at taxpayer expense, for neither Pick nor Sloan made more than token revisions. Insisting on 107 of the 113 projects for the Missouri and its tributaries, they managed to almost double the cost.[16] Congress allowed the number to stand when it passed the Flood Control Act in December. Section 9 of the Act authorized two hundred million dollars apiece "for the partial accomplishment of the works to be undertaken...," an infinitesimal fraction of what these projects are costing the public.[17]

Corps and Bureau projects invariably cost far more than their estimates. Congress is accustomed to that, but it did not anticipate that so much productive land would be inundated to irrigate poor land, or that the environmental damage would be so excessive. The Bureau's Garrison diversion project became especially controversial.

"Opposed by the Canadian government, conservationalists, hunters and the National Taxpayers Union," a compromise was reached early in 1985 when the $1.1 billion project was scaled down to irrigate half as much land, provide more water to municipalities, and preserve a national wildlife refuge.[18]

In North Dakota much of the prairie land is not suitable for irrigation and in South Dakota only about half of the one million acres Sloan planned to irrigate were later found to be irrigable.[19] Growing crops on some areas adversely affected by the Garrison project would be like trying to grow crops in Alaska's permafrost region, this author was told while reviewing slides of the project in the early 1970s.[20]

Project failures of the past in the Dakotas, Montana, and Wyoming prompted Sloan to make a provision in his plan for remedial measures to improve them.[21] He succeeded mainly in making worse the problems of unsuspecting farm families. When the old Riverton (Wyoming) project was revamped with a view to irrigating 100,000 acres instead of 42,000, financially qualified World War II veterans were invited to draw lots to establish 104 farms. Within a few years it proved to be an invitation to disaster. In 1953 Congress had to pass legislation to relocate the disadvantaged families to lands in Idaho, Arizona, California, and the Columbia Basin, so poor was their Wyoming land.[22] Several years of hard work and the expenditure of thousands of dollars in hard cash was the lot of these unfortunate farmers, 78 of whom had left for reclamation projects in other states by 1955.[23] Relocation presumably was accomplished under the Farm Unit Exchange Act.[24]

Wyoming has never had much potential for the development of irrigated agriculture other than for hay and grain. Under reclamation law as first conceived, it was entitled to federal projects based on the sales of public lands as were all the arid and semi-arid states. Furthermore, its wealth of oil and coal resulted in royalties that by law were shared with the reclamation fund. So it got its share of projects, including several that watered alkaline soils. Its most successful project probably is the Buffalo Bill, but it took a half century to make it so. Originally known as the Shoshone project, the Bureau took it over in 1905 from private entrepreneurs operating under the Carey Act of 1894. By 1964 the Buffalo Bill had cost the government almost

$24 million.[25]

The Bureau had better luck in Colorado, but it cannot claim all the credit for its successful Colorado-Big Thompson Project. Conceived by Coloradoans long before the federal government was looking for ways to put people to work in the 1930s, it was promoted principally by Charles Hansen of the Greeley Tribune. Supplemental water for irrigated agriculture in the South Platte Valley was its main purpose, but Hansen and others also saw a potential to develop hydroelectric power to serve Greeley, Fort Collins, and other Front Range cities in Northern Colorado.[26]

To expedite their project the Northern Colorado Water Users Association was formed.[27] Composed of representatives of farm, ranch, and local governmental groups, the association lobbied for and got the project with passage of the Interior Department Appropriation Act of August 9, 1937, in which the Bureau was authorized to begin work as soon as repayment of "all costs of the project" was assured by appropriate contracts with a water conservancy district or other acceptable water users' association, duly organized under Colorado law.[28] The association became the nucleus of the Northern Colorado Water Conservancy District which in 1938 negotiated a contract with the government to pay no more than $25 million for a project estimated at that time to cost $44 million.[29]

The Colorado-Big Thompson project, designed to serve 615,000 acres of farmland with supplemental water and to provide electricity at modest rates to Front Range cities, cost $164 million by the time it was fully operational in 1957.[30] The acreage limitation does not apply. The rationale for lifting it was based on the contention that the water was supplemental to a non-federal irrigation system then in operation on farms relatively few of which exceeded 160 acres.[31]

The Pick-Sloan projects that were constructed concurrently with the Colorado-Big Thompson project suffered by comparison. By the time Truman's Hoover Commission report was published in 1949, the original cost estimates of the former had tripled and Pick-Sloan's pie-in-the-sky was in ill repute. The six-billion-dollar, poorly put together projects disturbed the Commission's natural resources task force and its water resources projects task force. The natural resources task force criticized the Corps as well as the Bureau.

Operations had commenced "in the face of uncertainties." There was a lack of "basic data." "Planning was not undertaken in the proper order." The plan had not been "sufficiently evaluated in terms of the national interest." It lacked a "complete program for the valley as a whole."[32] Truman tried to pull the disparate parts together and so did Congress, but two dozen federal bureaus and agencies tied to one or more aspects of the Pick-Sloan plan could not be coordinated with the Bureau-Corps combine in command.[33]

The Bureau and the Corps are construction-oriented. As such, they want to build. In the upper Missouri Basin where about four and a half million acres were under irrigation, the Bureau could claim to have irrigated but 550,000 by 1940. With the Pick-Sloan projects it hoped to irrigate almost five million more. Since 1903 the Bureau's irrigation ventures in the Missouri Basin had not been impressive enough to attract much public support. The Milk River project in Montana was a disaster that Secretary Lane had to deal with in 1913. The North Platte project in Wyoming served mainly Nebraska. The Buford-Trenton and Williston projects in North Dakota were written off in 1926 at a loss of $630,500. Several other projects were written off by Congress in 1952 at a loss of $6,674,000.[34] Reclamation Service Engineer Frank Weymouth had searched all of North Dakota lying west of the Missouri River for a feasible project in 1903. He thought the Lower Yellowstone River, two-thirds of which is in Montana, might do. The project, constructed in an area of alkali soil, was opened to settlement in 1908 and declared a failure in 1917.[35]

In the 1940s the Bureau was still spreading water on poor land. In June 1948, said the task force, the Bureau had under construction in the Missouri Basin "17 reservoirs and the associated irrigation works" designed to irrigate 406,000 acres of new land and to provide supplemental water to 660,000 acres then under irrigation.[36]

The Corps had under construction "six reservoirs..., 15 local flood protection projects, and 3 navigation projects."[37] Apropos those projects, the task force criticized the inadequacy of surface and groundwater data, soils and geologic data, stream sediment load, and other missing data. Scientists in the Geological Survey and the Soil Conservation Service had to be called upon to augment the Bureau's data.[38]

Looking at the astronomical cost of the Missouri Basin

projects, the task force said that "since nearly all of the initial capital for the planned development of the Missouri Basin, and a considerable part of the final cost, [would] be contributed by all of the people of the United States, the relation of the program to national interest must be considered an item of first importance."[39] The Bureau has never viewed its projects in this light; it maintains that the projects return the capital to the taxpayers by making available cheaper food and cotton products and by requiring the irrigators to pay project and water delivery costs. It does not publicize the fact that many of its clients are in arrears and that subsidies for recent projects are nearing 100 percent.[40]

In viewing the implementation of the Pick- Sloan plan in 1948, the task force saw no evidence of efforts to equalize the opportunity for employment in the Upper Missouri Basin, thereby mitigating some of the social and economic distress so much a part of life in a region that was rapidly losing its inhabitants to states with better opportunities and a kinder climate. Both the Bureau and the Corps, oriented as they are to creating and maintaining projects successful from the standpoint of engineering--not facilities for promoting industrial development and urban planning--prompted the task force to say: "It would seem that regional conservation and development is not being looked upon as a dynamic process of indefinite duration, but is an emergency objective, which will drop out of focus until another emergency arises."[41] Quoting the Department of Agriculture it said: "'Making water available to a semidesert or subhumid area does not of itself guarantee successful development. Sound social and economic engineering is as essential to the success of such projects as is adequate engineering of the physical...plant.'"[42]

The task force then turned its attention to raw materials and food production in a subhumid area where a probable rainfall of 27 inches annually had made dryfarming successful, except in years of drought. Would those farmers take to irrigated agriculture? It would mean a reduction in the size of many farms were they to abide by the 160-acre limitation. After years of dry farming, would they adopt the techniques irrigated agriculture requires? These and other questions the Bureau left unanswered when it insisted that North and South Dakota and eastern Nebraska-- where half of the "proposed new irrigated acreage" was to be located--must "look squarely to new lands and stabilized agriculture resulting from irrigation, if the production of food and clothing" was to keep pace with the "growing population of the United States and depletion of soil fertility in the Eastern states."[43] It was an old song often heard. The task force was not convinced. "This is a position not yet factually supported," they said.[44]

In 1944, 29 percent of the "irrigable land on completed reclamation projects in the West was unused," according to the Bureau of Agricultural Economics.[45] Yet, William E. Warne, Assistant Commissioner of Reclamation, stated in January 1945 that the Bureau was proposing "nothing less than the full development of the water and related resources of the West."[46] "In view of this ambition," said the task force, "not only an evaluation of present projects in terms of the national scene is needed, but a means of looking over <u>critically</u> future projects of a similar nature."[47] [Emphasis added]

A critical look at the Missouri-Souris region might have disclosed that it was not the place to put a project and a properly designed survey might have disclosed insufficient support for one. On the basis of a "small sample survey" of farmers in the region, the Bureau maintained that a majority of them were in favor of the project.[48] The Bureau is fond of small sample surveys; skillfully used they can justify a project that should not be built. When the reclamation fund ran out of money from the sales of public lands, the Bureau had had to devise other means to obtain funding. With a small sample survey it could convince Congress of a project's desirability. If the Bureau can show significant support for a project, Western congressmen are likely to get Congress to fund it; funding--even a well-timed congressional authorization--can produce votes at election time in project states.

Pushing the Missouri-Souris project proved to be a serious mistake. The names of the congressmen who participated have been forgotten, leaving the Bureau to bear the brunt of adverse criticism.[49] In Sloan's hurry to produce a grandiose plan for the Missouri Basin he neglected to make a thorough study of the soils to be irrigated. Later much of the project in North and South Dakota was reduced in size. Especially was this necessary in the loop of the Souris River in North Dakota, and the Redfield region of South Dakota.[50] As a consequence Sloan had to accept a drastic reduction in the size and cost of these project units.[51] The chronology of events is of interest.

In 1957 the Missouri-Souris unit was substantially cut back to accommodate the Garrison unit, estimated at that time to cost $695 million.[52] In 1965 Congress mandated that water delivered from the Garrison unit be restricted to the irrigation of nonsurplus crops and that fish and wildlife be protected in accordance with the Fish and Wildlife Coordination Acts of 1946 and 1958.[53] (During the Reagan administration Congress withdrew the surplus crop restriction.) In 1975 the displeasure of the Canadian government regarding the impact of the Garrison unit on the Souris, Assiniboine, and Red Rivers was before Congress and so were environmental concerns on this side of the border. Another substantial cutback in the unit was made in 1985.[54] The task force had been fully justified in 1949 in urging a critical look at such projects.[55] Apropos the outcome of the Pick-Sloan projects, the task force wondered whether farmers in semihumid areas would be willing to pay for irrigation works and water to irrigate their crops? Would the remaining crop lands compensate for the bottom lands inundated by a Bureau reservoir?[56]

The Bureau's planning was backward, said the task force. Big dams and other large engineering structures had been "planned without reference to multiple demands for the same water, and without knowledge of the likely over-all pattern of social and economic development." Multiple-purpose projects are supposed to serve without undue conflict the needs of navigation, flood control, power production, irrigation, domestic and industrial users; they must, therefore, be designed to accomodate droughts as well as periods of normal and above normal precipitation. The task force feared the projects would invite a test of constitutionality. The fact that the projects had been planned "in many of their phases without adequate data on soil fertility, irrigability, water amount and quality, consumer acceptance of irrigation, and basic economic data," was especially disturbing.[57]

Henry Hart in The Dark Missouri was as critical of the Missouri Basin projects as the task force. Of more than a hundred projects on the Pick-Sloan list, Congress initially appropriated funds for eight. Eight years later, after the expenditure of five million dollars on surveys, the Bureau learned that only two of the eight projects were satisfactory for irrigation and flood control; two were of doubtful value. Conditions such as soil suitability justified rejection of the remaining four.[58]

Large reservoirs in relatively flat country may inundate up to several hundred thousand acres of land--often prime farm land. The Bureau's message to potential irrigators is convincing at the outset, and relatively few farmers reject it initially. It is later that they learn how much land they stand to lose, and it is then that the Bureau and the Corps run into opposition. Floods the farmers would like to be without, and irrigation would be nice to have in years of little rain, but it was not the Upper Missouri Basin farmers who pressured Congress to pass the Flood Control Act of 1944; it was the politicians.

The Bureau was to find in the subhumid states a resistance to irrigation it had not anticipated. The farmers there were a different breed from those the Bureau was accustomed to. They were more self-sufficient; more innovative. Suspicious by nature of government interference, many of them banded together to build their own irrigation systems when drought struck during the early 1950s. It would take years to get wheat farmers off their tractors and into hip boots to maintain ditches on the Bureau's projects. Many of those farmers have since accepted irrigation as a concommitant of fashionable farming, but there are still a few strongholds of embattled resisters, holding off the Bureau and the Corps.

Inasmuch as the Corps' projects on the Missouri preceded the Bureau's, it was the Corps that used force majeure to pry Indians from their homes.[59] The Bureau, however, has little to offer those 900 dislocated Indian families, over half of whom are Sioux. Corps dams have "inundated more than 202,000 acres of Sioux land," said Michael Lawson in his definitive and thoroughly documented study of the Missouri River Sioux.[60] Forced to move from their rich river bottom lands to the empty prairies, they have neither the capital nor the will to start over again. So that cities can maintain their industrially developed river properties with a minimum of flooding the Indians have had to give up their timber lands and their hay meadows; their grazing lands and their homesites.[61]

Although the Missouri dams are reducing the number of deaths attributable to floods, they are not reducing property damage.[62] Apparently they have not even given the boost to the economy that was anticipated. A recent article in U. S. Water News, referring to South Dakota, states that "For years, sidewalk political analysts at coffee shops and diners across South Dakota have complained about how the state has been shortchanged by the federal government for the loss of thousands of acres of productive land flooded by four massive Missouri River dams." Of the four Pick-Sloan dams in South Dakota, which account for a loss of about a half million acres, Oahe Reservoir has inundated 319,000 acres.[63]

Agricultural economist Jay Leitch, in his study for South Dakota officials, estimated a personal income loss of $378 million over the past 25 years. Other losses, estimated in 1985 dollars on an annual basis, include $27.5 million in retail trade; $1.1 million in sales tax, mostly attributable to the 1,225 jobs that could be expected to exist if the dams had not been built. Leitch estimated tremendous losses to the cattle industry, $52.6 million from Oahe alone with its inundation of 319,000 acres. With the cattle industry went 835 jobs. South Dakota officials now maintain that the state would be better off had it developed the "river's hydropower on its own, rather than letting the federal government do it."[64] Other similarly impacted states are likely to agree. With good reason the Hoover Commission task force took a dim view of the Pick-Sloan plan as the answer to the needs of the Upper Misssouri Basin states.

The failure of the Missouri River dams to protect flood-prone properties has not been lost on the Corps, however. For the past two decades it has been amenable to the virtues of non-structural remedies such as flood-plain zoning and flood-proofing of structures as a means to protect lives and property.[65] Regrettably what the Bureau and the Corps have learned from their mistakes in the Upper Missouri Basin comes too late for that damaged region.

NOTES

1. Andrews and Sansone, supra, 182. Full citation, 3, note 14.

2. Ibid., 182-83; 53 Stat. 1196, 43 U.S.C., sec. 485h(e); Leland O. Graham, Some Aspects of Federal-State Relationships in California Water Resources Development (Mimeo., 1961), 175-178.

3. Andrews and Sansone, supra; 53 Stat. 1196, U.S.C., sec. 485h(e).

4. Ibid., including sec. 485h(d) and all of the annotation for Section 9, the "Repayment" provision.

5. Leveen and King, supra. Full citation 3, note 29.

6. 58 Stat. 887; 33 U.S.C sec. 701-1.

7. Warne, supra, 25-28. Full citation, 3, note 26.

8. Ibid., 28-29.

9. Marian E. Ridgeway. The Missouri Basin's Pick-Sloan Plan: A Case Study in Congressional Policy Determination (Urbana: University of Illinois Press, 1955) 161-62.

10. Ibid., 162.

11. Michael L. Lawson. Damned Indians: The Pick-Sloan Plan and the Missouri River Sioux, 1944-1980 (Norman: University Press, 1982) 15-16. Sloan expected to irrigate 4.8 million acres of land, and to produce annually four billion kilowatt-hours of power with his $1.26 billion structures on the Missouri and its tributaries.

12. Although the proposed nine-foot channel has not been considered to be part of the Pick plan, and it was not authorized until 1945, it was very much at issue when the Pick and Sloan plans were being discussed in 1944. Also see Rufus Terral, The Missouri Valley (New Haven: Yale University Press, 1947) 120-24. For more on Pick's plan, see Lawson, supra, 12-13.

13. Henry C. Hart, The Dark Missouri (Madison: University of Wisconsin Press, 1957) 132; Ridgeway, supra, 158-60.

14. Chairman of the House Flood Control Committee Will Whittington, a Mississippi congressman, is quoted in the Congressional Record, November 22, 1944, p. 4123, as saying: "With repeated floods, especially from Sioux City to St. Louis, there can be no question but what the dominant interest along the Missouri River Basin is flood control."

15. Hart, supra, 127-129; Ridgeway, supra, Appendix D, 340.

16. Lawson, supra, 19.

17. 58 Stat. 891.

18. Dale Russakoff, "Ending an Irrigation Dispute/North Dakota plan signed," Washington Post Weekly, February 4, 1985. A map of the project area, as originally planned, accompanies the article. Dean Whiteway, Canadian House of Commons, expressed concern in 1975. See Congressional Record, June 20, 1975, p. 20,005, regarding anticipated impact of Garrison Diversion Project on Souris,

Assiniboine and Red rivers.

19. Lawson, supra, 185.

20. Included in the Garrison project are the lands in North Dakota extending westward from the Red River of the North about two-thirds of the distance across the state, and in South Dakota the lands along its northern boundary. See Hart, supra, 163, Fig. 13.

21. For description of the Pick-Sloan plan see Senate Document 80, 75th Congress, and here and there in Hart, supra, 155-163.

22. Hart, supra, 159. 67 Stat. 566.

23. Hart, supra, 159.

24. 67 Stat. 566.

25. T. A. Larson. History of Wyoming (Lincoln: University of Nebraska Press, 1965) 355- 56. Professor Larson covers in detail Wyoming's various irrigation projects.

26. Marshall Sprague. Colorado/A Bicentennial History (New York: Norton & Company, 1976), 167; Mary L. Geffs, Under Ten Flags/A History of Weld County, Colorado (Greeley, Colorado, 1938), Chapter XV.

27. Charles W. Howe, et al, "Innovations in Water Management...," in Scarce Water and Institutional Change, ed. by Kenneth D. Frederick, 1986, at p. 171-180; Charles W. Howe, "Project Benefits and Costs from National and Regional Viewpoints: Methodological Issues and Case Study of the Colorado-Big Thompson Project," Natural Resources Journal, Vol. 27, No. 1 (Winter 1987), 9-10.

28. 50 Stat. 595. See also Federal Reclamation and Related Laws Annotated, Vol. I, 565.

29. Hart, supra, 157; Howe, et al, supra, 183-199; Howe, supra, 9-10.

30. Howe, et al, supra, 181-183; Howe, supra, 9-10.

31. Act of June 16, 1938, Ch. 485, 52 Stat. 764; Montgomery and Clawson, supra, 144. Full citation, 3, note 4.

32. U. S. Commission on Organization of the Executive Branch of the Government, Herbert Hoover, Chairman. Task Force Report on Natural Resources (Washington, D.C., 1949) Appendix L, 108.

33. Ibid.

34. Hart, supra, 114.

35. Ibid., 112.

36. U. S. Commission on Organization..., supra, 118.

37. Ibid.

38. Ibid.

39. Ibid., 119.

40. John Fogarty, "A Bill to Make Farms Pay More for U. S. Water." San Francisco Chronicle, March 19, 1981.

41. U. S. Commission on Organization..., supra, 121.

42. Ibid.

43. Ibid., 121-123.

44. Ibid., 123.

45. Ibid., 122.

46. Ibid., 123.

47. Ibid.

48. Ibid., 122.

49. Ridgeway, supra, 298.

50. Hart, supra, 162.

51. Ridgeway, supra, 86.

52. Lawson, supra, 185.

53. 79 Stat. 433.

54. Russakoff, supra.

55. U. S. Commission on Organization..., supra, 123.

56. Ibid., 134.

57. Ibid., 136-137.

58. Hart, supra, 162-169.

59. U. S. Commission on Organization of the Executive Branch of the Government. Task Force Report on Water Resources Projects, Washington, D.C., 1949, Appendix K, 40.

60. Lawson, supra, 27-29. Note impact on four Indian reservations in South Dakota, page 28; Anon., "S.D. wants payback from Pick-Sloan," U. S. Water News, May 1988, 24. Governor George S. Mickelson noted that the state had lost over 520,000 acres..."including almost 180,000 acres on... Indian reservations."

61. Lawson, supra, 29.

62. Gilbert F. White. Flood Hazard in the United States: A Research Assessment (Boulder: University of Colorado, Institute of Behavioral Science, 1975) 30.

63. Anon., "S.D. has damage estimate for Missouri R. dams,"

U.S. Water News, Aug. 1987, 9.

64. Ibid.

65. White, supra, 22; Earl J. Baker and Joe Gordon McPhee. Land Use Management and Regulation in Hazardous Areas: A Research Assessment (Boulder: University of Colorado, Institute of Behavioral Science, 1975) 90-91. Under the Water Resources Development Act of 1974, the Corps can consider "non-structural" alternatives to the extent of moving structures out of floodplains when funded by congressional authorization; National Science Foundation. A Report on Flood Hazard Mitigation (Washington, D.C., September 1980), 61. (The Bureau is listed here as Water and Power Resources Service, a name given it during the Carter administration but abandoned during the Reagan administration.) For a useful reference on non-structural measures, see Colonel Gerald E. Galloway's "A Review of the Use of Non-Structural Measures in Flood Damage Reduction Activities of the Departments of Agriculture, Army and Interior," U.S. Water Resources Council, Washington, D.C., July 1980.

5
Games Bureaucrats Play

The previous chapter explored the problems of Bureau-Corps jurisdiction over the development of irrigation and flood control projects in the Missouri River Basin. Although the Corps of Engineers has become amenable to flood-proofing flood-prone areas with non-structural methods, competition with the Bureau of Reclamation to build new projects is endemic. As in the Missouri River Basin, Bureau and Corps projects in Western states tend to overlap from the planning stage on up. Other federal agencies guilty of such overlapping are the Department of Agriculture, the Bureau of Indian Affairs, Bonneville Power Administration, and the Southwestern Power Administration. Although the Bureau and the Corps are the two principal construction agencies in the West, the others also are in competition for jurisdiction over projects.[1]

Speaking of Bureau-Corps overlapping, duplication, and competition, the Bureau's regional director Richard Boke said in 1947:

> ...Each has a mandate from Congress, and each is properly aggressive for its own job and its own jurisdiction.
>
> The legislative tactics of both agencies are similar. Each seeks authorizations from the same Congress to plan and ultimately construct the same dams, or, if not the same dams, different dams to perform the same services. Each has a measure of success even to the point of

securing identical authorizations for the same dams in the same streams.[2]

In four decades Congress has done little to discourage this kind of competition despite several efforts in the Executive Department to merge the Bureau and the Corps. About all that can be said in Congress' favor during the present era of astronomical deficits, crop and water subsidies, over-production, and surplus crops produced with cheap irrigation water, is its present restraint in funding new projects. However, Congress is not stopping the Bureau from "counting the production of surplus crops as a benefit of some of the new water projects that individual members of Congress are currently promoting," editorialized the Fresno Bee in April 1988.[3]

Figuring the benefits and costs of a proposed project is a complicated process. It is difficult to allocate costs in planning multiple- purpose projects: they are theoretical and rather loosely arrived at. Though the procedures have been refined over time, the statement of the Hoover Commission's Water Resources Task Force is still germane: "Material presented to Congress regarding allocations is frequently either so inadequate or so technical that judgements are seriously hampered."[4] When benefits are overstated as they were by the Bureau for the Missouri Basin projects in 1944 (2.57 to 1) or construction costs far exceed estimated costs or adverse economic impacts such as those in South Dakota become apparent,[5] the Bureau has further burdened the taxpaying public.

The reason federal construction agencies tend to overstate the benefits and understate the costs is obvious; if they don't their chance of getting congressional authorization for a project would be nil unless Congress decided the Nation's well-being would be jeopardized if it were not built. The Water Resources Task Force suggested the following questions be incorporated in irrigation policies to avoid the kind of problems associated with the Missouri Basin and other major projects it examined where benefit-cost analyses were in error:

a. Is the loss in land values resultant from flooding bottom lands plus the cost of irrigating new lands, commensurate with the value of land reclaimed?

b. Should irrigation projects be initiated if they do not appear likely to produce revenues adequate to provide for self-support and eventual self-liquidation?

c. Would it not be wiser to spend equivalent monies on soil conservation projects on farms and on upstream tributaries in lieu of spending them on large downstream projects; in other words, is it more economical to preserve the land we have than to reclaim the land we have lost?[6]

Apropos the last question the Task Force recommended a "Shift of emphasis from development of channelized water to water conservation in connection with land use and soil conservation."[7] Apropos the second question it recommended a "return to the policy of requiring local contributions."[8] Despite the games that have been played by the Bureau, the Corps, and the Department of Agriculture to get pet projects authorized and funded, progress has been made in the improvement of benefit-cost assessment methods and the projects are being more carefully scrutinized for social, environmental, and economic impacts.

A few examples of how the games are played are nevertheless of interest. In 1949, during the year the first Hoover Commission report appeared, the Central Arizona Project was under consideration by the House Subcommittee on Irrigation and Reclamation. The Bureau's V. E. Larson testified that the project was feasible. California Congressman Clair Engle, in disputing Larson's statement, quoted a Bureau of the Budget report that said, "the project as proposed is economically infeasible under existing reclamation laws."[9] Larson was relying on legislation extending the repayment period for power facilities in connection with this multiple-purpose project. Construction costs of irrigation facilities are interest-free; construction costs of power facilities are not. By prolonging the repayment period Larson increased benefits over costs sufficiently to make the project feasible and assure the Bureau's power-company clients a competitive rate for the sale of power.

Said Rep. Engle to Larson, "You have had to change the reclamation laws, have you not...to make this a feasible project; is this not true?"[10] Not only was Larson caught short on this question, but Engle made him admit that the benefit-cost ratio for CAP reflected gross crop returns instead of net returns.[11]

Two years before the Central Arizona Project was authorized in 1968, the Bureau was in a battle with environmentalists for the damsites it needed for the project. David Brower, an experienced hand at finding flaws in Bureau proposals, wrote in an open letter to Secretary Stewart Udall: "You remember our proving how bad their arithmetic about the reservoir evaporation was a few years ago--how in the Echo Park battle they were awarded a rubber slide rule for stretching the truth. They are still at it. Now they claim they need two cash-register dams (their term) in Grand Canyon...."[12]

The two damsites--Bridge Canyon and Marble Gorge--were cited by John Baldwin for "Analytical Deficiencies" in the benefit-cost analysis.[13] Charles Howe and William Easter raised the issue of opportunity costs, the existence of which they feel should be reflected in the benefit-cost analysis. In addition to the three classes of costs associated with interbasin transfers--"direct construction, operating, and maintenance costs"--there should be included in the analysis "the opportunity costs of both the land involved in the project site or sites and the water in the area of origin, and the external costs imposed on parties removed from the project site." "External costs," they continue, "may stem from water quality degradation, or they may take the form of a loss of incomes to immobile resources in regions which 'lose out' competitively to those receiving new water."[14] They cite the Central Arizona Project among others where such costs should have been included. A benefit-cost analysis that reflects all the true costs as well as the anticipated benefits can be a useful tool. If it overstates the benefits and/or understates the costs it can be "A Tricky Game."[15]

Subsidy programs, another arena of game-playing, operate on an international scale and are defended as essential by many countries. Canada and the United States opposed them at a recent meeting on free trade. In reporting the meeting for the Associated Press, Barry Schweid wrote:

> Already on the summit agenda was a U.S. joust with the Europeans over agriculture subsidies. The U. S. delegation, probably joined by Canada, will seek an end of all agricultural subsidies, but the idea is meeting stiff resistance from France and West Germany....With countries around the world spending $150 billion to $200 billion on farm subsidies, Canadian Prime Minister Brian Mulroney said, "It is very important that all of us,

including Japan, recognize that these subsidies to agriculture are trade-distorting in nature (and) eventually protectionist."[16]

The Bureau is aware that subsidy programs benefiting its clients are under fire nationally, but when the Acreage Limitation Branch in Denver showed progress in enforcing the Reclamation Reform Act of 1982 to limit their abuse its Branch Chief was transferred to another position. What appears to have precipitated the transfer was his candid acknowledgement to Congressman Sam Gejdenson, author of a bill to reform the irrigation subsidy program, that the annual westwide subsidy on Bureau projects is $2.2 billion, not the $534 million his superiors in the Secretary's office would like the public to believe.[17] For cumulative costs since 1902, the Secretary's office reported $9.8 billion; the Bureau in Denver reported $24.4 billion.[18] According to the report of the Congressional Budget Office sent to Gejdenson on October 12, 1988: "Using BuRec data but adjusting its procedures results in estimates of the cost of providing the irrigation subsidy ranging from $33.7 billion to $70.3 billion...."[19] (See Appendix B for entire report.)

Six relatively recent projects demonstrate the cost of the Bureau's subsidized projects. They carry price tags up to $130 an acre-foot of water in 1981 dollars.[20] The subsidies on them have been estimated at: 97.8% for the North Loup Division of the Pick-Sloan Missouri Basin project; 96.4% for the Pollock-Herreid Unit of the Pick-Sloan project; 95.0% for the Frying Pan- Arkansas River project in Colorado; 94.5% for the Auburn-Folsom Unit of the Central Valley Project; 92.3% for the Oroville-Tonasket Unit Extension of the Chief Joseph Dam Project in Washington; 92.2% for the Dallas Creek Participating Project in Colorado.[21]

By 1977 Bureau projects were irrigating about one-fifth of the 50.2 million acres under irrigation in the 17 contiguous Western states.[22] It is questionable and also controversial whether land that has been successfully dryfarmed should be irrigated but the Bureau and some congressmen have a stake in enlarging the government's water and power domain. Western congressmen find it expedient to obtain seats on House and Senate Interior committees, especially the subcommittees that deal with water and power.

The goal of politicians is to get elected: to promise projects to regions of constituency support brings campaign contributions and votes. Politicians who make it to Congress from the West must woo their Eastern counterparts if their special-interest legislation is to pass.[23] An examination of political contributions from agribusiness at any given time will show which non-Western congressmen are obligated to cooperate with their Western counterparts in the pursuance of new irrigation projects and interbasin water transfers.

The Bureau, no less than Western congressmen, displays an intense interest in reclamation projects it wishes to undertake. Suggestions for enabling legislation may emanate with the Commissioner, or they may emanate within one of the Bureau's regions. The Commissioner presents the project proposals to the Interior secretary who clears them with the Executive Office of the President.[24] Such proposals are then presented formally by the Secretary of the Interior to the president of the Senate and the speaker of the House. The Water and Power Resources Subcommittee, as the name suggests, has jurisdiction over federal water projects in the House; its counterpart in the Senate is the Subcommittee on Water and Power.[25] These committees prepare the reclamation legislation, giving due weight to the desires of the Bureau. Lobbyists for a particular project or program add another aspect to the process; indeed, the lobbying may extend to the administration in power, and to Congress. Typically the legislation reflects a compromise, often so poorly worded that those who implement it will be at a loss to make it function as intended.

A case in point is the Central Valley Project, a state project in the planning stage before it was taken over by the federal government in 1935 and assigned to the Corps of Engineers.[26] Soon afterward it was transferred to the Bureau. It was reauthorized in 1937, and at various times thereafter. One of its most controversial aspects involves fish and wildlife conservation. Predating the passage of the CVP Act is the 1934 Act to "promote the conservation of wild life, fish and game."[27] The Bureau has wobbled back and forth on whether its projects are subject to fish and wildlife conservation. At times it views the CVP Act's wording and intent as if the Act and subsequent reauthorizations were contracts: unless Congress spells out in each one precisely what it must do to conserve fish and wildlife habitats, it is not obligated to do anything.

After the Fish and Wildlife Coordination Act was passed in 1946, the Bureau's obligations became somewhat clearer. A memorandum by Acting Solicitor J. R. Armstrong in 1954 should have put the controversy to rest. Said Armstrong: "...the terms of the Coordination Act authorizing allocations for wildlife conservation are applicable to those portions of the Central Valley Project, the construction of which was begun after August 14, 1946,"[28] the date of passage of the Coordination Act.

Armstrong's opinion was given more than lip service in September 1976 during a congressional hearing before the Subcommittee on Water and Power Resources.[29] Notwithstanding congressional acceptance of fish and wildlife conservation as an established purpose of CVP, a regional solicitor in the Sacramento office issued a memorandum on April 14, 1977, stating that "without further Congressional legislation, the Bureau of Reclamation may utilize CVP water for fish and wildlife purposes only in those instances where such use has been authorized by Congress...and where such use would not otherwise infringe upon presently authorized functions."[30] [Emphasis added.] At a public hearing in August congressional leaders learned that "because of the Bureau's unwillingness to meet water quality objectives in the [Sacramento-San Joaquin] delta during 1976 and early 1977, the State Water Project was required to release 172,000 acre-feet to make up the Bureau's share of delta outflow."[31] The Bureau does not stand on firm ground when it ignores the needs of the Delta to which it committed the federal government in 1935, or the needs of fisheries protected by fish and wildlife legislation. Although it is trying with innovative structures to mitigate damage from dam and diversion projects in California and perhaps elsewhere, it is apparently too early to expect much in the way of favorable results.[32]

In general the pattern of compliance of federal construction agencies with fish and wildlife legislation is not impressive. From time to time Congress has requested the Government Accounting Office to investigate the violations. GAO reports cite specific projects where Fish and Wildlife Service recommendations were bypassed.[33] Unfortunately fish and wildlife do not have an aggressive defender on the administrative level such as the irrigators have in the Bureau of Reclamation. Interior solicitors tend to read into Bureau contracts very little protection for fish and wildlife, apparently with little opposition from Interior's office of the Assistant Secretary of Fish and Wildlife and Parks.

When the Bureau conceives a water project it emphasizes the recreational advantages. Fishing will improve and waterfowl habitats will be enhanced. "Duck Grounds on West Side To be Protected," reads the caption of a Fresno Bee article written in 1937 when Friant Dam was getting underway. The caption was based on the statement of the Bureau's acting commissioner: "We consider this one of the most critical spots for water fowl preservation in the nation, and Fresno may be assured that we will not overlook any opportunities of furthering the interests of this phase of our valuable wild life resources."[34] The remark was in response to a suggestion from Fresno's city attorney who had wondered whether it was possible "to file a claim to a portion of the first stored flood waters [in Millerton Lake] which could also be sent down the river to be used for flooding at least part of the present duck club lands [near Los Banos] in order to preserve the flight of ducks down the Pacific Coast."[35] The Bureau was amenable to temporary releases of water but an act of Congress was required for a firm supply, an act that did not materialize until 1954.[36] The annual delivery of 50,000 acre-feet is not enough, except in wet years when releases at Friant Dam flood the Grasslands. In 1985 Interior's Office of the Solicitor undertook to define the legal issues in a lengthy opinion, duck club owners having rejected selenium-laced wastewater from local farms.[37] Since then the Grassland Water District board has argued the pros and cons of wastewater augmentation, officially rejecting it, and at a recent meeting voting to rescind the rejection.[38]

What concerned San Joaquin Valley duck hunters as well as Fresno's city attorney in 1937 was the river's inability to flood duck habitats near Los Banos when Friant Dam was completed. Water destined for the Delta which periodically flooded Merced County grasslands was to be diverted to the Friant-Kern and Madera canals following completion of the dam in December 1942. By 1953 the canals were in operation, cutting off the annual floodwaters upon which waterfowl were dependent. The project also destroyed the native salmon population.[39]

Soon after selenium was identified as the cause of waterfowl death and deformation at Kesterson in 1983, U. S. Fish and Wildlife scientists investigated conditions at the Grasslands. For years the aquatic inhabitants had been exposed to selenium and other contaminants carried in the drainwater from upgradient irrigators. Because some fresh water had been supplied and the drainage had an outlet to the river it had taken longer for the problem to materialize. Essentially the San Joaquin River was serving the same purpose as the San Luis Drain which flowed to the Kesterson ponds.

Much of the contaminated drainage from irrigated agriculture on the west side of the San Joaquin Valley travels via tributary streams and sloughs, or seeps into subsurface groundwater, constituting most of the San Joaquin River's flow below Friant Dam. In a presentation to Los Banos area residents in October 1984, a Fish and Wildlife Service retiree called the River the "lower colon of California." He described it as a "stinking sewer contaminated with salts, heavy metals, trace elements, and the residue from the annual application of hundreds of tons of insecticides, herbicides, and fertilizers."[40] Once the salmon runs in the San Joaquin exceeded 100,000; now they are down to "5 or 10 thousand, mostly supported by hatcheries, with no natural spawning in the San Joaquin itself."[41] The process by which drainwater gets to the river, and prior to July 1986 how it got to Kesterson via the San Luis Drain is described by Mike Beno in Ducks Unlimited:

> ...To someone standing on the surface, it all looks like a few ditches and culverts. But the guts of the setup is underground. It resembles the leaching field of a septic system, though one which operates in reverse--water is cxtracted, not injected. Perforated pipe is buried in a parallel pattern, on gravel beds, six to eight feet deep. The lines converge at a sump in a corner of the field. The system pulls excess water from root zones and leaches salts downward and away.[42]

Although the 75,000-acre Grasslands had been getting 50,000 acre-feet annually, supplementing the fresh water inflow were "at least 28,000 acre-feet of tile drain water."[43] Loaded with selenium and other soil constituents, it was creating a Kesterson-type disaster. In March 1985, Felix Smith in the Sacramento office of the Fish and Wildlife Service wrote his superior in Portland spelling out what must be done to save the wildlife and mitigate the damage to the habitat:

> At this time every effort must be made to obtain good quality water, equal in quality to native upper San Joaquin water for all lands/habitat used by migratory birds. In addition, every effort must be made to reduce the amount of selenium-laden waste water being generated by the agricultural community. However, the effects of other metals or chemicals must not be overlooked.[44]

The Fish and Wildlife Service has about 22,000 acres of wetlands in easements in Merced County.[45] By 1984 some duck club owners who had granted easements to FWS began to fault the program. Agricultural wastewater from the surrounding farms was destroying a wildlife habitat to the extent that it had become noticeable. In May, Lloyd Carter, then with the Fresno Bee, learned from Jeff Kerry of the California Waterfowl Association that he had written Region II's Richard Myshak regarding the poor quality of the water, the decline in the area's wildlife, and the absence of frogs and fish.[46] Kerry had asked Myshak whether government officials knew that the area was deteriorating. Myshak's response, which was noncommital, was guarded due to the potential for litigation the problem presented.[47]

The acquisition of conservation easements to preserve wetlands from the plow is a federal program in which the Fish and Wildlife Service interacts with local, state, and federal agencies such as the Bureau. The sum of money per acre that FWS can offer owners of the wetlands is based on a careful appraisal after consultations with all affected individuals and agencies. When irrigation tailwater or drainwater entering the wetlands is tainted, the wetlands soon lose their value as a wildlife habitat and the owners end up with severely damaged land and water.

Supposedly safe levels of total dissolved solids (TDS) and boron have been established for irrigation drainage entering the Grasslands, but some irrigation districts are known to exceed them and also may be exceeding recently established selenium standards. Self-monitoring, which the Bureau is reluctant to police, will probably continue to be lax. Fish and Wildlife Service administrators have reason to be worried about their easement program which was designed to preserve migratory bird flyways. Bureau projects had so increased the value of wetlands for agricultural development that owners were selling out to the highest bidder when the Service initiated this program. By paying owners of wetlands a few hundred dollars an acre for easement rights, FWS hoped to retain them for migratory birds and local waterfowl.

Earl James Foster, an experienced appraiser with FWS from 1971 to December 1985, transferred to the Portland office in 1977 to participate in the program. Among the easements he handled in the Merced County Grasslands was the 985-acre cattle ranch and duck club of James and Karen Claus. When their cattle began to sicken and wildlife to disappear, Claus discussed his observations with Foster. Foster investigated, and learned more than his superiors wanted him to know about an issue that was becoming increasingly sensitive. Warned to develop "amnesia" over water quality issues, he was suspended several days without pay.[48] Foster, who followed official guidelines in making appraisals, told this author that appraisers need more than Public Law 91-646 and the 1973 "Uniform Appraisal Standards for Federal Land Acquisitions" to guide them; they need water quality data pertinent to each parcel they appraise.[49] He mentioned a 1979 report on water quality Roy Leach did for the Soil Conservation Service.[50] The report showed that irrigation tailwater and tile drainage flowing into the Grasslands exceeded on numerous occasions the recommended 2500 parts per million total dissolved solids and the 8.0 parts per million limit for boron.[51] Selenium, though known to be causing bird loss at Kesterson by 1983, had not been quantified when Foster ran into difficulties with his superiors.

Several years earlier Leach had similar difficulties, though not with his superiors in the U. S. Department of Agriculture. During preparation of his report and while seeking funds from the Environmental Protection Agency to continue the investigation, Leach was approached by the attorney for the Grasslands Water District and told, according to UPI reporters: "'If anybody from EPA showed up on any of my tours or I had more correspondence with them, I'd have stronger dealings with the [GWD] board. In other words, I was history....'"[52]

Duck clubs in the Merced County Grasslands appear to be

owned mostly by well-to-do outsiders who hunt waterfowl and who, since selenium was identified, have demanded water of better quality from the Grasslands Water District which historically has had contracts with irrigators to accept their agricultural wastewater. Region I of the Fish and Wildlife Service, hoping to steer clear of trouble with the Bureau which supplies the irrigation districts with water, chose to tell Foster to "go along with the assumption that the GWD was providing specification water to landowners"[53] of whom Robert James Claus was one. Foster soon found himself in the middle of a tense situation in which he was out of favor with his superiors and his superiors were out of favor with Claus. Claus, fed up with bureaucratic gameplaying and the obvious deterioration of his ranch caused by Kesterson, as well as the irrigation water that did not meet specifications, filed claims against FWS and the Bureau and a petition to the California State Water Resources Control Board to close Kesterson.

Although the Board complied in February 1985, the gameplaying continued. Only the principal players changed. When Board member Ken Willis resigned five months later he told a reporter that the Kesterson cleanup order was "'the toughest decision the board had to make, because of the inordinate pressure that was put on the board to try to be more lenient.'"[54] Observers who followed the proceedings know that Willis did not exaggerate. Evidentiary hearings were dominated by agribusiness representatives, mainly from Westlands Water District. The governor was sympathetic to their entreaties. Board members quickly got the message that they would not be reappointed to their well-paid positions. Three of them succumbed to politicking. But as Willis said when the abatement order was under consideration, "'nobody's going to get reappointed to this board if they do the right thing.'"[55] No one was.

Willis, since his appointment in 1982, had been one of the board's most effective members in carrying out the board's water-quality mandate under the state's Porter-Cologne Act. He saw the board's problems in enforcing that Act against agribusiness and refrained from blaming them on the Bureau.[56] Many observers of state and federal actions since Kesterson have little doubt that in bureaucratic game playing, agribusiness has the upper hand in California. Of apparent advantage to agribusiness firms and water and/or irrigation districts are several law firms that are staffed with former Interior Department solicitors and assistant attorneys. The expertise those former government attorneys possess is useful to agribusiness in playing the subsidy game.

NOTES

1. U. S. Commission on Organization of the Executive Branch, supra, 40. Full citation, 4, note 59.

2. Ibid., 41.

3. Editor, "Double-dipping at the well," Fresno Bee, April 4, 1988.

4. U. S. Commission on Organization..., supra, 18.

5. Ibid., 23; Anon., "S.D. has damage estimate for Missouri R. dams" and "S.D. wants payback from Pick-Sloan," supra. Full citation, 4, notes 60 and 63.

6. U. S. Commission on Organization..., supra, 14.

7. Ibid., 47.

8. Ibid.

9. U. S. Congress. The Central Arizona Project. Hearings before a House Subcommittee on Irrigation and Reclamation, Committee on Public Lands. 81st Cong., 1st sess. Part I, Serial No. 11 (Washington: Government Printing Office, 1949) 425.

10. Ibid.

11. U. S. Congress. The Central Arizona Project, supra, 424. Bernard Shanks, "Dams and Disasters: The Social Problems of Water Development Policies" in Bureaucracy vs. Environment, John Baden and Richard L. Stroup (eds.) (Ann Arbor: University of Michigan Press, 1981) 108-123.

12. David Brower. Open letter to The Hon. Stewart L. Udall, Secretary of the Interior, "1902 Bureau methods don't add up in 1966." Ad in the New York Times, June 9, 1966.

13. John H. Baldwin. Environmental Planning and Management (Boulder: Westview Press, 1985), 238.

14. Charles W. Howe and K. William Easter. Interbasin Transfers of Water (Baltimore: Johns Hopkins Press, 1971), 105-106; William K. Easter (Economist, Bureau of the Budget) "Interbasin

Water Transfers--Economic Issues and Impacts," p. 194-98 of Proceedings, 4th American Water Resources Conference. AWRA.

15. Conservation Foundation Letter, "Cost-Benefit Analysis: A Tricky Game" (December 1980) 1-8.

16. Barry Schweid, "U.S., Japan talks on free-trade pact seen as possibility," San Francisco Examiner, June 18, 1988, A7.

17. Michael Doyle, "Lawmakers leery of reclamation shuffle," Fresno Bee, June 13, 1988.

18. Doyle, "Water subsidy cost grossly under estimated," Fresno Bee, October 14, 1988.

19. Congressional Budget Office, "Procedures for Estimating the Subsidies Associated with Bureau of Reclamation Irrigation Projects," U. S. Congress, n.d., p. 1.

20. U. S. Comptroller General. Federal Charges for Irrigation Projects Reviewed do not Cover Costs (Washington, D.C.: U. S. General Accounting Office, 1981), Cover.

21. Ibid., 36-37.

22. Daniel J. Bernardo and Norman K. Whittlesey, "The Historical Setting for Irrigation in the West" in Energy and Water Management in Western Irrigated Agriculture edited by Norman K. Whittlesey (Boulder: Westview Press, 1986), 13; Donald Worster, "A Dream of Water," Montana, Autumn 1986, 73.

23. Richard F. Fenno, Jr., Congressmen in Committees (Boston: Little, Brown and Company, 1973), 92.

24. Warne, supra, 23. Full citation, 3, note 23.

25. Andrews and Sansone, supra, 264. Full citation, 3, note 13. Fenno, Jr., supra.

26. Act of August 30, 1935, 49 Stat. 1028, 1039.

27. Act of March 10, 1934, ch. 55, 48 Stat. 401.

28. J. Raual Armstrong, Memorandum of Acting Solicitor Armstrong, November 15, 1954. See also, Act of August 26, 1937, ch. 832, 50 Stat. 844, Note 25.

29. U. S. Congress. Water Supply for Grasslands Water District, Central Valley Project, California. Hearing before the House Subcommittee on Water and Power Resources, Committee on Interior and Insular Affairs. 94th Cong., 2d sess. Serial No. 94-78 (Washington: Government Printing Office, 1976), 242.

30. Charles R. Renda, Regional Solicitor, to Field Supervisor,

Division of Ecological Services, Fish and Wildlife Service, Sacramento, Memorandum of April 14, 1977.

31. U. S. Department of the Interior. Public Hearing on the San Luis Unit Task Force, Fresno, California, August 3, 1977. Page 74 gives 130,000 acre-feet. By the end of September the figure was 172,000 acre-feet. See Ronald B. Robie, "Water Issues Facing California" in Paul W. Gates (ed.), Four Persistent Issues (Berkeley: University of California Institute of Governmental Studies, 1978), 38.

32. Letter and enclosure from Assistant Regional Director Lawrence F. Hancock to Nancy Foster, National Marine Fisheries Service, July 1, 1988, re: Cooperative Agreement of May 20, 1988; Warne, supra, 179-80; Glen Martin, "Paradise Lost/Why California fishing isn't what it used to be," from "This World," San Francisco Chronicle, December 4, 1988, 12, quoting William Keir, who heads the California Advisory Committee on Salmon and Steelhead Trout.

33. U. S. Comptroller General. Improved Federal Efforts Needed to Equally Consider Wildlife Conservation with other Features of Water Resource Developments (Washington, D. C., 1974).

34. Anon., "Duck Grounds on West Side To Be Protected," Fresno Bee, June 28, 1937.

35. Ibid.

36. P.L. 674, 68 Stat. 879; Contract dated September 13, 1956 between U. S. A. and the Grassland Water District. See also subsequent contracts 14-06-200-3447A and 4658A; An historical account of interest is by Phillip E. Jones, and others, draft of April 1, 1947, "Land and Water Utilization In the Westside Grasslands Area of San Joaquin Valley."

37. Opinion of Principal Deputy Solicitor Horn, dated November 18, 1985.

38. Russell Clemings, "Grassland board rescinds cutoff of drainage water," Fresno Bee, November 23, 1988.

39. Jones, and others, supra.

40. William Sweeney, "Central Valley Project and the Public Trust Doctrine/Some Questions Which Should Be Asked -- and Answered," Statement presented at meeting on "The Use of Agricultural Drainage Water On Private and Public Wetlands For Waterfowl" at Los Banos (California) Fairgrounds, October 6, 1984,

page 2.

41. Ibid., 4.

42. Mike Beno, "Deadly Quiet," Ducks Unlimited (September/October 1984) 96.

43. Felix E. Smith to Fish and Wildlife Service regional office, Portland, Memorandum of March 14, 1985, re: Selenium in the Greater Grasslands Area, San Joaquin Valley -- A Discussion," with attachment.

44. Ibid.

45. Ibid., Attachment, page 9.

46. Lloyd G. Carter, "Wildlife and the land," Wire Service Dispatch/McClatchy News Service, May 10, 1984.

47. Ibid.

48. Lloyd G. Carter, "Claus seeks damages over federal appraisal of land," Fresno Bee, November 21, 1985; Earl James Foster, telephone conversation with the author, October 27, 1985.

49. Foster telephone conversation, Ibid.

50. Roy Leach. Water Conveyance Pollutants into the Grassland Resource Conservation District (U. S. Department of Agriculture: Grassland Resource Conservation District and Soil Conservation Service, 1979).

51. Ibid., 9, 16.

52. Lloyd G. Carter and Gregory Gordon (for United Press International), "Chemicals causing defects, death in Valley wildlife/Grasslands district targeted," Sacramento Union, August 16, 1984.

53. Earl J. Foster, Senior Appraiser, USFWS, Portland, Statement to Stephen D. Lunsford, Special Agent, Office of Inspector General, U. S. Department of the Interior, taken in January 1985, but not used in Report of Investigation Summary, Case No. 5VI 025.

54. Lloyd G. Carter, "Ex-board member calls Kesterson decision 'toughest,'" Fresno Bee, August 11, 1985, B2.

55. Ibid.

56. Ibid.

6
"Big Money Buys Big Clout . . ."[1]

During this century much of the land in California's Westlands Water District was converted from sheep pasture--about all it was good for without water--to farms irrigated primarily with surface water supplied by the Bureau of Reclamation's San Luis Unit of the Central Valley Project.[2] In the 1950s when groundwater was the irrigators' source of supply, the land sold from $100 to $500 an acre; in 1984--although inflation was a contributing factor--appraisals on those lands were between $3,000 and $6,000 an acre.[3] Subsidized water had made them valuable. Lands that can produce agricultural crops are said to be fertile even though they may require tons of pesticides, herbicides, fertilizers, and soil amendments to make them productive. In an Interior Department draft environmental impact statement, Westlands reported annual applications of approximately 500,000 pounds of herbicides and 1,400,000 pounds of pesticides.[4]

The origin of this productivity and the degradation of water quality it entails goes back to the late 1950s when funding of the San Luis Unit of the Central Valley Project appeared imminent. At that time western and southwestern San Joaquin Valley growers were agitating for water projects. The latter pressed for a state project; Westlands and other westside districts had sought and were about to get a federal project. Both groups embraced the concept that commingled waters to be stored in a reservoir behind a dam financed jointly by federal and state governments should not be subject to a federal acreage limitation. The San Luis Act of 1960 included the acreage limitation for federal water recepients much to Westlands' distress.

In western and southern San Joaquin Valley the largest landowners are oil companies and Southern Pacific Railroad. In 1988 the latter was selling off its holdings in Westlands Water District.

In 1959, Southern Pacific owned over 200,000 acres in San Joaquin Valley; Standard Oil over 218,000; other oil companies a total of over 348,000. Private land-owners with more than 1000 each held about 1,324,000 acres.[5] During congressional hearings preceding passage of the 1960 Act a Southern Pacific official intimated that his company would not comply with the acreage limitation.[6] Later, Southern Pacific and others among Westlands' landowners found a way to get around that hated and much debated proscription.

When the San Luis Act was passed, over half of Westlands' lands was in ownerships exceeding 5,000 acres and at least 68 percent of its lands were affected. After the District began receiving water in 1968, 351,425 acres were placed under cleverly contrived recordable contracts. By 1976, about 100,000 acres had been sold.[7] Very little of that land was sold to farmers who wished to reside on the land; mainly it was sold to the non-resident members of the early landowner families and to investors. To avoid selling off excess land within the required ten-year period Westlands' attorneys made those sales look legal enough to meet the requirements of a federal policy that promotes agribusiness, often to the detriment of small farms. Landowners operating outside acreage limitations are called "paper farmers." Their names appear on 160-acre parcels of land over which they have little control. In 1984 a paper farmer told a reporter that her sister's husband had persuaded members of the family "into putting nearly 1,000 acres of his farmland in their names to evade federal restrictions..."[8] The paper farmer's sister admitted that she had "asked her parents and sister to hold the land 'because we needed names because we had so much land.'"[9]

In a report to the California Assembly that analyzed agricultural land ownerships of various of Westland's water users, an ownership unit is defined as one that is in a "single name, or unique set of names, appearing on a grant deed (or equivalent instrument)," i.e., "a group of individuals who own land as tenants in common."[10]

Supporting the definition the author of the report quoted an excerpt from the California Real Estate department's manual.[11] Standard practice in the real estate industry as well as in the field of agricultural economics was followed by the report writer in providing to the state legislature this timely analysis of land ownerships among various large landowners in a 49,000-acre segment of Westlands Water District.

In California as a whole, "about half of all farm land is leased and half is farmed by the owner"; in the 49,000-acre segment of Westlands analyzed for the California Assembly, an "overwhelming majority of land ownership units [leased] their land to the business that actually [farmed] it."[12] Neither the landowners who leased excess lands to agribusiness corporations or to individual farmers, nor the lessees of those lands were subject to acreage limitations until the Reclamation Reform Act of 1982 was passed.

Irrigation districts organized under California's 1887 Irrigation District Act operate on a one-member/one-vote basis. Water districts such as Westlands permit one vote for each dollar of the assessed value of a member's land. In the San Joaquin Valley, "land ownership patterns are characteristically corporate and large-scale."[13]

When the San Luis Act was passed in June 1960, anticipation of a bright future for small-scale farming ran high. The selling of excess lands, it was said, would create 6100 farms from the 1400 separate ownerships then of record, and provide employment to 26,100 persons on farms and 43,500 "in collateral industries by 1990."[14] In 1978, "67 percent of the farms were over 320 acres, and...99 percent of the land was tied up in these large farms."[15] "Where giant [farming] corporations are the norm," said University of California's Professor Dean MacCannell, "we find poverty, inequality, ignorance and a full range of related social pathologies."[16] MacCannell cited Westlands as a prime example. Ten to 21.1 percent of the farm workers at Westlands were living "below the poverty line" in 1980, he said. "In other words, the people of the Westlands are the poorest of the poor in California."[17] LeVeen and King averaged the unemployment in agribusiness counties from January 1982 to December 1984 and found it double the statewide rate.[18] "Despite the alleged economic benefits of subsidized water...Unemployment in these areas has reached persistent, catastrophic levels."[19]

The counties studied by LeVeen and King are among the

richest in the state, but their towns in the agricultural belt are among the shabbiest. Mendota with a population of six thousand is "listed among the 20 poorest communities in California in spite of the wealthy landowners who control much of the Westlands [Water District]," wrote John Flinn in the San Francisco Examiner in March 1985.[20] In Mendota unemployment is part of life for farm workers reported the California Farmer in May. The article mentioned that unemployment payment figures for 1984, a fairly good year, had totaled nearly $8 million.[21] Richard Gonzales, manager of Mendota's Employment Development Department office, when interviewed during May 1985, emphasized that the applicants for unemployment payments are mainly permanent residents, not migrant workers who flock to Mendota and other nearby towns and then move on toward Arizona when the crops are harvested.[22]

Although the permanent farmworker employees in these San Joaquin Valley towns appear to have the experience to farm their own lands if available to them, reclamation law requires applicants for subsidized water to have "capital" sufficient to maintain a farm.[23] However, had the Bureau enforced the provision requiring farmers to live on or near their lands,[24] the outlook for the Valley's Hispanic farmworkers might now be a promising one. But that provision, perhaps unenforceable given that the Bureau has always been subject to Interior Department dictates, has had very few proponents in a political arena that includes some of the largest landowners in the West.

Successful farming requires knowledge of and dedication to the land. Ann Scheuring's The Tillers is a series of success stories of California farmers who did not need a lot of land to make a good living, nor did they all have cheap federal water.[25] In time, some of those farmers acquired enough land to worry about the acreage limitation, and one of them worked briefly for an agribusiness concern. He did not view that kind of farming as efficient.[26] The degree of efficiency attained on many small farms probably does exceed that of many agribusiness operations.

Agribusiness spawns financiers not farmers. For example, there are the Wolfsens with gigantic holdings outside as well as inside Westlands Water District. Some of their lands have selenium, arsenic, and boron problems.[27] The patriarch of this early family, Lawrence

Christian Wolfsen, "arrived in Merced County in 1881 as a German immigrant," wrote Lloyd Carter in the Fresno Bee.[28] In 1929 Wolfsen's sons, Henry B. and Lawrence C., formed a partnership and expanded "the modest-sized family ranch near Merced into one of the west's largest agricultural complexes, acquiring many thousands of acres," engaging in "western valley water politics," and serving on "numerous irrigation district boards."[29]

The Wolfsen brothers' heirs are identified in the report for the California Assembly as participants in the following operations: Wolfsen Land & Cattle Co., a Corporation doing business in Stanislaus and Merced Counties (12,304 acres); Wolfsen Brothers, a Partnership doing business in Fresno County (2,012 acres); Romero Ranch, Inc., a Corporation, doing business in Merced county (38,000 acres); Simon Newman, Inc., a Corporation, doing business in Merced County (54,195 acres); M. C. Wolfsen Ranch, a California Limited Partnership, doing business in Glenn County (15,481 acres); Wolfsen Feed Lots, Inc.; and Santa Nella Development Company.[30] The family's 9,579 acres in Westlands Water District is farmed under the name Timco, "an acronym formed from the names of the two operating divisions: Turner Island Farms and Murietta Farms."[31] In Table 6, which shows the eight largest farm operators in the 49,000-acre drainage study area, Timco tops the others with 9,579 acres. Of the 53 farming operations active in the study area 48 had other lands outside the area, including lands in the 600,000-acre Westlands Water District.[32]

Timco has 15 partners, none with more than a 2/15th interest. Total farmland stands at 13,408 acres. Crops raised are cotton, wheat, barley, corn, and sugar beets.[33] Westlands' field crops as a whole follow much the same pattern. Figures for 1983 show 230,307 acres in cotton; 49,045 in wheat; 21,004 in barley; 6,645 in corn; 5,203 in sugar beets. All of these crops, including 21,719 acres in alfalfa, could be better raised elsewhere than the San Joaquin's selenium valley. Highly water consumptive, they are in the main surplus products. Cotton was Timco's main cash crop out of an estimated total of $18 million in 1984.[34]

In 1983 Timco "idled a significant portion" of its land to participate in the commodity programs of the U. S. Department of Agriculture, designed to reduce surpluses of cotton and grain which had led to low "commodity prices and high costs for government storage of the surplus." Known as the "Payment in Kind" or PIK program, it has netted the participants a tidy sum. In return for idling land that year, Timco and Wolfsen Land & Cattle Company received over $1 million.[35] PIK appears to have benefitted mainly the rich, among whom are large landowners in California.

In 1986 owners of J. G. Boswell Co. "received $13.7 million in government payments."[36] Boswell also received $5.2 million "through first-handler and inventory programs," the outgrowth of 1985 legislation to protect cotton growers when prices dropped drastically as a result of foreign competition for the cotton market.[37] Foreign investors in agribusiness operations also profit from these subsidized programs--among them the crown prince of Liechtenstein who received $2.2 million one year from his investment in another surplus-producing state.[38]

Inasmuch as over production and subsidized crops contribute to the federal deficit as well as to water shortages--80% to 90% of Western water supplies are committed to agriculture--LeVeen and King recommend that Congress "enact a prohibition against use of subsidized water to grow surplus crops."[39] In Arizona, where users of Central Arizona Project water anticipate a drastic reduction in agricultural use, especially for low-income surplus crops, reallocation of water to meet the needs of urban growth is being accomplished by the state.[40] California, unlike Arizona, is not short of water; it is short on innovative legislation to manage this resource with a view to future needs, including periodic droughts.

At present any bill introduced in Congress to modify federal project water priorities is likely to face strong opposition from San Joaquin Valley congressmen such as Tony Coelho and Charles Pashayan, Jr. John Krebs, Pashayan's predecessor, feels his defeat in 1978 can be attributed to his refusal of a campaign contribution that was tied to specific legislative action. In "Big money buys big clout," two UPI reporters describe the circumstances. When Krebs returned an agribusiness donor's check for $1,000, the donor and another of the Valley's agribusiness growers allegedly raised $27,000 to get Pashayan elected.[41]

With the availability of irrigation water from the San Luis Unit in the 1970s, small-scale farmers began to demand enforcement of the acreage limitation so they could buy excess lands. Among the landowners they approached was Southern Pacific which then owned about 106,000 acres in Westlands Water District. Southern Pacific declined, and so did other large landholders who were approached. Knowing the Bureau of Reclamation would not interfere, they sold instead to other large landholders and to syndicates. Robert Jones, in an article for the Los Angeles Times entitled "Small Farmers in Land Battle with Corporations," wrote in February 1976:

> "...Landowners have been given wide latitude by the Bureau of Reclamation to choose the purchasers of their land, and the sales have gone almost exclusively to syndicates which combine many 160-acre parcels into farms nearly as large as the original."[42]

Governor Jerry Brown told the farmers who wished to purchase land from Westlands and other large landowners that the state government was "willing to shoulder its share of the burden and willing to join with the federal government in trying to redeem the promise of the Reclamation Act of 1902."[43] From his deputy director came a scathing indictment of Westlands' policies in a report that enumerated the findings of several state agencies. But the Bureau was "content to maintain the status quo."[44] U. S. Senator Gaylord Nelson, during a congressional investigation in Fresno in 1976, angrily denounced those landowners: "There are people out there not intending to farm, who do not farm at all; not a damn one ever farms at it.... That circumvents the whole intent and purpose" of the law.[45] By 1976, Nelson and Brown were too late on the scene to reverse the direction reclamation law had taken in California. Circumventing the law on behalf of Westlands was Ralph Brody, an expert in water law. With a salary that exceeded that of Jerry Brown, or the president of the University of California, or the chief justice of the California Supreme Court, Brody "used his influence derived from his backing by the landowners, and his knowledge of water law to wheedle numerous administrative changes in the 160-acre limitation. The cumulative effect has been to substantially weaken the law."[46]

Brody had come to Westlands from Governor Pat Brown's office where he had been chief deputy for the Department of Water Resources and Brown's special counselor on water issues during 1959 and 1960 while Brown was getting the State Water Project underway.

Brody's education included a law degree and a bachelor's degree in political science when he went to work for the Department of Agriculture in 1938. Before going into private practice he served from 1944 to 1952 in the Sacramento office of the Interior Department's regional solicitor where he handled Bureau of Reclamation matters. While working for Brown in 1960 he was appointed chairman of the California Water Commission, a body that advises Congress on state water policy. That same year he became manager-chief counsel for Westlands but continued to serve on the Commission until 1966 when Reagan became governor. Brody retired as manager-chief counsel in 1977 at a salary of $81,500, thereafter serving Westlands for three years as a part-time consultant at $45,000.

Brody not only wheedled administrative changes in the acreage limitation but he wheedled enough water to serve considerably more land than provisions of the San Luis Act provided. Rights to the use of water by the Bureau's clients are obtained by the Bureau from the states. These rights for irrigation water are allocated on the basis of beneficial use as required by the Reclamation Act of 1902. The amount of water a project is expected to require is determined in the planning stage. Project projections for the San Luis Unit anticipated that Westlands, in addition to existing groundwater supplies which would increase when withdrawals were reduced, would require an annual delivery of 704,000 acre-feet. When Brody came on board he demanded and got the figure increased: a water service contract for annual deliveries of 1,008,000 acre-feet was signed in June 1963.[47] The difficulties of Bureau personnel in negotiating with Brody are all too apparent in memos to the Bureau's central files in Sacramento and in stray copies that found their way into Brody's personal files, now in the Water Resources Center Archives, University of California (Berkeley). In this instance the Bureau's negotiators gave up on getting Brody near the 704,000 acre-feet figure and forwarded the contract to their superiors with the figure left blank.

Since Brody's departure, Westlands' managerial and legal staff (including outside counsel) continue to exhibit an awesome capability to negotiate successfully with Interior secretaries and Bureau personnel despite the adverse press coverage that followed the Kesterson disaster. Among the issues seized upon by the press are overly generous donations of time and money to government officials and candidates. "Big money buys big clout for West Side's polluting growers" reads UPI's caption wherein it is stated that campaign donations from westside growers between 1978 and 1982 totaled $1,456,425 and that they had flown Reagan and George Deukmejian around during the 1980 campaign.[48]

Westlands has been much in the news since the Kesterson disaster which it blames entirely on the Bureau. But the Bureau is not responsible for the condition of irrigation water after it leaves the point of delivery, nor does the Interior Department deem it obligated to assume the expense of cleaning up Kesterson. In May 1987 the westside water and/or irrigation districts were advised by Interior Solicitor Ralph Tarr that they are to reimburse the federal government for the cleanup costs.[49] Since then Westlands and its allies have been pursuing new friendships with a view to congressional action to relieve them of their obligation.

"Westlands leads lawmakers to water," is the caption of a July 1988 article about growers inducing congressmen to visit California and deliver speeches for which they can by law accept honorariums that do not exceed $2,000. March 12, representatives Tom Bevill (Alabama) and John T. Myers (Indiana) were guests of Westlands and two organizations. The latter each contributed $1,000 to each of the guests; Westlands contributed $2,000 to each. Travel expenses were divided among the three.[50] What is intriguing about this article is the timing of Bevill and Myers' visit, not the fact that each departed with $4,000.

Early in 1988 the Bureau proceeded to comply with the Kesterson Reservoir cleanup deadline ordered by the California State Water Resources Control Board (No. WQ 87-3) by letting bids for the onsite disposal facility favored by the Board. Westlands and the Land Preservation Association, one of the associated organizations mentioned above, opposed it as environmentally damaging and too expensive. Neither Westlands nor LPA have the scientific expertise to assess the environmental impacts of onsite disposal or the so-called less expensive experimental alternatives.

February 15, 1988, a lengthy letter to the Editor of the Fresno Bee from LPA's Stephen Hall glorified the experimental methods the Bureau had been paying for but which had failed to reduce the selenium sufficiently to protect migratory and local bird populations.

Disparaging the onsite disposal alternative ordered by the State Board, Hall said the estimated onsite disposal costs of $10 to $25 million for the first phase (which included removal of the selenium-contaminated mud and placing it in the onsite disposal pond) were unrealistic and would more likely be $60 million.[51] February 29, Henry Voss of the California Farm Bureau Federation sent a memorandum prepared by his natural resources director to Secretary Donald Hodel, with copies to numerous legislators, including Senators Wilson and Cranston and Representative Coelho.[52] Paramount in those letters of Hall and Voss was a strategy to force the State Board to reopen hearings; on behalf of Westlands they wanted the Board's cleanup order held in abeyance and the experiments continued for several more years.

Until the method and the cost of the cleanup are determined, Westlands apparently can escape paying its share; therefore it was to Westlands' advantage to stall the Board's order until it could be modified to permit further delays in cleaning up the Kesterson mess. Taxpayers will indeed be lucky if they escape picking up the tab for the millions of dollars that are being funneled into experiments that, even if successful, Westlands and other irrigation districts can be expected to shun as financially infeasible for private sector use.

March 7, the day the bids for onsite disposal were to be opened, a meeting in San Francisco, called at the behest of Hall, was going on in the conference room of the Natural Resources Defense Council. With Hall were Jerald Butchert (manager of Westlands) and Dan Nelson (representing the San Luis Water District). Others present represented various environmental organizations or were unaffiliated. Hall spoke at length on behalf of Westlands. Hall wanted all of the environmental organizations to assist in diverting the Bureau from its stated intention of awarding to the low bidder the contract to remove the selenium-contaminated mud from the Kesterson ponds.

Among those present at the meeting was a scientist who represented the Environmental Defense Fund. Previously EDF had been useful to Westlands in dealing with Congress, as had several other environmental organizations. But EDF was the organization mentioned by Butchert at a December 1986 meeting of the National Water Resources Association that had accomplished for Westlands what Westlands' staff could not have accomplished.[53] All others present declined to cooperate with Westlands in frustrating the decision of the State Board to proceed with onsite disposal. Several hours later a low bid of $8.3 million was announced by a Bureau spokesman--far short of the $10 to $25 million that Steve Hall and Westlands would have the public believe. Whether or not onsite disposal should have been allowed to proceed in the manner agreed upon between the Bureau and the State is open to question, but that is not the issue here. What is at issue is the manner in which certain congressmen took it upon themselves to intervene on Westlands' behalf.

March 8, with Chairman Bevill presiding, hearings of the Subcommittee on Energy and Water Development of the Committee on Appropriations included discussion of the high cost of cleaning up Kesterson with the onsite disposal method requested by the State Board. The $8.3 million low bid was ignored when addressing the Bureau's original sixty million dollar estimate.

The Bureau has never been enthusiastic about onsite disposal, preferring to conduct experiments that might cost less and be of more use in cleaning up selenium-contaminated sites at other refuges in the West. It has made a number of estimates that have since proved unrealistic and considerable cynicism is evident in the remarks of environmentalists. Said Hal Candee (an attorney for NRDC) in July 1988: "We remain very concerned that the Bureau of Reclamation obtained a congressional intervention in March and an amended order from the state board this spring based on predictions of cost figures that are now shown to be totally unrealistic."[54]

It may well be that the Bureau instigated the congressional intervention. However the instigators may have been Steve Hall on behalf of Westlands, or Bevill and Myers on behalf of Westlands. Or it may have been Secretary Hodel. March 12, Bevill and Myers spent the day at Westlands touring San Joaquin Valley where they were honored at lunch and dinner, and given the opportunity to make "brief speeches." They departed with $4,000 each.[55] March 24, Bevill, as chairman of the subcommittee, and Myers as ranking minority member, wrote to Hodel a letter that falls in place with the apparent intentions of Westlands Water District, the Land Preservation Association, and the California Farm Bureau Federation:

> You have indicated in your March 23, 1988, letter that you intend to proceed with the clean-up of Kesterson Reservoir on April 1, 1988, in the absence of contrary directions by Congress.
>
> We appreciate that you feel obligated to keep your commitment to the State Water Resources Control Board and to appropriately carry out the directions of Congress. However, it is the intention of this Subcommittee to provide no funds for the on-site disposal method in the FY 1989 Appropriations Act and to reprogram the amount appropriated for construction of the on-site disposal facility at the Kesterson Reservoir in the FY 1988 Appropriations Act pending further review of this matter.
>
> You are therefore instructed not to award contracts or take other actions to proceed with construction of the on-site disposal facility until this issue has been considered by Congress. As we indicated earlier, we feel the Department should immediately proceed to request reconsideration of the cleanup method by the Central Valley Regional Control Board, as appropriate.
>
> We wish to emphasize that the Subcommittee is concerned about environmental values, but there appear to be more effective and less costly options to cleaning up Kesterson Reservoir than the on-site disposal method.
>
> We trust you will comply with our request.[56]

Hodel responded by authorizing regional director Dave Houston to explain the Department's position to State Board chairman W. Don Maughan and to request that he schedule a hearing to reconsider Order No. WQ 87-3.[57] Maughan complied. A hearing was held June 23, 1988, followed by an order on July 5, permitting the Bureau to continue with its experiments but requiring it to fill ephemeral pools of selenium-tainted water accessible to waterfowl.

NOTES

1. Gregory Gordon and Lloyd Carter, "Big money buys big clout for West Side's polluting growers," San Francisco Examiner, August 13, 1984, A6.

2. California Agricultural Technology Institute, "Perspective," Update, July 1988, 2.

3. Gordon and Carter, supra.

4. U. S. Department of the Interior/Water and Power Resources. Draft Environmental Impact Statement, "Acreage Limitation/Westlands Case Study," Appendix F, 1980, F1-9. This DEIS should not be confused with Interior's "Westwide" DEIS.

5. Angus McDonald. The San Luis Reclamation Bill (New York: McGraw Hill, 1962) 7.

6. Ibid., 31.

7. Ellen Liebman. California Farmland: A History of Large Agricultural Landholdings (Totowa, New Jersey: Towman and Allanheld, 1983) 156.

8. Anon., "How 'paper farmers' got around water law," San Francisco Examiner, August 13, 1984, A7.

9. Ibid.

10. Don Villarejo, California Insitute for Rural Studies. Agricultural Land Ownership and Operations in the 49,000 Acre Drainage Study Area of the Westlands Water District (Assembly Office of Research, 1985) 5.

11. Ibid.

12. Ibid.

13. Merrill R. Goodall, John D. Sullivan, and Timothy DeYoung. California Water: A New Political Economy (Montclair and New York: Land Mark Studies. Allanheld, Osmun/Universe Books, Allanheld, Osmun and Co. Publishers, Inc., 1978) 20-21, 95-100.

14. Ellingson, supra. Full citation, 3, note 26.

15. Leveen and King, supra, 13. Full citation, 3, note 25.

16. Ibid., 14, quoting MacCannell.

17. Ibid., 15, quoting MacCannell.

18. Ibid., 16.

19. Ibid., 15-16.

20. John Flinn, "Farmers angry, looking for help after decision to cut off water," San Francisco Examiner, March 17, 1985, A1, A20. (Examiner staff writer Lynn Ludlow contributed to the reporting.)

21. Mike Henry, "Specter of Lost Jobs Haunts Mendota's Farm Community." California Farmer, May 18, 1985, 7.

22. Ibid., 8.

23. Act of December 5, 1924; 43 Stat. 702.

24. Reclamation Act of June 17, 1902; 32 Stat. 389.

25. Ann Foley Scheuring. Tillers: An Oral History of Family Farms in California (New York: Praeger Publishers, 1983).

26. Ibid.

27. Lloyd G. Carter, "Selenium in Tulare Lake Basin/Readings compare with Kesterson findings in '83," Fresno Bee, August 6, 1985, A-1. This lengthy article is based on interviews with scientists involved in drainwater evaporation pond studies.

28. Lloyd G. Carter, "Threatened farmland in hands of wealthy few/Wolfsen biggest in area," Fresno Bee, March 11, 1985, B1.

29. Ibid., B1, B3.

30. Villarejo, supra, 17-18.

31. Ibid., 12, 16.

32. Ibid., 12.

33. Ibid., 35.

34. Ibid., 16. See also Westlands' annual Production Reports, available at the District's office, 3130 North Fresno Street, Fresno 93703.

35. Villarejo, supra, 18.

36. John Johnson, "Boswell got $13.7 million from US in '86," Fresno Bee, April 15, 1987, B1.

37. Ibid.

38. Anon., "This money does grow on trees," Oakland Tribune, January 8, 1987, B6.

39. Leveen and King, supra, 156.

40. William E. Martin and Helen M. Ingram. Planning For Growth in the Southwest (Washington, D.C.: National Planning Association, 1985), 6.

41. Gordon and Carter, supra.

42. Robert A. Jones, "Small Farmers in Land Battle With Corporations/Firms Violate Intent of Law, Group Claims," Los

Angeles Times, February 16, 1976, Part II, 1, 4; Mary Louise Frampton, "The Enforcement of Federal Reclamation Law in the Westlands Water District: A Broken Promise," 13 U. C. Davis Law Review (1979) 95-105.

43. Jones, Ibid.

44. George L. Baker, "Family Farming vs. Land Monopoly/ Westlands' Ralph Brody--the $81,500 public servant." California Journal, September 1976, 293-96, at 295.

45. Ibid., 194.

46. Ibid., 293-96.

47. U. S. Bureau of Reclamation Region II Central Files, Memorandum of San Luis Liaison Engineer [Edgar Price] to "The Files" dated June 6, 1962; H. N. Britten, Chief, Water Marketing Branch, Memorandum for the Files dated July 30, 1962, and another dated August 9, increasing the figure to 782,500 acre-feet; Memorandum of Repayment Specialist [signed A. D. Harvey] to Central Files dated September 14, 1962, with postscript by R. G. Howard, Regional Supervisor of Irrigation, stating: "We had been prepared to offer a compromise in terms of water quantities; however, we felt the District's request was so far out of line that there was no point in offering any concession above our estimate of 782,000 until the District showed some indication of moving below its new demand of 1,006,000...." [In that figure it is not clear whether the figure 7 has been written over the figure 6. A "clean draft of contract, complete except for water quantities" was thereafter prepared and submitted to the parties for review, according to Howard.] The signed contract is numbered 14-06-200-495A.

48. Gordon and Carter, supra.

49. Pat McNally, "Speaker emphasizes farmers' part in Kesterson cleanup," Merced Sun-Star, May 9, 1987, 3.

50. Jeanie Borba and Michael Doyle, "Westlands leads lawmakers to water," Fresno Bee, July 10, 1988, A1, A8.

51. Stephen K. Hall, Executive Director, Land Preservation Association, Fresno. "What's the best solution at Kesterson?" Fresno Bee, February 15, 1988, B11.

52. Henry J. Voss, President, California Farm Bureau Federation, to Honorable Donald Hodel, Secretary of Interior. Letter of February 29, 1988, enclosing three-page statement of William I.

DuBois, Natural Resources Director of CFBF. In addition to Cranston, Wilson, and Coelho, Voss sent copies to Ken Maddy, Jim Costa, and Rusty Areias (California state legislators), Bill Jones, Dale Duvall, David Houston, Don Maughan, and Karen Vercruze; a blind copy was sent to William Crooks, Executive Officer, California Regional Water Quality Control Board--Central Valley Region.

53. Robert Gottlieb. A Life of Its Own/The Politics and Power of Water (San Diego New York London: Harcourt Brace Jovanovich, 1988), 218.

54. Russell Clemings, "Contract signed for first phase of Kesterson cleanup." Fresno Bee, July 7, 1988, B1, B3.

55. Borba and Doyle, supra.

56. Tom Bevill and John T. Myers to Honorable Donald P. Hodel, Secretary. Letter of March 24, 1988.

57. The State Board held the hearing on June 23, 1988, for consideration of a Draft Order dated June 22, 1988. The Board's decision followed on July 5, 1988, permitting the Bureau to continue its experiments, but requiring the Bureau to fill in all the ephemeral pool areas "to convert these areas to upland habitat or implement an alternative which accomplishes the same result." When the Bureau let a contract to a University of California (Riverside) team to proceed with an experiment entailing volatilization of the selenium, having abandoned the wet flex experiment of the Lawrence Berkeley Laboratory, it had not anticipated the Board's order to fill the ephemeral pools. Such success as it might have had with Frankenburger's volatilization method was in any event some 14 or more years in the future according to one Bureau scientist. That the Bureau chose to contract out the research to LBL and UC Riverside rather than to the Geological Survey appears to be shortsighted in light of recent research by Ronald Oremland and his team of scientists.

7
Dead Birds and Dispossessed Ranchers

The spread of selenium in wildlife refuges throughout the West should not have taken the Bureau of Reclamation by surprise. Its existence had been publicized in periodicals and its locations mapped by geologists, the latter as late as 1974. In soils it "may be derived (1) from parent material weathered from the underlying rock; (2) from wind- or water-deposited seleniferous materials; (3) from ground or surface water, by precipitation; (4) from volcanic emanations brought down by rain; and (5) from sediments derived from mining operations."[1] Selenium is a trace element which the Bureau of Mines calls a metalloid.[2] How it got into the San Luis Drain from the alluvial fans on the east side of California's Coast Range to Kesterson National Wildlife Refuge has been graphically described by Theresa Presser in a paper she wrote with Harry Ohlendorf entitled "Biogeochemical Cycling of Selenium in the San Joaquin Valley."[3] Presser is a research chemist with the Geological Survey who worked with Ivan Barnes during their field investigations and Ohlendorf is a wildlife research biologist with the Fish and Wildlife Service.

When Alice Howard of Oakland, California, undertook to edit the 1985, '86, and '87 proceedings of Selenium and Agricultural Drainage: Implications for San Francisco Bay and the California Environment, she made a thorough search of the literature on selenium and also contacted living scientists who were known for their work in that field. This chapter draws on material supplied by

Howard as well as public statements of various scientists who spoke at the symposiums and whose professional papers have added significantly to the literature. It also draws on newspaper articles by journalists who made a study of selenium and managed to combine deadlines with indepth reporting.

The San Luis Drain carried selenium-laden drainwater via conduits on 8,000 acres in Westlands Water District to Kesterson Reservoir in gradually increasing amounts between 1978 and 1982 when it began averaging about 7,000 acre-feet annually. The ill effects of that drain water on fish and the wild aquatic birds that nested at the refuge having by 1982 become evident, scientists in the Fish and Wildlife Service began their studies, first on mosquitofish, and in 1983 on aquatic birds. In September 1983 the public learned about the deaths and deformities of resident and migratory birds; in December the Bureau of Reclamation held a selenium workshop in Sacramento, and in February 1984 it participated in an agricultural wastewater workshop at the University of California in Davis. Through excellent news coverage--especially by the Sacramento, Fresno, and Modesto Bee--the ill effects of selenium are now well known.

Selenium is present in some of the vitamin/mineral products formulated by pharmaceutical companies. In minute quantities it is beneficial to human and animal health; in amounts that exceed safe levels, it is poisonous and may cause death. "There is a very narrow range between deficiency and toxicity," said one authority.[4] An extreme case in a high selenium region in Oregon caused a rancher's death in 1973. Tom Harris, who wrote the story following a seven-month investigation of selenium in 1988 to update his 1985 investigation for the Bee, interviewed doctors as well as the families who had learned too late the dangers of selenium to human and animal health.[5]

Where selenium is prevalent in the West farm animals early became the subject of studies. Post-mortem examinations have shown lethal deterioration of the liver, heart, lungs, stomach, intestines, gall bladder, kidneys, spleen, pancreas, and adrenals. The landmark study of University of Wyoming's Professor O. A. Beath and Irene Rosenfeld, published in 1946 by the University of Wyoming Agricultural Experiment Station and in 1964 by Academic Press, confirms the damage to vital organs on experimental animals given selenium in their food.[6] Manifestations of alkali disease and the blind staggers were discussed in detail by Colorado State University Professor Charles G. Wilbur when he spoke at the Bureau's December 1983 workshop at which time he also discussed the Beath-Rosenfeld investigations.[7]

"Alkali disease shows a more chronic and progressive degenerative disease than the blind staggers," said Dr. Wilber. "In alkali disease, the devastating injury is in the heart and the liver."[8] In the blind staggers, all the organs are affected.[9] During the Sacramento Bee's investigation, reporter Tom Harris found that hundreds of "cattle, horses, sheep and swine--in at least five Western states--are sick, dead or dying from the same kind of selenium poisoning that has killed or deformed thousands of waterfowl and aquatic organisms in and around Kesterson Wildlife Refuge."[10] They die mainly from eating plants "that naturally accumulate deadly levels of the trace element," selenium, wherever it is prevalent.[11] The buildup of selenium in the aquatic food chain at Kesterson was rapid and lethal.

Elsewhere a study of poultry showed that the "embryo of the chick is extremely sensitive to selenium toxicity. Hatchability of eggs is reduced by concentrations of selenium in feeds that are too low to produce symptoms of poisoning in other farm animals."[12] Like the canary in the mines, hatchability of eggs has been used as an indicator that the poison may be present.

An overdose of selenium in humans is harder to diagnose. Farmers handling selenium-tainted grain are advised to minimize their exposure; their symptoms may go away. Dr. Arthur Kilness, based in Rapid City, South Dakota, has had years of experience in diagnosing selenium poisoning. He objects to its use as a "human food supplement" and worries about its misuse as a livestock supplement.[13] "Veterinarians know little more than most physicians about the toxic nature or effects of selenium poisoning, often misdiagnosing its symptoms as those of selenium deficiency, a more well-known livestock condition, and worsening matters by prescribing selenium injections or feed supplements."[14]

Forty-five years ago, some forty cases of human selenium toxicity were reported in medical journals, principally caused by handling grain and consuming products raised in South Dakota's selenium-contaminated areas. In 1985, Tom Harris and his colleague, Jim Morris, identified a 35,000 square-mile area in North and South Dakota and Montana where springs, stock ponds, marshes and waterfowl refuges are laden with selenium, much of it from irrigation drainage.[15]

Forty years ago members of over 100 families living in seleniferous areas of South Dakota, Wyoming, and Nebraska were found to have "an abnormally high incidence of more or less serious damage to the liver, kidneys, skin, and joints and digestive disorders were common" and that 95 percent "of the subjects had selenium in the urine."[16] J. David Love, a widely known geologist who recently retired from the Geological Survey, had collected these and other data on selenium for a proposed study of the selenium problem in arid states in 1949, but nothing came of it because the Department of Agriculture declined to undertake the project despite the seriousness of the problem.[17] Love's "conservative estimate" of the magnitude of the problem "confronting the economy of the western United States" follows: "In Montana, approximately 30% of the state has at the surface seleniferous rocks that are actively or potentially poisonous. The figure for Wyoming is 20%, for Colorado 30%, for the northern half of Arizona 20%, for the northern half of New Mexico 40%, for Utah 25%. In short, thousands of square miles of land in these regions are now, or may become poisonous to livestock that graze there and to human beings that live there, and crops that are raised there may be poisonous."[18]

Because it was expedient to please certain congressmen some of the Bureau's projects were constructed in the very worst areas such as Senator Kendrick's Casper-Kendrick project near Casper, Wyoming.[19] Understandably Love worries about the consequences of such projects as the Kendrick which drains into the North Platte River. On maps accompanying Love's 1949 research proposal he identified selenium regions in 15 of the 17 contiguous Western states.[20] Although his findings and those of other investigators were available to Bureau dam builders they were not utilized in siting subsequent projects during the planning process.

The San Luis Unit of the Central Valley Project represents another example of the Bureau's acquiescent response to a project proposal. Build now and worry later seems to be its motto. As a consequence of the Kesterson disaster Bureau personnel have done a lot of worrying: selenium has brought the Bureau's engineering and design mistakes to public attention. March 15, 1985, Interior secretary Hodel had Kesterson closed with considerable fanfare at a public hearing called by Congressman George Miller to assess the extent of "Agricultural Drainage Problems and Contamination at Kesterson Reservoir." The irrigators were outraged. With assistance from several environmental groups they got their water back two weeks later with the proviso that they plug their drains to Kesterson by June 30, 1986.[21] In 1984 at least one Bureau official had suggested termination of irrigation water to growers responsible for the selenium-tainted drainwater flowing into Kesterson; when deliveries were reinstated he of course had to go along with Hodel's reversal. Privately Bureau personnel may agree with their critics that marginal land should not be watered; publicly they must support the secretary's decision. The alarming number of deaths and deformities of birds attributed to selenium in agricultural drainwater in ponds at Kesterson did not lead Harris and Morris to investigate only Bureau projects as implied by their article captioned, "Toxic chemical threatens West/Massive projects for water blamed," but most of their samples of water, mud, and plant life were obtained at wildlife refuges dependent upon the runoff and drainwater from the Bureau's projects. They had those projects in mind when they said that the widespread "poisoning is similar to that which is forcing the federal government to close the Kesterson National Wildlife Refuge in the San Joaquin Valley after it suffered the most severe outbreak of bird deformities ever recorded in the wild,"[22] but they were no less concerned about the natural origins of selenium in those arid states along the northern tier of their investigations.

Although not as spectacular as at Kesterson where dead and deformed birds continue to be found, the annual migratory bird census of the Fish and Wildlife Service for 1985 was "the lowest it had been in the 30 years the counts have been made."[23] To what extent selenium is responsible is not known. Ducks on the Pacific Flyway had declined 20 percent from the previous year, and on the Central Flyway, 30 percent. Destruction of their habitats undoubtedly has taken a heavy toll. Not only have these wetlands been drastically reduced in size by the farmer's plow, but they are "being tainted by increasingly saline water and lethal contaminants."[24] In urban areas wetlands are being reduced in size by residential and industrial development. In 1977, with a view to reversing this nationwide trend, President Carter issued Executive Order 11990. In his statement accompanying the order he said in part:

> Recent estimates indicate that the United States has already lost over 40 percent of our 120 million acres of wetlands inventoried in the 1950's....In order to avoid to the extent possible the long and short term adverse impacts associated with the destruction or modification of wetlands and to avoid direct or indirect support of new construction in wetlands wherever there is a practical alternative, I have issued an Executive order on the protection of wetlands.[25]

Wetlands are areas inundated by water for periods long enough to support vegetation and aquatic life. A 1965 publication of California's Department of Water Resources calls them swamp lands. Under the Swamp Land Act of 1850, two million acres of Central Valley swamp lands were deeded by the federal government to the state. In San Joaquin Valley, all but a few thousand acres were soon sold to private parties.[26] The high incidence of botulism among bird populations is frequently attributed to their shrunken and overcrowded habitats. So is avian cholera. Although the reduction of wetlands by the farmer's plow may be largely responsible for the overcrowding of water fowl that leads to epidemics, recent research suggests that their diseases may be "directly or indirectly related to elevated selenium levels."[27]

The authors of "Biogeochemical Cycling of Selenium..." have estimated that a "minimum of 1000 migratory birds (adults, embryos, and chicks) probably died or were seriously malformed during 1983-1985 as a result of feeding on food-chain organisms with elevated Se concentrations" at Kesterson.[28] During 1983-1984 avian cholera claimed the lives of thousands of birds and that fact provided an irresistable temptation to Interior Department spokesmen to play down the seriousness of the situation. But Carla Bard who chaired the State Water Resources Control Board from 1979 to 1982 countered with public statements and a letter to the new chairman of the Board. In the letter she reminded the Board that as early as July 9, 1962, the Bureau was warned that bioaccumulation of toxic material could prove lethal to "'fish, birds or mammals (including man).'"[29] In an address to graduating students at UC (Berkeley) in May 1985, Bard charged that the Bureau had ignored "thousands of pages of documents and reports from public and private sector scientists warning of the environmental and public health threats inherent in the discharge of agricultural drainage wastewater into a wildlife refuge."[30] In January 1985 she had appeared before the State Board on behalf of the ranchers living next to Kesterson, so concerned had she become for their health and welfare.

Although assistant director Lawrence Hancock and senior scientist Edwin Lee in the Bureau's Region II office were concerned for the health and welfare of residents living near the Kesterson ponds, they were not in a position to do more than sympathize with their plight. Officialdom in Washington disclaimed liability, offered no compensation, and failed to alert the residents to potential selenium poisoning from exposure. Although Fish and Wildlife Service officials in Washington were quick to react to the dangers to personnel working at Kesterson they did nothing to mitigate the dangers to the Freitas families living next to the Kesterson ponds. Unlike FWS personnel the families were not provided masks and protective clothing. As ranchers with cattle and sheep to tend they were subjected to the dust and fumes of the noxious-smelling ponds as they went about their daily chores. Unaware at first of the danger to their health, they began to experience such symptoms as Dr. Wilbur had mentioned: "severe respiratory irritation, occasional dermatitis, nausea, nervousness, and gastrointestinal disturbances."[31] For FWS personnel the following precautions were required: "(i) preemployment physical examinations to screen out employees with asthma, allergies, known sensitivity to selenium, chronic respiratory disease, gastrointestinal disturbances, or disorders of the liver or kidneys, (ii) training to recognize selenium toxicity symptoms, (iii) the use of goggles, respirators, frequent changes of clothing and showers, and (iv) regular monitoring of blood and urine selenium levels...."[32]

The Freitas ranch is at the east end of Gun Club Road which cuts through the middle of Kesterson Reservoir from the west. Janette Freitas has read enough about selenium to fear its effects on her family, especially her young grandchildren and her daughter-in-law who has asthma. (The young, the ill, and the elderly are known to be more susceptible to selenium poisoning.) But finding homes for three ranch families at locations where they could continue their cattle business required time. One June night in 1985 when sleep evaded Janette--as it often did from worry and the incessant noise from the FWS hazing program to frighten birds away from the Kesterson ponds--she began writing down what transpired after the Bureau of Reclamation decided to take part of their ranch for its master drain as the San Luis Drain was then called:

> This whole nightmare started in 1968 when the Bureau of Reclamation came to us and said they needed our property in connection with the San Luis Unit of the Central Valley Project. I told them we were not interested in selling any part of our property. They said they would return when they had more information.
>
> I believe it was about a month later when they returned with what they described as "good news." They led us to believe we would benefit from the master drain because the water would be of such good quality that it could be used to irrigate; that if we chose to do some farming, something could be worked out so that we could use the water.

With cheap federal water, crops are more profitable than cattle. As irrigation water became available from the Central Valley Project in California, and from other Bureau projects in the West, grazing lands succumbed to the plow. Ranchers became farmers with the turn of the federal water tap. The Freitas family did not find this alternative attractive. Janette recalls telling the Bureau's representatives again: "We are not interested in selling any part of the ranch. We need it all if we are going to continue in the cattle business."

The Bureau was in a tight spot in 1968: provision for constructing the drain had been made in 1962, but the cost-sharing arrangement with the state had not materialized. The state had gone as far as studying two reservoir sites, abandoning one because of "political opposition."[33] The other--the less desirable Kesterson site--was for sale, and therefore readily available, a condition of importance to the Bureau in view of a suit by irrigators for compliance with the 1960 Act. To obtain additional land needed for the reservoir, the Bureau instituted condemnation proceedings.

Janette Freitas told this author that Bureau officials did not tell her they planned to take the land by right of eminent domain. Several weeks after their second visit she received a phone call from her banker who informed her that almost 800 acres of the ranch "had been condemned." The bank had been advised of condemnation proceedings by the Bureau because the ranch had been put up as collateral in obtaining loans. Janette did not receive a copy of the condemnation papers until several days had passed. They were to receive $200 an acre for one parcel and $250 an acre for another parcel--very low figures they thought for land as good as theirs. They engaged an attorney who obtained a higher figure. Janette tells what transpired after the condemnation papers were received:

> From that time on there was no further communication from the Bureau. Two or three months went by. Our cattle were in the field when a crew of men started taking down the fences. Of course that told us to move them.
>
> Then started the construction of the drain. First there was the mess of heavy equipment parked and blocking our driveway. Many truck loads of gravel were hauled in to build Gun Club Road up about five feet higher than it was. While they were doing that the school bus driver refused to pick up my children. Because we couldn't get out of the ranch on Gun Club Road, we had to use 4-wheel drive pickups and go through the fields to school and to town. It took us 45 minutes longer.
>
> One day I found out that the construction crew had hooked a temporary telephone to our phone line. When I asked the supervisor why they did that without asking, he said they had to have a phone in case someone got hurt; it was the law. The phone company had told him it would take two or three months before they could run another line out there.

Janette's reference to the "master drain" instead of the San Luis Drain has been explained. However, this concrete-lined drain should not be confused with the old San Luis Canal which runs parallel at this point. During construction of the drain and the 12 cells that comprise Stage One the Bureau built a picket fence to separate its newly acquired property from the Freitas ranch but apparently did not keep it in repair. Continuing her account, Janette said:

> The years that the floods came the water would be over the top of the pickets for two or three months. After it went down there would be one or two miles of fence to mend. They never once helped with repairs. When it comes to something they want such as using our ranch to drill test holes they came around all smiles.
>
> On January 9, 1985, we gave them permission to drill nine more test holes no more than 230 feet deep. After they had been drilling several weeks, my husband, just kidding, asked if they had hit oil. The man said, "no," we are at 400 feet, and getting pretty white sand. After checking our copy which said to the depth of 230 feet, I called Merced County Health Department to see what kind of a permit they had. They had not obtained one for that well, or any of the other eight wells they drilled on our property. Merced County shut them down.[34]

Almost 800 acres of the Freitas ranch, the Kesterson estate, and other smaller parcels of private property--purchased by the government in 1968--became Kesterson National Wildlife Refuge in July 1970 when it was turned over to U. S. Fish and Wildlife Service for conservation and management of wildlife. Twelve cells or seepage ponds, constructed partly on land acquired from the Freitas family, began receiving water in 1972.[35] Initially that water was mostly surface flows from local sources and the Delta-Mendota Canal, providing a relatively safe habitat for warmwater game fish. Californians have become accustomed to fish kills, but when waterfowl and livestock began to sicken and die, ranchers became alarmed. Moreover, they were disturbed by unexplained flooding of their lands. When Charles Schwab reported water standing on his property "adjacent to ponds 1, 3 and 4 of Kesterson Reservoir," the state's Central Valley Regional Water Quality Control Board suspected seepage from the reservoir.[36]

About the same time, James and Karen Claus, owners of

Kesterson Gun Club and a cattle ranch bordering the ponds, began requesting the Fish and Wildlife Service to clean out its section of the San Luis Canal. It had become "so clogged with silt and tules that it became virtually impossible to move water along it," said Claus in a formal claim filed in 1983. (During one summer Claus had shared the expense of cleaning out the clogged canal with Grassland Water District at a cost to him of $5400.) The total amount claimed for damage resulting "from a continuous process that began approximately 36 months ago" was $32,250.[37]

The Fish and Wildlife Service did not respond so Claus filed a second claim in January 1984. Because the quality of water he was receiving was poor, he alleged that he was damaged to the extent of $955,000.[38] He also filed a claim against the Bureau for $986,250.[39] Damages were itemized in both claims. Unsuccessful in gaining redress through these claims, Claus sought relief in the courts. Thwarted by Justice Department attorneys who relied on "sovereign immunity" and the government's "protected discretionary functions" in opposing his suit, Claus got the message. In 1987 he accepted $102,500 for 90 acres of his ranch and the Schwab brothers accepted $165,000 for 180 acres.[40] The Freitases who sustained far more extensive damages thought the government would compensate them without going to court. In September 1986 they learned that to settle with them could leave the government open to suits from other landowners along the San Luis Drain.[41] In 1987 they filed suit; in mid-April 1989 the case was still unsettled.

Seepage from Kesterson to the Freitas ranch was excessive because specifications for construction of the ponds were not adhered to. A clay layer of adequate thickness was to have been left intact so that most of the water would evaporate. When this author learned that about 60 percent of the water was seeping from the ponds, a search was made for all reports, engineering specifications, maps, and photographs relating to construction. Although Bureau personnel were most helpful in locating this documentation, they had not been around when the work was done. No one with whom seepage was discussed disputed that bulldozers probably had pierced the clay layer during construction. Neither did they shed any light on why that was permitted to happen.

Initially the state was to have participated in the construction of the evaporation ponds as well as the drain which was to have extended to the Delta. Therefore, the Department of Water Resources had been a participant since 1962 in planning and designing the facility, completing its investigation after the state abrogated the commitment to a joint facility that was to serve the state project as well as the San Luis Unit of the CVP. Ironically the Bureau and DWR had referred to their evaporation ponds facility as the "Kesterson enhancement area." Prior to construction, which began in 1969, they accumulated an impressive fund of knowledge about the area. They had performed every conceivable kind of test to determine where the ponds should be located in order to avoid excess seepage, how deep they should be, what the effect of the hydraulic head would be on groundwater movement, et cetera. They knew that the range of infiltration could be as low as 0.0001 feet per day or as as high as 12.0 feet per day with average infiltration as high as 4.3 feet per day. The challenge before them was not insurmountable, as reflected in the positive tone of the report which DWR prepared.[42] In 1973 the acting regional director of the Bureau reported to its Denver office the completion of the evaporation ponds and the drain and commended the contractor who did the work.[43]

By 1986 the damage to the Freitas ranch caused by Kesterson was "not reversible over any reasonable period of time."[44]

Between July 1981, when Schwab reported standing water on his property, and September 1983, when the Kesterson disaster became front page news, Bureau scientists engaged in geohydrologic investigations, wrote a memorandum to the central files describing where they had run their seepage tests--they reported nothing that might explain standing water on Schwab's property--and prepared the "Technical Report" required in the process of obtaining a permit to discharge agricultural wastewater.[45] The report is dated July 1983 and directed to the California Regional Water Quality Control Board, which had been letting the Bureau use Kesterson for drainwater since the late 1970s. Selenium added a new dimension to the Bureau's problems for it could not get a permit. In addition it had prompted Claus to put pressure on the Regional Board to stop using Kesterson for drainwater, and ultimately on the State Water Resources Control Board when the Regional Board did not respond. But for the discovery of selenium in the drainwater, it seems likely that the water-logging of contiguous ranches would have been passed off as due to other causes, leaving the victims with little hope of recovery, meager as it may be.

NOTES

1. Hansford T. Shacklette, Josephine G. Boerngen, and John R. Keith. Selenium, Fluorine, and Arsenic in Surficial Materials of the Conterminous United States. U. S. Geological Survey Circular 692 (Washington, 1974), 2-3.

2. Charles G. Wilber, "Some Thoughts on the Toxicology of Selenium," a paper delivered at the Conference on Toxicity Problems at Kesterson Reservoir, December 5-7, 1983, at Sacramento, California (Lafayette, California: Ecological Analysts, Inc., January 1984). See also Wilber's Selenium/A Potential Environmental Poison and a Necessary Food Constituent (Springfield, Illinois: Charles C. Thomas, Publisher, 1983).

3. Theresa S. Presser and Harry M. Ohlendorf, "Biogeochemical Cycling of Selenium in the San Joaquin Valley, California, USA," Environmental Management, Vol. 11, No. 6, 805-821.

4. Tom Harris, "Human Use of Selenium Under Study," Sacramento Bee, March 16, 1984, quoting Dr.Richard Burau, professor of soil science and environmental toxicology, University of California (Davis). Presser and Ohlendorf, supra, 817 wherein they discuss human tolerance and the need to minimize the likelihood of selenium exceeding a safe level.

5. Harris, "Selenium: The Poisoning of America," Sacramento Bee, December 4, 5, 1988; as noted by Harris the use of dry weight analysis was recommended by scientists he consulted, but not by federal and state nutritionists. The preference of FDA for making wet weight analyses has caused some controversy locally.

6. Rosenfeld and Beath. Selenium: Geobotany, Biochemistry, Toxicity, and Nutrition, New York, 1964.

7. Wilber, supra, Conference paper, p. 2-7.

8. Ibid., 6.

9. Ibid., 4-5. See also K. R. Van Kampen and L. F. James,

"Manifestations of intoxication by selenium-accumulating plants," in Effects of Poisonous Plants on Livestock, R.F. Keeler and others (eds.) (New York: Academic Press), 1978.

10. Harris, "Selenium poisoning threat over five Western states," San Francisco Examiner, Sept. 9, 1985, B1.

11. Ibid.

12. Wilber, supra, Conference paper, p. 7.

13. Harris, "Human Use of Selenium Under Study," supra.

14. Harris, "Selenium poisoning threat...," supra, B4.

15. Ibid.

16. David Love to W. H. Bradley, Chief Geologist, U. S. Geological Survey, memorandum of February 25, 1949, in response to request for a "Suggested Research Program on Geology and Related Studies of Poisonous Rocks," a nine-page transcript and a series of maps showing the locations of seleniferous rocks in arid states. (Love received the "Scientists of the Year" award from the Rocky Mountain Association of Geologists in December 1986 and earlier that year he was the subject of John McPhee's three-part article, "Annals of the Former World," in New Yorker magazine, February 24, March 3 and 10, 1986, which subsequently was published as a book. Love retired from the Geology Survey after 40 years of service, but continues to work in his office at Laramie, Wyoming.)

17. Lloyd G. Carter, "Geologist says '49 selenium plan killed," Fresno Bee, February 9, 1987, B1.

18. Love to Bradley, "Suggested Research Program...," supra.

19. Reisner, supra, 232-33. Full citation, 3, note 28.

20. Love to Bradley, "Suggested Research Program...," supra. See also Marvin A. Crist, "Selenium in Waters in and Adjacent to the Kendrick Project, Natrona County, Wyoming," Geological Survey Water-Supply Paper 2023 (Washington: USGPO, 1974).

21. Virgil Meibert, "U. S. lifts ban on Kesterson/Agreement with Westlands District will keep irrigation water flowing," Oakland Tribune, March 29, 1985, in which Hodel's spokesperson Carol Hallett credited the Oakland chapter of the Sierra Club, among others, with providing support for lifting the ban on the March 15, 1985 closure. Jeanie Borba, "Groups ask Hodel to reconsider/Conservation, consumer organizations oppose water cutoff," Fresno Bee, March 26, 1985, listed the groups as Sierra Club,

National Resources Defense Council, Consumers Union, California Rural Legal Assistance [Foundation], and Pacific Coast Federation of Fishermen's Associations.

22. Tom Harris and Jim Morris, "Toxic chemical threatens West/Massive projects for water blamed," Sacramento Bee, September 8, 1985, A1. Presser and Ohlendorf, supra, state: "The USBR has about 220 projects or units from which irrigation return flows discharge into refuge areas or into receiving water bodies used for drinking- water supply, irrigation, or recreation" and cite two Interior Department reports for 1985 and 1986 at pages 816, 820.

23. Lloyd G. Carter and Gregory Gordon, "Valley ducks periled by pollution," San Francisco Examiner, August 14, 1984, D1. Third in a series researched and written by this UPI team.

24. Harris and Morris, supra, A17.

25. Jimmy Carter, "Statement by the President Accompanying Executive Order 11990," 42 Fed. Reg. 26961 (1977).

26. California Department of Water Resources. San Joaquin Valley Drainage Investigation/ San Joaquin Master Drain, Preliminary edition (Sacramento: January 1965), 12.

27. Harris and Morris, supra, A17.

28. Presser and Ohlendorf, supra, 814.

29. Carla Bard to Chairwoman Carole Onorato and Members of the State Water Resources Control Board, letter of January 21, 1985.

30. Carla Bard, "Kesterson Disaster/A Betrayal of Public Trust," commencement address to the College of Natural Resources of the University of California, Berkeley, May 18, 1985, p. 4. See also Tom Harris, "Selenium cover-up hinted/US allegedly kept quiet on Kesterson," Sacramento Bee, April 11, 1985, A1, A22.

31. Wilber, supra, 15.

32. Bard to Onorato, supra, 3.

33. James N. Luthin. Final Report on Seepage from Reservoir Sites in the Dos Palos and Kesterson Areas/Western Merced County, June 8, 1966, p. 1. Dr. Luthin, a consultant for the California Department of Water Resources, prepared this and other reports during the period the state was cooperating with the Bureau in a plan to build a master drain that would serve both state and federal irrigators.

34. Written statement of Janette Freitas dated September 28, 1985.

35. U. S. Bureau of Reclamation. Kesterson Reservoir- First Stage Technical Report in Support of Report of Waste Discharge to the California Regional Water Quality Control Board, Sacramento, July 1983, 1-7 and Appendix D, 5.

36. Ibid, 17. Initially the ponds had been designated "seepage ponds" or "cells."

37. Robert James Claus, "Claim for damage, injury, or death" dated November 1, 1983, directed to Richard J. Myshack [sic], Regional Director, USFWS, Region I.

38. Robert James Claus, "Claim for damage, injury, or death" dated January 11, 1984, directed to Richard J. Mycshack [sic]. Regional Director, USFWS, Region I.

39. Robert James Claus, "Claim for damage, injury, or death" dated January 11, 1984, directed to U. S. Bureau of Reclamation, Department of the Interior.

40. Federal Defendants' Memorandum in Support of their Motion for Summary Judgment, James Claus and Karen E. Claus vs. United States of America, et al, Civil No. S84-1309 LKK, U. S. District Court, Eastern District, California; Russell Clemings, "US settles two Kesterson claims," Fresno Bee, November 6, 1987.

41. Lloyd G. Carter, "US buyout of Freitas ranch near Kesterson dim for '86," Fresno Bee, September 22, 1986, B4.

42. California Department of Water Resources. Use Aspects of San Joaquin Valley Drainage Investigation. June 1970, 147-157.

43. U. S. Bureau of Reclamation, Acting Regional Director, Mid-Pacific Region, to Chief, Division of Water Operation & Maintenance. Memorandum of December 17, 1973.

44. Skibitzke Engineers & Associates, Inc., Tempe, Arizona, report to Mr. and Mrs. Frank Freitas, January 31, 1986.

45. H. L. Dillingham, Physical Science Technician, to Central Files. Memorandum of January 10, 1983; Kesterson Reservoir - First Stage Report, supra, which also has a copy of Dillingham's memorandum.

8
Irrigation-Induced Problems in the Arid West

February 5, 1985, California's State Water Resources Control Board issued Cleanup and Abatement Order No. 85-1 for Kesterson National Wildlife Refuge. Among the Board's concerns was the status of the food chain at the reservoir. For example, "Food chain organisms at Kesterson contain 50 to 100 times the normal concentration of selenium."[1] Initially the warnings by scientists failed to deter the Bureau of Reclamation in its desire to burn the vegetation as an alternative in fulfilling cleanup requirements of the state's order. Burning was specified as an alternative in the Bureau's closure plan, transmitted with a press release dated July 5, 1985,[2] notwithstanding Merced County's refusal to issue a permit. Apparently the Bureau had not taken seriously the County's stand that it "would not issue a permit for burning because of the potential for harming public health from particulate matter in the smoke."[3] It will be recalled from the previous chapter that Dr. Wilber, at a conference on toxicity problems convened by the Bureau in December 1983, warned against "selenium inhalation or contact of the skin to dust or fumes."[4]

When the Fish and Wildlife Service ordered its Kesterson crew to wear protective clothing and gas masks, it was worried about the possible presence of gas as well as dust. Anaerobic conditions which may produce gas are most likely to do so on hot, windless summer days, Geological Survey scientist Marc Sylvester explained to the author.

At a University of California symposium in March 1985, Geological Survey scientist Ivan Barnes expounded on the dangers of selenium, including its gaseous forms. "I know enough about the chemistry of selenium that I would be very hesitant to live there or work there," he said in referring to Kesterson. Selenium is ten times as toxic as arsenic and "can harm humans with little warning," added Barnes.[5] A University of California (Santa Cruz) team did some preliminary work on this aspect of selenium toxicity which resulted in a draft report in 1986 for the State Water Resources Control Board.[6]

Selenium warnings by Geological Survey scientists and investigative articles by newspaper reporters have irked key bureaucrats in Sacramento and Washington, D.C. Interior Department officials in the Reagan administration preferred that people not know so much about wildlife deformities and the prevalence of selenium. Very few government scientists have risked the ire of Interior by publicly stating that selenium-bearing soils are prevalent in most Western states where irrigation is practiced, and that "the selenium problem in the San Joaquin Valley should have been anticipated."[7] It was Barnes' address at the Selenium Symposium which Tom Harris covered for the Sacramento Bee that prompted the Bee's four-month investigation of selenium in water, mud, algae, plants, and aquatic life at refuges receiving irrigation drainwater. Chemical analyses of samples Harris and his colleague Jim Morris brought back confirm their allegations that federal water projects appear to be largely responsible for the increase in selenium dissemination which has had a deleterious effect on cattle, fish, and waterfowl where prevalent in higher than acceptable concentrations.[8]

Barnes had named nine other states where problems with selenium were likely: North and South Dakota, Wyoming, Utah, Colorado, Arizona, New Mexico, Oregon, and Nevada.[9] Harris and Morris traveled thousands of miles through 12 states, taking samples that when analyzed led them to become especially alarmed by conditions at Salton Sea National Wildlife Refuge in California; Imperial National Wildlife Refuge across the Colorado River in Arizona; New Mexico's Bosque del Apache National Wildlife Refuge; Utah's Desert Lake and Stewart Lake waterfowl management areas; Montana's Bowdoin, Freezeout Lake, and Benton Lake national wildlife refuges; Idaho's Deer Flat National Wildlife Refuge; and South Dakota's Belle Fourche and Cheyenne River habitats upstream from Oahe Reservoir. Selenium in a catfish taken from Stewart Lake in Utah measured 12,768 parts per billion.[10] The damage to wildlife habitats--those convenient receptacles for agricultural drainwater--will take years to mitigate.

By 1931 it was known among soil scientists that selenium poisoning was caused by the "consumption of grain and other vegetation grown upon definite soil areas."[11] H. G. Byers, who began making chemical analyses of vegetation in affected areas of South Dakota in 1928, was instrumental in getting underway a cooperative study in which Department of Agriculture personnel played a significant part. Results of investigations in Montana, Wyoming, the Dakotas, and Colorado, published in 1935, received widespread coverage in scientific journals. Subsequently studies were made by other investigators, principally in the southwestern states. In 1961 the Interior Department, with the cooperation of the Geological Survey and the Department of Agriculture published a reference work covering selenium problem areas in 15 of the 17 contiguous Western states based on a bibliography of 212 listings.[12]

As early as 1935 it was apparent that drainage from irrigation projects in seleniferous areas of the West was something to beware of. Byers reported 1200 parts per billion of selenium in the drainage water of the Bureau's Belle Fourche irrigation project in South Dakota. In 500 samples of Pierre shale from the general area he detected selenium in every one.[13] Determining the selenium in soils is much less complicated than determining the selenium in water, and it is usually given in parts per million. In 1941 Byers and H. W. Lakin--another scientist specializing in soil constituents--published the results of their California samples of Cretaceous shales from Southern California northward to the vicinity of Maxwell in Colusa County, a distance of 400 miles. In their San Joaquin County samples, selenium tested as high as 29 parts per million.[14] Byers' method of analysis permitted detection of selenium in soils in amounts as low as 0.1 ppm.[15]

Selenium in water is difficult to measure because its solubility varies with pH conditions. In alkaline waters of the West pH values are above 7 and selenium occurs "in part at least, as selenate," said investigators in 1961. This "selenate selenium," they said, "would be soluble, available to vegetation, and readily transported in ground waters." In acid waters pH values are below 7 and "selenium, if present, would be...quite stationary, and presumably of low availability to plants."[16] Geological Survey scientists have for years accurately measured selenium in water but the amount of selenium in the Bureau's samples was more often than not measured inaccurately until the GS was asked to do much of the sampling and to supervise such sampling as the Bureau did undertake.

In California the Bureau began sampling for selenium in June 1981 at which time it found 451 parts per billion in San Luis Drain water.[17] Far in excess of the upper limit for the survival of aquatic life established by the Environmental Protection Agency, it should have been reported to the State Water Resources Control Board as well as to the Fish and Wildlife Service. According to Bureau and FWS personnel, the latter was informally advised either late in 1981 or during the Spring of 1982. Unaccompanied by a memorandum transmitting the data, neither party seems to remember the date. In querying government personnel for further details this author was told that the Bureau had hoped to first obtain a waste discharge permit before divulging the seriousness of the situation.

The detrimental effect of agricultural drainage on receiving waters already was considerable when selenium was added to the list of destructive constituents and identified as toxic. In California a waste discharge permit usually is processed through a regional board. In this proceeding two regional boards were involved: the regional board for the Central Valley and the regional board for the San Francisco Bay Area. Therefore, the Bureau's application for a permit was to be processed by the state board. Former state board chairman Carla Bard recalled in 1984 that the Bureau had requested a preliminary permit in August 1980.[18] California's water boards have done what they can--perhaps more than they should--to oblige the Bureau. However, it is imperative that the Bureau supply the technical information necessary to set discharge requirements for Bureau projects, and that its clients, the water contractors, assume responsibility for the quality of drain water released to receiving waters.

A function of the state board that particularly disturbs the

Bureau is the state board's power to modify water rights permits when changing circumstances require a reallocation of water for beneficial uses other than irrigation water. It is now apparent that the deleterious effects of both state and federal water projects on California fisheries and the ecological damage to the Sacramento-San Joaquin Delta and San Francisco Bay must be mitigated. In the Delta, this means the retention of more water for fisheries and salinity control and less for water-project customers, including the Bureau's clients. Not only has the Bureau been unsuccessful in transporting Westlands' drainwater to the Delta, but it may not get all the water its largest and most powerful client is demanding.

Westlands describes its district as covering "some 603,000 acres of excellent farmland in Fresno and Kings Counties between Mendota and Kettleman City."[19] Its present drainage system serves 42,000 acres of which some 8,000 had conduits to the San Luis Drain which terminated at Kesterson Reservoir. From that small acreage Westlands reported drainwater discharges of 7,160 acre-feet in 1981; 6,380 in 1982; and 8,186 in 1983.[20] In three years selenium in that drainwater destroyed Kesterson. To understand the enormity of the impact of tile drainage on receiving waters from Westlands alone it is important to know that Westlands planned to expand its drainage systems to serve 300,000 acres. Another destructive soil constituent in Westlands' drainwater is boron. If it is not removed from the root zone of plants it destroys the productivity of the plants; to flush it from the root zone requires about twice as much water as for other salts which also are detrimental to plant growth.[21] Three salt-resistant, boron-tolerant crops account for 83 percent of Westlands' agricultural production: cotton, barley, and tomatoes.[22] San Joaquin Valley's boron problems have been the subject of scientific articles and reports for many years and recent investigations have enabled scientists to quantify the extent of the selenium problem.[23]

When the Bureau, the state's Department of Water Resources, and the State Water Resources Control Board completed their interagency drainage report in 1979, nitrogen removal was considered imperative and unforeseen problems with other pollutants were anticipated. However, they assumed that the beneficiaries of the federal and state water projects would cooperate by treating their drainwater to the extent required to maintain water quality standards in receiving waters. That the director of this Interagency Program, Louis Beck of DWR, may have had some reservations about that cooperation is indicated in his transmittal letter which accompanied the IDP report. Said Beck to the recipients of the report which included Westlands: "...the most important prerequisite to implementation of the Recommended Plan is the support of the agricultural community in the San Joaquin Valley. When this support is expressed, particularly in regard to paying a fair share of drainage program costs, the State and Federal Government can proceed."[24]

Another aspect of the report was the assumption that the Fish and Wildlife Service would have funds to monitor its Valley wildlife refuges. "A comprehensive monitoring program will be initiated to observe the effects of the discharge on the receiving waters," said the authors.[25] Funding did not materialize and by 1981 bass and other species were beginning to die at Kesterson along with virtually all aquatic inhabitants, except mosquitofish. The miracle of their survival has baffled scientists.

After the Bureau communicated the results of its 1981 sampling program to the Fish and Wildlife Service in Sacramento, staff scientists Drs. Harry Ohlendorf and Michael Saiki initiated a small-scale investigation of their own. Using Volta Wildlife Refuge as a control site--it is located near Kesterson--they examined mosquitofish samples from both refuges for trace metals and organochlorine pesticides. They found a hundred-fold difference for selenium, but for other trace metals and organochlorine pesticides, the amounts were practically identical. Mosquitofish samples from Kesterson showed 30 $\mu g/g$ (parts per million) by weight; mosquitofish samples from Volta showed 0.3 $\mu g/g$ (ppm).[26]

In 1983, coots, ducks, grebes, and stilts--because of their prevalence at Kesterson--were selected for study. All ingest fish, invertebrates, and aquatic vegetation as food items. What Ohlendorf and Saiki wished to determine was whether "birds nesting at the Kesterson ponds were experiencing reproductive problems," whether "concentrations of selenium and heavy metals occurred in the various components of the Kesterson ecosystem," and whether their findings compared with findings in "suitable control areas."[27] From April to August samples were taken and observations made. Following the birds through the breeding season, they found 20 percent of the 350 nests under study had at least "one deformed embryo or hatchling" and "about 40 percent contained at least one dead embryo. The externally visible abnormalities included deformed or missing eyes, beaks, wings, legs, and toes." Coot nests contained the highest percentage of abnormalities. Of 563 eggs examined, "246 contained dead embryos and 97 contained deformed embryos."[28]

By June 1983 enough was known about the condition of waterfowl at Kesterson to call for action. "There is deep concern" that someone or some agency "should be monitoring agricultural waste water and its component parts in selected areas of the San Joaquin Valley," wrote environmental assessment specialist Felix Smith to the Region I director in Portland, Oregon. Smith cited sources of information on selenium and urged the acquisition of funds for a detailed study.[29] A "Concern Alert" was prepared in the Sacramento office of the Fish and Wildlife Service and distributed. The copy sent to the Bureau was responded to by Donald Swain who charged that there were "several inflamatory statements" in it that concerned him.[30] It is not clear how a memorandum that mentioned no names nor in any manner identified persons in the Service or the Bureau could be considered inflamatory in the sense Swain charged. However neither "Concern Alert" nor Smith's entreaties to his superior in Portland produced the desired effect. Several months passed while the regional directors in the Service and the Bureau pretended the problems at Kesterson were not urgent. Late in September, Smith, with the approval of his wife and children, leaked the Ohlendorf-Saiki findings to the press.[31]

It is not unusual for a scientist to be harassed when his or her research calls for decisions administrators are reluctant to make. It is therefore particularly gratifying to report that the National Parks & Conservation Association chose Smith "as the 1985 Western Regional winner of the coveted Stephen T. Mather Award."[32] (Mather had the distinction of serving as the first director of our National Parks, earning a reputation as their "wily" defender.) According to the Association, Smith received the award for "the role he played in alerting the public" to the contamination occurring at Kesterson. Said the president of the Association in presenting the award:

> Environmental managers increasingly must contend with myriad pressures upon the resources they manage.

> Often they are asked to forsake protection of a resource for the convenience of short-term priorities and expediencies. The Mather Award seeks to recognize and reward those capable individuals, such as Smith, who have unswervingly fought for the preservation of this nation's natural resources despite bureaucratic red tape and political demands.[33]

The Bureau, with its penchant for damming the West, has given Fish and Wildlife administrators and scientists a bad time for many years. Its dams have had disastrous consequences for fisheries in Western waters and now selenium-tainted drainwater threatens the food chain of aquatic life. Within that context Smith strives to save what is left of the West's fish and wildlife resources. Swain's mission since 1970 when he became chief of the Bureau's Water Quality Branch/Planning Division, and later held titles embracing water quality and environmental planning, has been to bring agricultural wastewater to the Delta and San Francisco Bay. It is the one alternative out of 18 that is the "most economical and environmentally safe," Swain said at an agricultural wastewater workshop in February 1984.[34] Swain's is not the voice of reason in an era of scientists who, since the mid-1950s, have known that the solution to pollution is not dilution.

It has been indepth reporting on selenium by certain newspapers, along with the willingness of Interior Department scientists in the Fish and Wildlife Service and the Geological Survey to put their careers on hold, that prompted Congress to order the Interior Secretary to investigate selenium and other toxics at wildlife refuges throughout the West. Damage at Kesterson does not appear to be reversible. Its condition was allowed to deteriorate further while contracts were let to study the deterioration instead of cleaning it up. Our troubled wildlife refuges deserve a better fate.

Two fact-finding studies dealing with the condition of national wildlife refuges emerged in late 1985 and early 1986. The 1985 study, prepared mainly by Geological Survey personnel, confirmed most of the Sacramento Bee reporters' findings. The 1986 study was prepared by the Fish and Wildlife Service. Both studies are considered drafts, but the latter had been around in one form or another before the most recent draft was released in April 1986. Entitled Contaminant

Issues of Concern, it classifies the refuges in three categories of seriousness,[35] and, although it credits refuge managers and biologists with being "the first to recognize when problems have occurred in refuge wildlife populations,"[36] their observations seem to have been left out of the refuge assessments. Neither William Horn (Assistant Secretary for Fish and Wildlife and Parks) nor Robert Broadbent (then Assistant Secretary for Water and Science) were disposed to attract attention to the Bureau's dilemma. Despite evidence in the GS study that supports most of the Harris and Morris allegations, Broadbent in a press release announcing the study is quoted as saying: "We cannot substantiate the sweeping generalizations stated or implied in the newspaper articles regarding widespread adverse effects of selenium."[37]

Each of the 23 sites is treated separately in the GS study[38] and some of the sites coincide with those in Contaminant Issues of Concern. Nine are seriously affected based on the following criteria: fish with 2500 parts per billion (dry weight) or more of selenium; algae and eggs with 1000 ppb (dry weight) or more; soil, sediment, and mud with 1500 ppb (dry weight) or more; water with 10 ppb or more. The nine sites are: Yuma Valley and Imperial National Wildlife Refuge, Arizona; Salton Sea National Wildlife Refuge, California; Imperial Valley, California; Benton Lake National Wildlife Refuge, Montana; Bowdoin National Wildlife Refuge, Montana; Fallon and Stillwater National Wildlife Refuges, Nevada; Poison Canyon, New Mexico; Angostura, South Dakota; Belle Fourche, South Dakota.[39] Kesterson and the Merced County Grasslands in California were omitted because they were not among the 23 sites investigated by Harris and Morris.

Geological Survey scientists placed the seriousness of their findings in Classes A through D. FWS scientists used the designation "Category." For example, Category A reads: "On-site, direct evidence indicates the need for in-depth monitoring and analysis of impacts."[40] GS Class A reads: "Areas where existing information indicates reason for concern and the need for further analysis of associated impacts."[41]

The GS selenium toxicity standard is 1500 parts per billion (dry weight) for mud. Mud brought back from Montana's Benton Lake and Bowdoin refuges by Harris and Morris was 7500 ppb and 3136 ppb, respectively.[42] Harris described what he saw at Bowdoin:

> Dust devils whirling near the south end sucked up towering columns of chalky-white dust.
>
> The shoreline had a telltale bathtub ring of salt crust around the edge.
>
> Thick clouds of brine flies hovered on or above the stagnant water.... It is a refuge in trouble....[43]

Drainwater and irrigation tailwater from the Bureau's Milk River Project "account for more than half of the lake's meager water supply," said Harris.[44] Although avian botulism is said to take an annual toll of from 300 to 1500 birds at Bowdoin,[45] selenium may be a contributing cause. The entire region is high in selenium, better left in place under undisturbed sod. Irrigated agriculture contributes to the condition of the refuges but even dry farming may be contributing in some areas.

Because "no testing to discover the kind of death and deformity of waterfowl that occurred at Kesterson has been done anywhere else in the nation," wrote Harris and Morris in 1985, the role of selenium in wildlife loss at national refuges is ill-defined.[46] Therefore the following disclaimer in Contaminant Issues of Concern seems inappropriate: "There have been no reported fish and wildlife die-offs, avian reproductive failures, or avian embryonic deformities that can be directly attributed to selenium...."[47] In an article for the Sacramento Bee, Harris presented evidence to the contrary.[48]

Over two million acres of Montana farmland contribute to the saline seepage, high in arsenic and selenium, that poisons lakes and wetlands in the state.[49] Benton Lake National Wildlife Refuge, where 7500 ppb of selenium were found in mud samples, is in Cascade County, a ranching and farming region since 1876. A recent compiler of the County's history, in commenting upon soil conditions, conceded that "Perhaps the Indian might have been right when he said white man turn too much of prairie upside down."[50] Seepage from surrounding farmland and tainted water from Muddy Creek which drains farmland served by the Bureau's Sun River Project appear to be the cause of problems at Benton Lake National Wildlife Refuge.[51] Said Harris and Morris:

> Millions of acres of native grassland that once held the water in place have been broken for cultivation, increasing tainted runoff and seepage. That drainage has

been increased greatly by irrigation that flushes salts and toxicants from the ground that otherwise would remain in place or be leached out slowly, and harmlessly, over hundreds of thousands of years.[52]

Freezeout Lake, about 30 miles northwest of Great Falls, is a former national refuge. Located in Montana's Teton County it is owned and managed by the state, except for a "435-acre piece of the main lake bottom which is owned by the Fish and Wildlife Service."[53] It is not listed in Contaminant Issues of Concern. Samples taken from drainage ditches "feeding into Freezeout Lake exceeded 1,400 ppb," wrote Harris and Morris.[54] Based on the "high concentrations of selenium in soils and sediments," GS scientists placed it in Class B. Like Benton Lake, it is in the area of the Bureau's Sun River Project.[55]

Harris and Morris were unable to elicit much information from most of the cattlemen they interviewed: adverse publicity interferes with the price of beef on the hoof when marketed. But rancher Mike Henry candidly supplied Harris with a detailed account of the illnesses that beset his family as well as his cattle and himself. Henry had not known the ranch was tainted when he bought it.[56]

Harris located reports[57] written 40 and 50 years ago that described how selenium migrated to receiving waters in semiarid parts of Montana and South Dakota. "Historically," wrote Harris, "the native grasslands used the available subsurface moisture and there were no seeps. But that land was broken for cultivation. When part of it lies bare for a season, to guard against overusing the soil's nutrient base, the moisture builds up and flushes out the heavy load of salts and toxic elements."[58]

Although South Dakota's wildlife refuges do not appear to be impacted by Bureau projects, project lands and water contain high levels of selenium. The Angostura Reservoir on the Cheyenne River in Fall River and Custer counties is about 50 miles southwest of Rapid City. It irrigates about 12,000 acres, mainly along the floodplain below the reservoir. The Belle Fourche River Project in western South Dakota irrigates about 57,100 acres. During the decade 1975-1985, GS scientists regularly sampled soil and water at these projects. Some springs had a maximum of 25 ppb of selenium; surface water had a maximum of 33 ppb. These figures far exceed the drinking water limit of 10 ppb. In 38 soil samples, the "maximum selenium concentration was 6,000 ppb and the median concentration was 2,000 ppb."[59] Samples taken by Harris and Morris contained: 2,128 ppb at Angostura and 6,832 at Belle Fourche.[60]

In Utah, a state where Mormons preceded the Bureau in large-scale irrigation projects, the Bureau's Emery County Project contributes to refuge problems. The affected refuge is the state-owned Desert Lake Waterfowl Management Area where TDS is of more immediate concern than selenium. Selenium measured at Desert Lake was not considered significant and it was placed in Class C.[61] Based on upper limit criteria used by the GS, selenium at Desert Lake did not equal or exceed the upper ninety-fifth percentile--a statistic "commonly used by geologists and soil scientists to define the normally-expected ranges of constituent concentrations in soils."[62] Two other Utah sites are affected by selenium, both of them located in the Middle Green River Basin. Vernal and Stewart Lake Wildlife Management areas are the impacted refuges. Although water and soil samples were not in the upper limits for selenium, fish tissue from smallmouth bass and carp had concentrations measured in 1978 and 1980 that ranged from 3400 to 4500 ppb (dry weight).[63]

The Fish and Wildlife Service erred in omitting the Nevada refuges near Fallon which should be in Category A. Although selenium contributes to the problems at these refuges, mercury is "one to four times the maximum suggested for human consumption," prompting the state to issue "a health advisory cautioning the public on the consumption of fish in the Carson River and Lahontan Reservoir."[64] Stillwater Wildlife Management Area contains approximately 144,000 acres, including Stillwater National Wildlife Refuge--a nonhunting sanctuary of 24,000 acres. Irrigation canals and water control structures, dams and earth plugs were constructed to provide a "nesting, resting, and feeding area for ducks, geese, and other migratory water birds."[65] Outside the management area are Fallon National Wildlife Refuge in Carson Sink and the state's Fernley Wildlife Management Area. When water was plentiful the Stillwater Management area had accommodated up to 300,000 migratory waterfowl.[66] Since 1960 water has not often been plentiful. GS scientists placed Stillwater in Class A "because of high concentrations of selenium and arsenic in water and high selenium concentrations in bird eggs."[67] Located in a closed basin and served largely by irrigation tailwater and subsurface drainage from the Bureau's Newlands Project, conditions at the refuges became desperate in 1987. Tom Harris described what he saw:

> A yard-wide band of death rings the massive, shallow and shrinking lake they call the Carson Sink, overwhelming evidence that the ecological system here is in complete collapse.
>
> Dead fish by the uncountable millions are washing up along the gooey shoreline, bobbing across the surface or decaying on the bottom, where bloating gases soon will pop great fetid masses more of them to the surface.
>
> Duck carcasses dot the shore....Knight-crested herons, egrets, grebes, geese, cormorants -- all are represented among the carcasses.
>
> It is a wretching, reeking sight.[68]

Several days later the San Francisco Examiner reported the kill had doubled to seven million[69] and the following week it published a feature story captioned, "Grim preview of the future at Carson Sink/Water projects are threatening wildlife all over the Western states."[70] Preliminary reports suggested that the high salt content of the water at the Nevada refuges caused the catastrophe, but later reports said that selenium, mercury, and boron were the main cause.[71] Not all the tui-chub perished immediately at the Nevada refuges; approximately seven million others survived for awhile in areas of ponded water that contained less salt until those areas also deteriorated. The birds perished from another cause. Preliminary tests showed they probably died of avian cholera.[72] Given that the habitat of birds and fish had been deteriorating rapidly from the lack of fresh water at these refuges, what is the outlook? The present status of the Newlands Project suggests that the outlook is not promising.

The project, named for the author of the Reclamation Act of 1902, was authorized in 1903 and completed in 1915. In 1926 the Bureau turned its operation and maintenance over to the Truckee-Carson Irrigation District, named for the California rivers from which the project draws its water. Raising the elevation of Lake Tahoe in conjunction with the project enabled the Truckee River to carry more water but it interfered with the migration of cutthroat trout and terminated their existence in Tahoe, Truckee, and Pyramid Lake waters; a planted variety was introduced but subsequent dams have been detrimental to it and also to native species such as the cui-ui. Pyramid Lake is located in a barren region where fish have been the main source of food for an otherwise impoverished Indian nation.

The history of the Newlands Project is reviewed in the Final Environmental Impact Statement for the Newlands Project Proposed Operating Criteria and Procedures (OCAP).[73] A 1973 court decision, Pyramid Lake Paiute Tribe of Indians v. Morton,[74] required the Interior secretary to fulfill certain fiduciary duties to the Tribe which included preventing the unnecessary waste of irrigation water within the Truckee-Carson Irrigation District. Contributing to the drawdown of Pyramid Lake were irrigators who did not hold rights to the water, further impairing the Tribe's fishing and recreation industry. Despite the court decision and Secretary Morton's warning that every acre-foot of illegally diverted water would have to be returned to Pyramid Lake, the illegalities continued.[75] Within a period of ten years approximately one million acre-feet of water were diverted and the lake's cui-ui were becoming extinct. In Carson-Truckee Water Conservancy District v. Clark (1984)[76]--a case in which the Tribe had invoked the Endangered Species Act--it was held that the "Secretary's obligations under the...Act supersede obligations under the Washoe Project Act [of 1956] and related federal reclamation laws."[77] The purpose of the Final Environmental Impact Statement was to propose operating criteria and procedures that reflected the intent of court decisions pertinent to water allocation from Bureau projects. The irrigators in TCID protested as was to be expected. Secretary Hodel accordingly scrapped the proposed criteria and had his staff prepare less restrictive OCAP. His press release of April 18, 1988, states:

> Instead of imposing detailed water conservation measures on either the Truckee-Carson Irrigation District (TCID) or its farmers to meet competing demands--such as water for endangered fish, Interior's new Operating Criteria and Procedures (OCAP) for the project establish rules and incentives for the district aimed at increasing the project's operating efficiency over the next five years.

***

During the five-year phase-in of the OCAP, Interior will step up its investigation of other ways to protect the cui-ui, including fishery studies, hatchery production, a pilot dredging project, rehabilitation of the Truckee River and translocating the cui-ui...."[78]

No one queried thinks that TCID will return to Pyramid Lake the million or so acre-feet of water it illegally diverted, nor are they optimistic about the outcome of Hodel's restorative measures for the cui-ui habitat. Apropos the latter, the taxpayer will be picking up the tab.[79] As to Hodel's concessions to the TCID irrigators, provided they conserve enough water to protect endangered species in Pyramid Lake, such additional water they conserve will be available to them "as water stored in Lahontan."[80] "This extra storage water," continues Hodel, "will be available to TCID to use as it sees fit under Nevada State and Federal Law." Hodel feels that his new OPAC package "deals with the farmer's right to farm as he sees fit and to have an irrigation system that provides him with his full entitlement of water at the headgate."[81] But what does it do for a region that is about to lose seventeen to eighteen thousand acres of wetlands in need of fresh water from the Newlands Project? Representative Barbara Vucanovich and others in Nevada consider the outlook for their wetlands "very serious."[82]

TCID irrigates approximately 63,100 acres with federally-subsidized water. Seventy percent of that acreage grows the highly water-consumptive, low income crop, alfalfa. Furthermore, according to the Pyramid Lake Paiute Tribe's consultant, only about 56,400 acres have legal rights to the water.[83] The high groundwater table attributed to project water serves the interests of some of the other irrigators and about 1,500 acres irrigated in 1985 received project water "without documented water rights."[84] Nothing in Hodel's package suggests that water without documented rights will be used to freshen the water in nearby refuges. More will be known about the future of Stillwater National Wildlife Refuge and other nearby refuges when the Geological Survey issues a report in 1989. A Bureau of Reclamation scientist with whom this author discussed the outlook is as unhappy about the prospects as Representative Vucanovich, but neither one is in a position to prevent the destruction of Stillwater.

NOTES

1. California State Water Resources Control Board. Cleanup and Abatement Order No. WQ 85-1, Finding No. 6, p. 1 of Appendix.

2. U. S. Dept. of the Interior. Kesterson Reservoir Closure and Cleanup Plan/SWRCB Order No. WQ 85-1 For Cleanup and Abatement of Kesterson Reservoir, July 5, 1985, Figure 5 and pages 29 and 38. Inasmuch as the Bureau's preferred cleanup procedures included burning in place, the several major burns that followed were thought by residents to have been authorized (this author was told).

3. U. S. Dept. of the Interior, Bureau of Reclamation. Preliminary Draft, Environmental Assessment for Preliminary Activities to Reduce the Nuisance to Human Health and Wildlife at Kesterson Reservoir, April 1985, p. 5-6.

4. Wilber, supra, 15. Full citation 7, note 1.

5. Ann Gibbons, "Toxic mineral widespread in state, experts say/Studies continuing of selenium's effect on wildlife and humans," Peninsula Times Tribune, March 24, 1985, A3, A4; Alice Q. Howard (ed.), Selenium and Agricultural Drainage: Implications for San Francisco Bay and the California Environment, Proceedings of the Second Selenium Symposium, March 23, 1985, Berkeley, 41-51.

6. Kenneth W. Bruland and Terence D. Cooke. Aquatic Selenium Speciation in California, Draft Report for State Water Resources Control Board submitted February 21, 1986. Bruland and Cooke are associated with the Institute of Marine Sciences, University of California (Santa Cruz). Additional information can be obtained from Ron Oremland, U. S. Geological Survey, Menlo Park,California.

7. Gibbons, supra.

8. Tom Harris and Jim Morris, "Toxic chemical threatens West/Massive projects for water blamed," Sacramento Bee, September 8, 1985, A1, A16-17, and September 9, 1985, A1, A15, A30.

9. Anon., "10 States Could Have Kesterson's Problems, "San Francisco Chronicle, March 25, 1985, 16.

10. Harris and Morris, supra, September 9, 1985, A16.

11. Horace G. Byers. Selenium Occurrence in Certain Soils in the United States with a Discussion of Related Topics, Technical Bulletin No. 482 (U. S. Dept. of Agriculture: Washington, D.C., August 1935), 2; M. S. Anderson, H. W. Lakin, K. C. Beeson, Floyd F.

Smith, and Edward Thacker. *Selenium in Agriculture*, Agriculture Handbook No. 200, Agricultural Research Service, U. S. Dept. of Agriculture, in cooperation with the Geological Survey (U. S. Dept. of the Interior: Washington, D.C., August 1961).

12. Anderson, *et al*, *supra*.

13. Anderson, *et al* *supra*, 4, 9, and 12, citing Byers, *supra*.

14. *Ibid*., 21-22. H. W. Lakin and H. G. Byers. *Selenium Occurrence in Certain Soils in the United States with a Discussion of Related Topics*, Sixth Report, Technical Bulletin No. 783 (USDA: Washington, D.C., 1941).

15. Anderson, *et al*, *supra*, 4.

16. *Ibid*., 12.

17. U. S. Bureau of Reclamation. *Kesterson Reservoir - First Stage Technical Report*, *supra*, Table 14. Full citation, 7, note 36.

18. California State Water Resources Control Board Administrative Record, File No. A-354, v. 22, December 7, 1984, testimony of Carla Bard, at page 42. U.S. Bureau of Reclamation, Mid-Pacific Region, in its San Luis Drain Chronology, dated January 18, 1985, page 13, gives the 1980 request as August 21.

19. Westlands Water District. *The Drainage Problem in the Western San Joaquin Valley*, 1984, 4, 8, 10 and map (Figure 2).

20. *Ibid*.

21. J. D. Oster, Glenn J. Hoffman, and Frank E. Robinson, "Management Alternatives: crop, water, and soil," *California Agriculture*, October 1984, 29-32.

22. U. S. Dept. of the Interior/Water and Power Resources, *supra*, Appendix F1-9. Full citation, 6, note 4.

23. Theresa S. Presser and Ivan Barnes. *Selenium Concentrations in Waters Tributary to and in the Vicinity of the Kesterson National Wildlife Refuge, Fresno and Merced Counties, California*, U. S. Geological Survey, Water Resources Investigations Report 84-4122 (Menlo Park, California, May 1984); Presser and Barnes, "Selenium Concentrations in Selected Sumps, Drains and Canals, Fresno and Merced Counties, California," Water Resources Division memorandum dated July 3, 1984, Office of the Regional Hydrologist, Menlo Park, California; Presser and Barnes. *Dissolved Constituents Including Selenium in waters in the Vicinity of Kesterson National Wildlife Refuge and the West Grassland, Fresno and*

Merced Counties, California. U. S. Geological Survey, Water Resources Investigations Report 85-4220 (Menlo Park, California, August 1985); S. J. Deverel, R. J. Gilliom, Roger Fujii, J.A. Izbicki, and J. C. Fields. Areal Distribution of Selenium and other Inorganic Constituents in Shallow Ground Water of the San Luis Drain Service Area, San Joaquin Valley, California: A Preliminary Study, U. S. Geological Survey Water-Resources Investigations Report 84-4319, Prepared in cooperation with the U. S. Bureau of Reclamation (Sacramento,California, November 1984). (Fields, a physical scientist, participated as an the employ of the Bureau.)

24 U. S. Bureau of Reclamation, California Department of Water Resources, and California State Water Resources Control Board. San Joaquin Valley Interagency Drainage Program/Agricultural Drainage and Salt Management in the San Joaquin Valley, June 1979, and transmittal letter of August 17, 1979.

25. Ibid., ch. 10, p. 12.

26. H. M. Ohlendorf, "The Biologic System," a paper delivered at a Conference on Toxicity Problems at Kesterson Reservoir, December 5-7, 1983, at Sacramento, California (Lafayette, California: Ecological Analysts, Inc., January 1984), 8-9.

27. Ibid., 9.

28. Ibid., 10-11.

29. Felix E. Smith, Memorandum of June 10, 1983, to FWS regional office in Portland, Subject: "Information Alert--Agricultural Waste Water (AWW) investigation - need for water/soil/vegetation/invertebrate monitoring."

30. The "Concern Alert" was sent to the Bureau's regional director by James J. McKevitt, Field Supervisor, Division of Ecological Services, Sacramento office of FWS, on or about July 8, 1983, and referred to Swain who responded July 23. Swain retired several years later but continued to work on the San Joaquin Valley Drainage Program as an employee of the California Dept. of Water Resources.

31. Deborah Blum, "Mineral is linked to bird deformities," Fresno Bee, September 21, 1983, A1, A14.

32. National Parks & Conservation Association, Letter and news release of May 18, 1985, to Felix Smith.

33. Ibid., News release, p. 2.

34. Agricultural Wastewater Workshop, University of California (Davis), February 22-23, 1984.

35. U. S. Fish and Wildlife Service. Draft, Preliminary Survey of Contaminant Issues of Concern, April 1986, 10-14.

36. Ibid., 1.

37. U. S. Dept. of the Interior Task Group on Irrigation Drainage. Draft, Preliminary Evaluation of Selenium Concentrations in Ground and Surface Water, Soils, Sediment, and Biota from selected Areas in the Western United States, December 6, 1985. Also see attached letter of December 10, 1985, of William P. Horn and Robert N. Broadbent to Honorable George Miller, Chairman, Subcommittee on Water & Power, Committee on Interior and Insular Affairs, House of Representatives, and attached news release dated December 11, 1985.

38. Ibid. Referred to generally as the "irrigation drainage report," it is based on data available at the time it was compiled. Each site reported by Harris and Morris is covered.

39. Ibid., 4-7. Sites placed in Class B are: Fairfield Bench, Montana; Freezeout Lake Wildlife Management Area, Montana; Bosque del Apache National Wildlife Refuge, New Mexico; Site adjacent to the Rio Grande, New Mexico; Edgemont, South Dakota; Laguna Atascosa National Wildlife Refuge, Texas; Cayo Atascosa, Texas; Vernal, Utah; Stewart Lake, Utah. In Class C are: Termo, California; Deer Flat National Wildlife Refuge, Idaho; Lower Rio Grande Valley National Wildlife Refuge,Texas; Desert Lake Waterfowl Management Area, Utah. Huntley, Montana, is in Class D. Using different criteria, Harris and Morris considered sites in Class C and Class D to be in serious condition. The GS did not.

40. U. S. Fish and Wildlife Service. Preliminary Survey supra, 4.

41. U.S. Dept. of the Interior Task Group, supra, Executive Summary, p. 2.

42. Harris and Morris, "Toxic chemical threatens West," supra, A16.

43. Tom Harris, "Refuge provides home for looming disaster," Sacramento Bee, September 9, 1985, 21.

44. Ibid.

45. U. S. Department of the Interior Task Group, supra, 60.

46. Harris and Morris, "Toxic chemical threatens West, supra, A17.

47. U. S. Department of the Interior Task Group, supra, 63.

48. Tom Harris, "Bird deformities found in 3 selenium-tainted sites," Sacramento Bee, August 15, 1987, A1, A28, with photograph of deformed pelican. Wetlands in Nevada, Utah, and the Tulare Lake basin in California are the principal sites referredto in the caption, but others now being studied are expected to have reproductive failures and deformities.

49. Harris and Morris, "Toxic chemical threatens West," supra, A17.

50. Cascade County, Montana. A Century in the Foothills 1876 to 1976/A History of the Eden Area (Eden Area Historical Committee, 1976), 13.

51. U. S. Department of the Interior Task Group, supra, 52, 55.

52. Harris and Morris, "Toxic chemical threatens West," supra, A17.

53. U. S. Department of the Interior Task Group, supra, 65.

54. Harris and Morris, "Toxic chemical threatens West," supra, A17.

55. U. S. Department of the Interior Task Group, supra, 66.

56. Harris, "Family's nightmare began life as a dream" in Howard (ed.), Selenium and Agriculural Drainage..., Third Selenium Symposium, 195-97.

57. Anderson, et al, supra; Harris used some of the referenced reports in writing his articles for the Bee.

58. Harris, "Selenium: Toxic slaughterhouse/Chemical preys on livestock," Sacramento Bee, September 9, 1985, A6. Dryfarming requires that plowed land in semiarid areas periodically lie fallow.

59. U. S. Department of the Interior Task Group, supra, 86, 90, 92.

60. Harris and Morris, "Toxic chemical threatens West," supra, A16.

61. U. S. Department of the Interior Task Group, supra, 112.

62. Ibid., 29.

63. Ibid., 113-17.

64. U. S. Fish and Wildlife Service, Preliminary Survey, supra, A-100.

65. Ibid. Also see U. S. Department of the Interior Task Group, supra, 70.

66. U. S. Fish and Wildlife Service, Preliminary Survey, supra, A-100; U. S. Dept. of the Interior Task Group, supra, 72.

67. Ibid., 74.

68. Harris, "Scientists try to find what is wiping out life at Carson Sink," Fresno Bee, February 15, 1987, A1. This article appeared in the Sacramento Bee under the caption, "Nevada's vast lake of death," and in the Oakland Tribune under the caption, "Polluted lake on its deathbed; wildlife dying."

69. Anon., "Cholera kill doubles to 7 million fish," San Francisco Examiner, February 20, 1987,B4. The caption is misleading. The cholera kill should refer to the waterfowl, not to the fish. Avian cholera is common at refuges where over-crowding and tainted water exists. In this heavily mined region, heavy metals such as mercury, chromium, cadmium, zinc, and lead, as well as selenium, arsenic, boron, and molybdenum may be contributing factors.

70. Jane Kay, "Grim preview of the future of Carson Sink," San Francisco Examiner, February 24, 1987, A1, A12.

71. Sam Whiting, "Grim Nevada Refuge For Migratory Birds," San Francisco Chronicle, August 20, 1988, A2.

72. United Press International, "Tests pin fish kill on salt, solids buildup," Fresno Bee, March 10, 1987, A5.

73. U. S. Department of the Interior/Bureau of Reclamation. Newlands Project Proposed Operating Criteria and Procedures, Final Environmental Impact Statement prepared by URS Corporation, December 1987.

74. 354 Fed. Supp 252 (D. D. C. 1973).

75. Robert S. Pelcyger (attorney for Pyramid Lake Paiute Tribe) to David G. Houston (Regional Director, Bureau of Reclamation), submittal letter for FEIS dated August 20, 1986 (FEIS, 5-262) p. 10, item 17.

76. American Indian Lawyer Training Program, Inc. Tribal Water Management Handbook (Published by the American Indian Resources Institute, 1987), ch. 5, p. 63. Case cited as 741 Fed. 2d 257 (9th Circuit, 1984).

77. Ibid. Act of August 1, 1956, Ch. 809, 70 Stat. 775.

78. U. S. Bureau of Reclamation, Mid-Pacific Region. Press

release of April 18, 1988, captioned "Interior Announces Incentives Plan to Ease Newlands Project Water Needs."

79. Ibid.

80. Donald Hodel, Secretary of the Interior, "Open Letter to the Water Users of the Newlands Project," April 15, 1988, p. 4, prepared and signed by Interior Under Secretary Earl Gjelde.

81. Ibid., p. 1.

82. Anne Pershing (ed.), "Wetlands concern Bryan, Vucanovich," Lahontan Valley News, Fallon, Nevada, April 20, 1988, p. 1.

83. Ali Shahroody (Stetson Engineers Inc.,) to Region II director David G. Houston, submittal for FEIS dated August 20, 1986 (FEIS 5-187), 1.

84. Ibid.

9
From Damaged Resources to Managed Resources

To read the history of irrigation is to read the story of salt. The authors of the Reclamation Act of 1902 knew that salt had destroyed civilizations in the Old World. Yet they did not address the problem of saline soils in their legislation. The Act does not prevent scientific investigation of soils to be irrigated with subsidized water paid for by the general public, but as engineers the directors of Interior's Reclamation Service preferred to build first and attend to problems later. The thought that the general public had a vested interest in the program that could not be realized unless the projects were successful probably never entered their minds.

Scientists in the Division of Soil Management, a bureau in the Department of Agriculture which was established in 1902, could have told the Reclamation Service which soils to avoid but they were not consulted. Service engineers were inclined to plant their projects where entrepreneurs and politicians wanted them. There wasn't an acre of public land in Arizona's first government-subsidized project.[1] Large landowners in the Salt River Valley saw in the reclamation program a cheaper way to irrigate their crops and their friends in the Interior Department saw a way to oblige them. After initiating the Salt River Project, the latter argued that since the land within the project was not in public ownership and private landowners wished to become beneficiaries of the program an association should be formed through which they could negotiate for federal irrigation facilities and water.[2]

George Maxwell, one of the authors of the 1902 Act, served as the landowners' legal counsel in forming the first Salt River Valley Water Users' Association. A meeting was held in Phoenix in August 1902, the articles of incorporation drafted in February 1903, and the contract between the association and the government formalized in June 1904.[3] With completion of Roosevelt Dam in 1911, a dependable supply of cheap water enabled the landowners to control the salt problem on their lands but, along with subsequent projects in the basin, the salt problem was passed on to Mexico via the Colorado to be resolved at astronomical expense by the United States government.

The Bureau of Reclamation project that has had a particularly devastating impact on Mexico's agricultural land in the lower Colorado River basin is the Wellton-Mohawk Unit of the Gila Project. Located in southwestern Arizona on both sides of the Gila River, the Bureau promised its farmer-clients healthy crops of high-income citrus fruits and salad greens--some of which have belatedly materialized at great expense to the farmers as well as the government. The lot of those first project farmers was one of hardship and despair.[4] By profusely irrigating cotton, hay, Bermuda seed, and wheat, some of them managed to stay in business; others found their land so salty they were forced to abandon it. Supposedly the Indians of prehistoric times who irrigated less salty lands farther up the Gila and the Salt abandoned their homes for similar reasons, for without huge reservoirs to store water they could not irrigate profusely to remove salt from the root zones of their crops. Such crops as are grown in the Wellton-Mohawk Service Area will continue to require huge applications of water. Treating that water after it enters the Colorado and before it enters Mexico costs one hundred times per acre-foot what the Bureau charges its Wellton-Mohawk clients.[5] A sane solution to so costly a project would be to abandon it and buy out the farmers. But the Bureau insists the project is a success with such in-house articles as "Crops are coaxed from a Sand Pile."[6]

Irrigation of marginal land drives up the value of that land for the owners but it has a devastating impact on water quality. In closed basins, or basins that do not offer a satisfactory outlet for irrigation drainwater, the irrigation of marginal land is likely to destroy the good land down-gradient. This is happening in California's San Joaquin Valley where salt and selenium were present long before the first settlers arrived in the late eighteenth century. To place in perspective the reality of irrigating lands in that Valley which covers an ancient saltwater sea, the San Joaquin Valley Drainage Program's manager, Edgar Imhoff, has had published the kind of indepth study other states with similar problems may wish to emulate. Written by Gerald Ogden,[7] long associated with the U. S. Department of Agriculture and more recently with the University of California (Davis), the study treats geology and climate change in relation to the land-use problems California experienced after irrigated agriculture was introduced in that Valley. Dr. Ogden states that the approximately 260 miles long and 130 miles wide Valley had been formed by the end of the Pleistocene Epoch. Covering an area of about 32,000 square miles, it represents "about one-fifth of the land surface of California." Within those "dimensions lay the valley floor that extended over an area of about 13,000 square miles" with a "transectional lobe" dividing the Valley north and south.[8]

The northern section or lower Valley began to experience water quality problems after the San Joaquin River, impounded behind Friant Dam, was channeled into the Friant-Kern Canal to irrigate land in Southern San Joaquin Valley. Except in wet years, and then only seasonally, very little fresh water moves down the river to the Delta. Recently the capacity of Friant Dam has been reduced to accommodate structural problems which will require extensive repair.[9] Unlike Hetch Hetchy's O'Shaughnessy Dam which Secretary Don Hodel wanted to remove, Friant, despite the damage it has done to lower San Joaquin Valley agriculture and the Delta, has not stirred the imagination of water resource planners and environmentalists. L. Douglas James' remarkable collection of essays in Man & Water posits that a "dam can be removed" though the factors that stand in the way are more likely to be "social than physical because the physical world is more easily changed back into a former state than are people."[10]

There is no excuse for the damage done to the San Joaquin Valley by the Bureau's San Luis Unit of the Central Valley Project for the land on the west side was known to be marginal. The irrigation and drainage system could have been sited in accordance with known soil characteristics. Department of Agriculture scientists, as early as 1919, had addressed the Valley's problem soils, classifying them "in terms of their agricultural potential."[11]

> ...Class 1 lands represented areas where soil texture, alkali accumulations and topography did not limit crop yield or discourage irrigation. They could produce high crop yields at reasonable costs for preparation, and could carry the costs for irrigation.
>
> Class 2 lands, flawed because of the presence of hardpan, roughness, alkali or other factors, could on the average carry the costs required for irrigation.
>
> Class 3 lands could not justify the costs of irrigation provided by regulated water supplies due to the presence of high concentrations of alkali, or the costs involved in land preparation or land leveling.
>
> Class 4 lands were considered of such poor quality that they could not produce cultivated crops, but were suited for use as flooded pasture.
>
> Class 5 lands were heavily alkaloid, shallow in depth, rough, underlain with hardpan, or steep, and were not considered cultivatable.[12]

Although the Bureau had tried to confine the San Luis Service Area to reasonably good land, it later succumbed to pressure from large landowners to expand the area. Bureau land classifications were not as restrictive as they needed to be to prevent damage to down-gradient areas. Class 1 was suitable for "sustained high production of any climatically adapted crop with minimum cost of management"; Class 2 was "Slightly less productive, adapted to fewer crops, and more difficult and costly to manage because of slight to moderate limitations in soil, topography, or drainage;" Class 3 "Restricted productivity, requiring difficult and costly management because of moderate to severe limitations"; Class 6 was "Unsuitable for irrigated cropping because of extreme limitations in soil, topography, or drainage." Classes 4 and 5 are not shown on the Bureau's land classification map.[13]

Ogden's timely report with its emphasis on salinity in a geomorphological setting has become available to decision makers and researchers at the same time as biogeochemical reports from Interior Department scientists. For California there are Geological Survey reconnaissance investigation reports on water quality, bottom sediment, and biota associated with irrigation drainage in the Tulare Lake, Lower Colorado River Valley (including adjacent areas in Arizona and Nevada), and Salton Sea regions.[14] Also pertinent to California are three GS Open-File Reports.[15] Not all the reconnaissance investigation reports are of equal merit but all contain basic data that can assist decision makers in attaining resource management goals such as safer habitats for fish and wildlife and improvement of water quality. In reading them one finds that irrigation practices commonly employed by project farmers are significantly contributing to the problems.

The Bureau promoted its reclamation program with dogma touted by the early irrigationists: They maintained enough had been written "to show that much more can be done with alkaline irrigation water than has hitherto been generally thought possible"[16] and all that they needed was "generous amounts of water."[17] Tile drains to remove wastewater were discussed by the irrigators and the Bureau's engineers, and even urged by engineers in the private sector but it was years before drains came into common use. When they did they created other problems, for usually there was no safe place for that drainwater. The Interior Department, now faced with an almost insurmountable problem at many wildlife refuges, must establish a policy that enables the Bureau to assist its clients in making a transition from excessive water use to conservative water use.

A first and very important step can be taken by the irrigators. Westlands Water District in California, faced with the closure of Kesterson Reservoir in June 1986, initiated in 1985 a water conservation and management program[18] which should be of interest to irrigation and/or water districts elsewhere. If Westlands' irrigators continue to cooperate and Westlands continues to issue progress reports, much can be learned from this program to conserve water and reduce dispersal of harmful soil constituents. Unfortunately, irrigators have not become accustomed to paying their way. Only two of the 21 irrigators who responded to Westlands' questionnaire, the basis of its progress report, said they "would be willing to help pay for the Program."[19]

In the San Joaquin Valley the salt problem, especially from boron, is enormous. Boron was not analyzed separately in the following example, but the high concentrations of salts that accumulated in ponds on the Freitas ranch three years after drain water began flowing into Kesterson Reservoir may be the main reason that the cattle and sheep died. According to the Merced County Division of Environmental Health, water quality samples from ponds on the ranch taken early in 1985 tested at two-and-one-half times the permissible amount for total dissolved solids; twice that permissible for sodium; and more than seven times that permissible for sulfates.[20] By 1986 portions of the ranch were so waterlogged and so polluted with salts as to be useless.[21]

By August 1986, salt buildup had reached astronomical concentrations--almost twice the saltiness of sea water. Pond samples taken by the Geological Survey on August 7 showed total dissolved solids ranging from 41,180 parts per million to 68,850 parts per million.[22] As the water that doesn't evaporate moves down-gradient to the San Joaquin River, which borders the Freitas ranch on the east side, salt grass has begun to replace the nutritive vegetation upon which several hundred head of cattle must feed.

Historically, Merced County, where Kesterson is located, had less serious salt problems than the other Valley counties, where they have been evident since the 1870s. University of California's distinguised pioneering Professor E.W. Hilgard discussed the problems in a landmark study begun in 1877 and published in 1886.[23] Another landmark study is the investigation of alkaline land and groundwater by W. C. Mendenhall and colleagues, published as a Geological Survey Water-Supply Paper in 1916.[24] Despite this early attention to salinity problems in San Joaquin Valley, "approximately 2 million acres of irrigated land" in Fresno, Stanislaus, Kings, and Kern counties had been badly damaged by 1915.[25] That the salinity problem on the west side of San Joaquin River did not attract much attention until later is because it had not attracted much development;[26] the land was poor in quality and groundwater was expensive to pump. Not even the Bureau saw this land as promising until technological developments and chemical-producing industries made marginal lands productive. The impacts of those developments on ground and surface waters, including impacts on human health, were not considered. Nor is the Bureau likely to get sufficient funding to deal with those impacts where its projects are at fault.

Historically, Bureau projects began with withdrawals by the Interior secretary of huge tracts of land. The withdrawals included lands to be irrigated--some of very poor quality--and the forested watersheds that held the sources of irrigation water. Where the land was privately owned, as it often was in the regions most suitable for agriculture, merely petitioning the Bureau for a project was not apt to be effective unless political clout was apparent. Oregon, for example, appears to have been less favored early in the century than one might expect, considering the withdrawal by the secretary of over two million acres by 1904.[27] When residents of Jefferson County looked to the Bureau for an irrigation project in 1913 they were ignored until 1938. When Wickiup Reservoir began filling in 1946 a long-awaited irrigation system was in view.[28]

The Bureau is not responsible for agricultural runoff at Malheur National Wildlife Refuge in eastern Oregon where large pockets of poor quality, problem soils exist. A three-year study by the Geological Survey and the Fish and Wildlife Service was begun there in 1986.[29] However, in the study plan it was suggested that Umatilla National Wildlife Refuge Complex, also in eastern Oregon, may be or may become impacted by Bureau projects and should be included in the Malheur investigation.[30] At the Malheur refuge selenium is less apparent than arsenic.[31] The Bureau's Klamath Project impacts California's Tule Lake on the northern border and the results of that investigation should appear in report form in 1989.[32]

Washington state has been the beneficiary of Bureau projects large and small but as yet none are identified as contributors of toxic drainwater to fish and wildlife refuges. The withdrawal of 4,700,000 acres of land by Interior from 1902 to 1904 is indicative of the Bureau's plans for this well-endowed and productive state.[33]

Idaho's selenium problems appeared minor in 1985 when Deer Flat National Wildlife Refuge near Nampa was given a Class C designation: "Areas where existing information does not justify concern." Since then American Falls Reservoir, another of the Bureau's early projects, has become a matter of concern. A reconnaissance report for the reservoir and service area is not expected before 1990.

Deer Flat was studied because Sacramento Bee reporters Harris and Morris, using different criteria, found reason for concern. (Geological Survey scientists did not agree.) Deer Flat is a 11,600-acre refuge surrounding 10,000-acre Lake Lowell, a Bureau reservoir. This part of the refuge was established in 1909; an area along the Snake River was added in 1939. Lake Lowell is typical of a Bureau impoundment, or any large impoundment associated with an irrigation or domestic water supply project. Known to be one of the "largest off-stream impoundments in the west," it supplies "about 137,000 acre-feet of irrigation water per year."[34] During early spring the reservoir is at capacity. As summer progresses, mud flats emerge. Although unsightly at times, such impoundments can offer important fish and wildlife habitats. Selenium and arsenic are common throughout the nation, and more so in Idaho than was previously thought, but they apparently have not seriously impacted this refuge where irrigation return flows supplement the water diverted from the Boise River. Lake Lowell Reservoir has been managed by the Bureau as part of the Boise Project since 1912.[35]

Montana's Sun River and Milk River projects have drainwater outlets to Benton Lake and Lake Bowdoin, respectively. The authors of the Sun River area reconnaissance investigation report did not blame the high concentrations of selenium on the Bureau's project despite the persuasiveness of their technical data. "To determine the relative proportions of constituents transported into the lakes by all sources, an extensive study of the water budget would be necessary,"[36] they said. Both lakes had benefitted from the greater than normal streamflow that occurred after Harris wrote about conditions at Bowdoin.[37] The authors of the Milk River area report acknowledged that weather conditions in "late 1985 and early 1986 raised the water levels in the refuge lakes and provided some partial flushing prior to the current study. As a result, concentrations of dissolved constituents analyzed in this study probably were diluted to some degree."[38] Persons familiar with selenium figures given as parts per billion in the Bee and other newspapers may want to compare them with figures in these reports which are given in micrograms per gram of dry weight. This can be done by multiplying the dry weight figures by 1000. Using Table 21 of the Milk River report as an example, selenium data on coots and avocets ranging up to 7400 parts per billion can be compared.[39] Inasmuch as the Milk River study area "overlies Cretaceous marine shales, which are known to contain relatively large concentrations of selenium and other trace elements in some areas,"[40] deformities among bird populations probably can be anticipated.

At Benton Lake where the maximum concentration of selenium in water reached 580 ppb, the authors of the Sun River area report hypothesized that saline seeps and springs around the lake could be the cause.[41] The bird eggs found near the lake had a maximum concentration of 68,000 ppb and the fish from the lake a maximum of 48,000 ppb.[42] The authors, however, seemed more concerned about the high concentrations of nitrate in groundwater which considerably exceeded the state's drinking-water standard; there are about 700 wells in the Greenfields Division of the Sun River Project supplying water for domestic use, some of them testing alarmingly high. Nitrate in groundwater not only is a public health concern but a geochemical concern because nitrate facilitates the movement of selenium and possibly other oxyanions in ground water.[43]

Concentrations of selenium in eggs and livers of birds nesting at the Kendrick Project in Wyoming are the highest found in this country to date: 160,000 and 170,000 ppb, respectively.[44] Kendrick is a sensitive issue with the Bureau and with Congress and neither seems to know how to deal with it. Like Kesterson, if any remedial measures are undertaken by the Interior Department they will be represented as voluntary.[45] Wyoming's Senator Kendrick wanted the project and apparently he also wanted his name on it.[46] Originally called the Casper-Alcova Project, funds for it were appropriated with a change of name in August 1937. The Act reserves to Colorado, where the North Platte River originates, rights to the natural flow.[47] Kendrick Project drainage is largely responsible for selenium found in water used for domestic purposes at Casper. More than 90 percent of the project service area is in alfalfa, other hay, corn fodder, and irrigated pasture.[48] According to geologist David Love, "Most of the service area is on seleniferous soil, even though the original acreage was cut in half because of selenium. Some of the seepage water from irrigation there is lethal. The Casper water supply is at the upper limit of human tolerance except during the irrigation season when it is higher...."[49]

Straddling the Green River in northeastern Utah near Jensen is the Stewart Lake Waterfowl Management Area which receives drainage from the Bureau's Jensen Unit of the Central Utah Project. Some years ago the Bureau must have had misgivings about the quality of water entering Stewart Lake from the drains it had constructed in connection with the project, for in 1978 it began sampling the water on a regular basis. Thirty miles southwest of Vernal is Ouray National Wildlife Refuge, also located on the Green, which does not receive drainage from the Jensen Unit.[50] What is especially impressive about the results of the reconnaissance investigation of irrigation drainage problems in the Middle Green Basin is the quality of the reporting. The authors present with easily understandable text, tables, and figures exactly what needs to be known about this impacted area where deformed embryos were found at Ouray. In fact, theirs is the only report by the reconnaissance teams that suggests human health is at risk for those who eat fish or waterfowl taken at either refuge, a topic of concern to the Congress that initiated the reconnaissance studies in 1985. The authors also reported the prevalence of uranium, boron, nitrate, and zinc, in that "order of severity."[51]

Unfortunately, Utah has very little land suitable for agriculture: a narrow strip west of the Wasatch Mountains referred to as the "Wasatch Oasis," and about 500 square miles in the Virgin and Santa Clara Valleys in the southwest corner of the state referred to as Utah's "Dixie."[52] Population growth is impinging upon the agricultural land in the narrow strip along the Wasatch Range so the Central Utah Project's customers will inevitably be urban dwellers. Land along the Middle Green was under irrigation many years before the Jensen Unit, which has about 4,000 acres in the service area but drains only about 750 acres.[53] However, selenium carried by drains, installed by the Bureau between 1974 and 1979, is highly concentrated.

Scheduled are other reconnaissance investigations into impacted regions for which reports can be anticipated: the Upper Sacramento River (California), the Gunnison River in Colorado, the Middle Arkansas River in Colorado and Kansas, the Angostura and Belle Fourche in South Dakota, the Bosque del Apache refuge in New

Mexico, the Riverton Reclamation Unit in Wyoming and, more recently, the Ute Reservation in southwestern Colorado where human health is at risk.[54]

Of the legal remedies available, the public trust doctrine now provides one of the most promising ways to control selenium and other contaminants. The doctrine has its roots in "ancient Roman law and the common law of England."[55] In the West it has been upheld in cases involving the beneficial use of water. In "Public Rights at the Headwaters," attorney John Thorson describes how Montana is utilizing the public trust doctrine in integrating public rights into its prior appropriation system; in facilitating stream access; in revising water permit requirements; in limiting private appropriation; and in controlling water leasing.[56] He discusses the doctrine in detail and cites various cases where the doctrine has been applied, including Idaho, California, and Montana.

In California an acknowledged legal scholar on the public trust doctrine is Professor of Law Harrison Dunning, University of California (Davis). His lectures and writings have been of particular assistance to Fish and Wildlife Service personnel in Sacramento who have used them in explaining what they perceive to be the role of the Service in applying the doctrine to instream flows:

> The United States Fish and Wildlife Service has long been concerned about instream flows and the need to protect and manage them for fish, wildlife, recreational and esthetic values. The growing public awareness and critical nature of water and its availability dictate that both the managers and the users of water exercise their roles in the public interest. We believe that the Public Trust Doctrine, judiciously applied, can be an effective tool for maintenance of instream flows and the management of the biological and ecological resources associated with these flows.[57]

The Bureau has opposed the doctrine because providing good water for aquatic life subtracts from the amount otherwise available to its massive irrigation projects. In California it intervened on behalf of the Los Angeles Department of Water and Power in the Mono Lake case, a lawsuit brought to prevent the Water Department from further lowering the lake by diverting stream flow in Mono Basin to

Los Angeles. It was not a popular position to have taken in California where the Owens Valley controversy of the early 1900s is still alive, but once taken the Bureau was implicated in the silencing of opposition in the Sacramento office of the Fish and Wildlife Service after the Service was asked by the State Water Resources Control Board to present its position on a water availability study on January 19, 1982. Felix Smith appeared on behalf of his superior, William Sweeney. Smith began his statement by mentioning the ecological studies of the Sacramento-San Joaquin Delta then being carried on by state and federal water agencies and listed the following authorities pertinent to the Service's involvement: the Fish and Wildlife Coordination Act, the National Environmental Policy Act, the Migratory Bird Treaty Act, the Migratory Bird Conservation Act, the Fish and Wildlife Act (1956), the Anadromous Fish Conservation Act, the Estuarine Protection Act, and the Endangered Species Act.[58]

The State Board had been concerned for some time about water quality and quantity problems in the Bay/Delta system when it scheduled the hearing to get reactions to the 1981 report prepared by its consultant. To the Bureau, a water availability study that suggested a more up-to-date method of modeling water quantity apparently posed the possible loss of some water to which it might not be entitled. To Smith and Sweeney, the hearing provided an opportunity to support the Board in determining the water needs for water quality improvement and fish survival. Said Smith:

> Fish species and ecosystems of the Bay-Delta System have continuously adjusted over geological time to natural environmental changes through evolutionary processes. To survive, a species must successfully compete within the system for necessary resources. Man's technology has enabled him to produce rapid environmental changes to which communities or organisms must adjust through the same evolutionary process, or be eliminated.
>
> It is within this context that we believe the Board has the responsibility to review and amend those water right permits which in any way modify Delta inflows, or Delta diversions or exports. The aim should be to provide, protect, or restore instream flows and water

quality and to protect and promote the public trust in fishery resources for all people and future generations.[59]

With the Mono Lake case in court and California's several area of origin acts attracting more interest than they had in the past, Smith's pronouncements were anathema to the Bureau and to the Interior Department solicitors who protect the Bureau's turf in and out of court. February 2, 1982, Mike Catino, Region II director, enunciated the Bureau's viewpoint to the Board.[60] Two months later Interior Department solicitors intervened on behalf of the Bureau. Robert Broadbent's protege, David Houston, then moving rapidly upward and soon to replace Catino, was put in charge of putting down Smith and seeing to it that other Fish and Wildlife Service personnel toed the line.

What went on thereafter can be described as government-by-solicitor. April 13, 1982, an assistant solicitor in Interior's Washington office prepared drafts of two letters to be put in final form by the office of the Assistant Secretary for Fish and Wildlife and Parks. These letters were to be sent to the State Board and the California Water Commission before whom Smith had presented his authorized statement on January 19 and April 2, respectively. The drafts charged that Smith's statement represented "no more than his personal views on the issues addressed" and should be stricken from the Board's and Commissions's hearing records and that Interior's position should be substituted as "part of the official record" of the Board and the Commission.[61]

To make a case against Smith and facilitate the future censorship of public statements made by Fish and Wildlife Service personnel, two sentences in Smith's statement were excerpted--one from the first page and one from the fourth--and juxtaposed so as to appear "totally contrary" to Interior's position.[62] Smith countered with a memorandum of protest to his superior, William Sweeney:

> ...The quote indicated on page 2 of subject memo are parts of 2 paragraphs taken out of context. This destroys their real meaning. They were lifted from our statement regarding the scope of the State Water Resources Control Board...Water Availability [study]...
>
> It is most unfortunate that the Solicitor's Office took this material as a direct quote without first looking

> into the facts. It looks like more shooting from the hip and very poor field investigation and findings of fact.[63]

April 29, Sweeney, responding to Smith's memo, wrote a tart letter to his boss, the Regional Director of the Fish and Wildlife Service whose office is in Portland, Oregon. Enclosing a copy of Catino's letter of February 2 to the Water Board, Sweeney called attention to paragraph three in which "Mr. Catino says 'It is important, therefore, for the Bureau to state, from the onset of this hearing and this study, that the United States disagrees with many of the legal conclusions reached in the [Board] consultant's study and endorsed in the Board's staff report.' Mr. Catino purports to speak for the United States (which presumably includes the Fish and Wildlife Service) in his statement." [Sweeney's emphasis; solicitors represent the United States but are supposed to maintain an impartial position in dealing with all Interior's various bureaus. Apropos the latter this author was told that their position is advisory.]

Problems experienced by Fish and Wildlife Service personnel in dealing with the Bureau have a long history in California for, as they see it, the Bureau's regional directors have the support of the regional solicitor and his staff of attorneys. During the Reagan administration this has been particularly noticeable and Sweeney had reason to be resentful. Protesting further he said:

> I wasn't aware that Mike Catino had been anointed and authorized to speak for the Fish and Wildlife Service.... I certainly don't agree with his position, and I'd be startled to learn that anyone else in the FWS agreed with it. If we're not supposed to testify on behalf of fish and wildlife interests, how does Bur Rec get away with testifying against those interests?[64] [Sweeney's emphasis.]

Within a month the director of the Fish and Wildlife Service in Washington, at the behest of Solicitor William Coldiron, gave the following command to all Fish and Wildlife personnel: "Past or present statements by Service employees which recognize the application of the public trust doctrine to California water rights allocation decisions are hereby disclaimed as being unauthorized by the Department."[65] Not only was the doctrine before the court but it was likely that the case would be decided in favor of preserving Mono Lake as indeed it was.[66]

Recent court decisions have cleared the way to wise management of natural resources. Especially is this true in California where Judge John Racanelli in United States of America v. State Water Resources Control Board eloquently enunciated the public trust doctrine and thereby strengthened the Board's position in reallocating water to meet changing needs.[67] Whether a majority of the Board can shed its subservience to the political whims of the governor in office remains to be seen. The Board has an able staff and an extraordinarily well-qualified chairman in Don Maughan. However, the Board is caught up in the politics of water in San Joaquin Valley where Kesterson and the drainage problem are not being resolved. The low spots in the Kesterson ponds have been covered with earth, inviting problems the extent of which are not now known. Contributing to those and other water quality problems are the huge pockets of selenium and salts on irrigated lands that are continuing to get their quota of water from the Bureau. Should the Bureau attempt to cut back on deliveries it is likely to be thwarted by state policy, enunciated in January 1986 by the governor's water resources director, David Kennedy, to keep that water flowing to west side valley farms.[68]

On the plus side, should the Board wish to pioneer a resources management program through the reallocation of water for beneficial use, it now has recent studies of Geological Survey scientists that show the extent of the sources of selenium in San Joaquin Valley and how it is mobilized and distributed. Some of the studies address the salt problem; others include toxicants in soils besides the ubiquitous selenium, especially boron; still others include the biochemical analyses by Fish and Wildlife scientists.[69]

Like the pilot project of Westlands Water District referenced in Note 18, the California studies alluded to in the previous paragraph are relevant to drainage problems in other irrigated areas of the arid and semi-arid West. Especially is this true of the Robert Gilliom report where he and his colleagues discuss how reducing the quantity of drainwater through the use of conservation methods in irrigating farmland can mitigate irrigation-induced surface and groundwater quality problems. Admittedly California's problems have come in for more scientific analysis than have the problems of other states. This need not be a deterrent. The various reconnaissance studies, some not yet published, provide enough biogeochemical data to justify the immediate undertaking of remedial measures. California's George Miller put the Department of the Interior on notice that a coverup of selenium problems related to reclamation projects throughout the West would not be tolerated, and decision makers now have at hand the data to get mitigation measures underway.

In interpreting some of the data in these reports, it will be helpful to have a copy of "Aquatic Cycling of Selenium: Implications for Fish and Wildlife," by Fish and Wildlife Service scientists A. Dennis Lemly and Gregory J. Smith.[70] As the title suggests, it describes how selenium reacts to varying ecological conditions and provides technical information and graphics that can assist persons in charge of refuges or pollution control mitigation efforts. Tables list wet and dry weight concentrations of selenium known to be hazardous to fish and wildlife under laboratory and field conditions. The processes that operate to remove the selenium from the system and "gradually reduce the residual contamination" when selenium inputs cease are described.[71] A supplemental reading list is provided.

Fish and Wildlife Service and Geological Survey scientists are passing through some difficult years but that has not deterred them from providing the best data of which they are capable, notwithstanding the aura of censorship in the Interior secretary's office. Decision makers in the afflicted states now have enough basic data from which to make extrapolations for foods the residents are likely to consume, not only those brought in by the fisherman and the hunter, but those grown in selenium-tainted soils.

NOTES

1. Gates, supra, 665. Full citation, 1, note 2.

2. U. S. Bureau of Reclamation. Third Annual Report of Reclamation Service (Washington: Government Printing Office, 1905), 54-55.

3. Ibid., 55.

4. Ernest Douglas (ed.), "Crops are coaxed from a Sand Pile," Reclamation Era, May 1965. For an overview of soil conditions and the kinds of crops grown, see: F. O. Youngs, W. G. Harper, and James Thorp, "Soil Survey of Yuma-Wellton Area," Arizona-

California U. S. Department of Agriculture, Bureau of Chemistry and Soils, 1929, prepared in cooperation with the University of Arizona; land classification maps in U. S. Bureau of Reclamation Land Classification Report Wellton-Mohawk Div., Gila Project (Yuma: July 1948, rev. March 1952); U. S. Department of the Interior/Bureau of Reclamation, "Supplemental Report of Payment Capacity/Wellton-Mohawk Division, Gila Project, Arizona," Region 3 (Boulder City, Nevada, March 1959), 4, 7; Wellton-Mohawk Irrigation and Drainage District, "Report of Productivity," Re-Examination Board, 2 vols. (July 3, 1973, Wellton, Arizona), vol. 1, for land taken out of production. With reference to project costs see Charles W. Howe, Natural Resources Economics (New York: John Wiley & Sons, 1979), 294.

5. Reisner, supra, 8. Full citation, 3, note 28.

6. Douglas, supra.

7. Gerald R. Ogden. Agricultural Land Use and Wildlife in the San Joaquin Valley, 1769-1930: An Overview. Prepared for the San Joaquin Valley Drainage Program (U. S. Bureau of Reclamation, Orders Nos. 7-PG-20-01610 and 7-PG-20-05910) March 1988.

8. Ibid., 2-3.

9. Rob Wells, "Dam loaded with cracks/Blame pinned on chemical reaction," Santa Rosa (California) Press Democrat, December 11, 1987.

10. L. Douglas James (ed.). Man & Water/The Social Sciences in Management of Water Resources (Lexington: The University Press of Kentucky, 1974), 212.

11. Ogden, supra, 24.

12. Ibid., 24-25. California Department of Public Works, Department of Water Resources Bulletin 29. San Joaquin River Basin Sacramento: State Printing Office, 1931).

13. U. S. Department of the Interior. Central Valley Project/Special Task Force Report on San Luis Unit (Washington, D.C.: USGPO, 1978), Appendix K, Plate 3. In addition to omitting two land classifications, 4 and 5, the map is drawn to imply there were no Class 6 lands. Originally there was a Class 5 containing 114,514 acres but an agreement among the various parties, including Westlands Water District, the Bureau, and the Interior Secretary resulted in omitting Class 5 and declaring 112,401 of the 114,514 acres as arable. Ibid., 283.

14. U. S. Geological Survey Water-Resources Investigations Report 88-4001, Reconnaissance Investigation of Water Quality, Bottom Sediment, and Biota Associated with Irrigation Drainage in the Tulare Lake Bed Area, Southern San Joaquin Valley, 1986-87 (February 1988); USGS Water-Resources Investigations Report, Reconnaissance Investigation of...Irrigation Drainage in the Salton Sea Area, California (in press); USGS Water Resources Investigations Report 88-4002, Reconnaissance Investigation of...Irrigation Drainage in the Lower Colorado River Valley, Arizona, California, and Nevada, 1986-87 (February 1988).

15. Roger Fujii, S. J. Deverel, and D. B. Hatfield, Distribution of Selenium in Soils of Agricultural Fields, Western San Joaquin Valley, California, USGS Open-File Report 87-467 (1987); Kenneth Belitz, Character and Evolution of the Ground-Water Flow System in the Central Part of the Western San Joaquin Valley, California, USGS Open File Report 87-573 (1988); Roger Fujii, Water-Quality and Sediment-Chemistry Data of Drain Water and Evaporation Ponds from Tulare Lake Drainage District, Kings County, California, March 1985 to March 1986, USGS Open-File Report 87-700 (1988).

16. Newell, supra, 258. Full citation, 1, note 36.

17. Ibid.

18. Westlands Water District. 1985-86 Water Conservation and Management Program/Review and Evaluation, prepared, in part, to satisty the requirements of Contract No. B-55748 with California Department of Water Resources (May 1987).

19. Ibid., 38.

20. Jeff Palsgaard, Merced County Division of Environmental Health, to Merced County Board of Supervisors member Al Goman, letter of February 25, 1985.

21. Skibitzke Engineers & Associates, Inc., groundwater report, supra. Full citation, 7, note 45.

22. David G. Houston, Region II director, USBR, to Frank Freitas, letter of September 8, 1986, enclosing water quality data supplied by USGS, Sacramento.

23. J. Letey, et al. An Agricultural Dilemma: Drainage Water and Toxics Disposal in the San Joaquin Valley (Berkeley: The Regents of the University of California, Division of Agriculture and Natural Resources, 1986), 14, 54.

24. W. C. Mendenhall, et al. Ground Water in San Joaquin Valley, California. USGS Water-Supply Paper 298 (Washington, D.C., 1916).

25. Robert L. Kelley and Ronald L. Nye, "Historical perspective on salinity and drainage problems in California," California Agriculture (October 1984), 5.

26. Ibid.

27. U. S. Bureau of Reclamation. Third Annual Report..., supra, 54.

28. Harold J. Eedemiller, "Irrigation of Jefferson County" in Jefferson County Reminiscences (Portland, Oregon: Binfords & Mort, 1957), 329-249. Eedemiller deals with the struggles and delays in getting the Bureau to build the North Unit Irrigation Canal and Wickiup Dam and Reservoir. County farmers had made various attempts to irrigate the region since 1872.

29. Identified as the Malheur Irrigation Study plan, it was submitted on or about May 15, 1986, by the USGS Interagency Team coordinator, Greg Fuhler, to the Bureau and the Fish and Wildlife Service.

30. Ibid., 26.

31. Ibid., 15.

32. U. S. Fish and Wildlife Service, Draft, Contaminant Issues of Concern, supra, A46-49. Full citation, 8, note 35. In the Bureau's Third Annual Report, supra, are details for potential development of projects which include the possibility of "lowering and draining Lower Klamath Lake." "Klamath River is the outlet of Klamath Lake, Oregon," states the report. "It flows through large swamp areas in Klamath County, Oreg., and by an overflow process feeds Little Klamath Lake" on the California border.

33. USBR, Third Annual Report, supra, 54.

34. U. S. Dept. of the Interior Task Group on Irrigation Drainage. Draft, Preliminary Evaluation of Selenium Concentrations, supra, 47-51. Full citation, 8, note 37.

35. Ibid.

36. USGS Water-Resources Investigations Report 87-4244, Reconnaissance Investigation of Water Quality, Bottom Sediment, and Biota Associated with Irrigation Drainage in the Sun River Area, West-Central Montana, 1986-87 (Helena, Montana, 1988), 57; USGS

Water-Resources Investigations Report 87-4243, Reconnaissance Investigation of...Irrigation Drainage in the Bowdoin National Wildlife Refuge and Adjacent Areas of the Milk River Basin, Northeastern Montana, 1986-87 (Helena, Montana, 1988).

37. Tom Harris, "Refuge provides home for looming disaster," supra. Full citation, 8, note 43.

38. USGS Water-Resources Investigation Report 87-4243, supra, 56.

39. Ibid., 69.

40. Ibid., 56.

41. USGS Water-Resources Investigations Report 87-4244, supra, 29, 64. Note also the prevalence of boron at this test site and also the one on page 63.

42. Ibid., 71 and 41, respectively.

43. Ronald S. Oremland, J. T. Hollibaugh, and others, "Measurement of Bacterial Selenate Reduction to Elemental Selenium in Anoxic Sediments" and "Dissimilatory Reduction of Selenate in Anoxic Sediments and by Anaerobic Bacterial Cultures," papers presented December 6 and 9, 1988, at the American Geophysical Union Conference in San Francisco.

44. USGS Water-Resources Investigations Report 87-4255. Reconnaissance Investigation of Water Quality, Bottom Sediment, and Biota Associated with Irrigation Drainage in the Kendrick Reclamation Project Area, Wyoming, 1986-87 (Cheyenne, Wyoming, 1988), 29, 31.

45. U. S. Department of the Interior/Office of the Solicitor, Pacific Southwest Region. Legal brief dated July 6, 1987, In re: California SWRCB File No. A-354, wherein it states: "In the Absence of a Clear and Unambiguous Waiver of Sovereign Immunity by Congress, No State May Subject a Federal Agency to Regulation under its laws." Interior takes the position that any mitigation measures it may undertake are purely voluntary. With reference to the reconnaissance reports herein cited, Secretary Hodel down-plays the seriousness of the selenium problem in a press release issued by Mitch Snow on May 10, 1988 (MP-88-18). Snow quotes Hodel as saying: "While it is clear from these reports that a new environmental problem of national proportions does not exist, it also is clear that some localized problems related to irrigation drainage water do

exist...." Of course it can be argued that the problem is not national, confined as it to sizeable areas of the arid and semiarid West.

46. Reisner, supra, 232-33.

47. 59 Stat. 595.

48. Ibid. For crops grown see USGS Report 87-4255, supra, 4. Full citation in note 44.

49. J. David Love to Alice Q. Howard, Oakland, California, letter of February 5, 1987. See also chapter 7, notes 16-18, 20.

50. USGS Water-Resources Investigations Report 88-4011. Reconnaissance Investigation of Water Quality, Bottom Sediment, and Biota Associated with Irrigation Drainage in the Middle Green River Basin, Utah, 1986-87 (Salt Lake City, Utah, 1988), 14, 24-25.

51. Ibid., 30; Tom Harris, "Congress calls hearings on selenium studies," Fresno Bee, December 18, D1.

52. Federal Writers' Project. Utah's Story (Salt Lake City: Utah State Road Commission, 1942), 20.

53. USGS Water-Resources Investigations Report 88-4011, supra, 29. Figure 7, page 21, shows irrigated land.

54. Tom Harris, "More tainted-water tests begin at wildlife refuges," Sacramento Bee, Feb. 18, 1988, A3, A4; Robert E. Brogden, E. Carter Hutchinson, and Donald E. Hillier. Availability and Quality of Groundwater Southern Ute Indian Reservation Southwestern Colorado, Geological Survey Water-Supply Paper 1576-J (Washington, D.C.: Government Printing Office, 1979).

55. Joseph L. Sax. Defending the Environment/A Strategy for Citizen Action (New York: Alfred A. Knopf, 1971), 163. Professor of Law Joseph Sax, University of Michigan, is a widely known authority on the public trust doctrine.

56. John E. Thorson, "Public Rights at the Headwaters," Journal AWWA (October 1986), 72-78. Thorson's article is one of seven presented under the caption, "Water Law in the West."

57. Felix E. Smith, "The Public Trust Doctrine, Instream Flows and Resources" (Sacramento: U.S. Fish and Wildlife Service, California-Nevada Area Office, March 1980), 2, quoting William D. Sweeney.

58. Felix Smith, "Sacramento-San Joaquin Delta Watershed Water Availability Study," p. 2 of statement to SWRCB, Jan. 19, 1982; Dendy & Associates, "Availability of Water for Appropriation in the

Sacramento and San Joaquin Rivers and Delta System," 1981.

59. Smith, Ibid., 7.

60. M. A. Catino, Region II director, USBR, to Carla M. Bard, Chairperson, SWRCB, letter of February 2, 1982.

61. Gary Fisher, Asst. Solicitor, Branch of Water and Power, Division of Energy and Resources, Department of the Interior. Memorandum of April 13, 1982, and drafts of two letters dated April 29, 1982, to Craig Potter, Special Assistant to the Assistant Secretary for Fish and Wildlife, Department of the Interior.

62. Gary Fisher to Commissioner, Bureau of Reclamation, memorandum of April 14, 1982, p. 2.

63. Felix Smith to Bill Sweeney, memorandum of April 28, 1982, p. 1.

64. William D. Sweeney to FWS Region I director, Portland, memorandum of April 29, 1982.

65. Robert A. Jantzen, Director, U.S.Fish and Wildlife Service, to Region I director, FWS, Portland. Memorandum of May 26, 1982, p. 2, as per instructions in Solicitor William H. Coldiron memorandum to Jantzen, April 23, 1982.

66. National Audubon Society v. Superior Court (1983) 33 Cal. 3d 419 [the Mono Lake Case] and United States of America v. State Water Resources Control Board (1986) 227 Cal. Rptr. 161, supporting Board in reallocating water.

67. Ibid., 227 Cal. Rept. 161.

68. Lloyd G. Carter, "Future of west side farming hinges on disposal of salt," Fresno Bee, Jan. 29, 1986.

69. USGS Water-Resources Investigations Report 88-4186 by Robert J. Gilliom and others, Preliminary Assessment of Sources, Distribution, and Mobility of Selenium in the San Joaquin Valley, California (Sacramento, California, 1989), and Notes 14, 15, 36, 44, and 50.

70. A. Dennis Lemly and Gregory J. Smith. Aquatic Cycling of Selenium: Implications for Fish and Wildlife (Washington, D.C.: U.S.Dept. of the Interior/Fish and Wildlife Service), Fish and Wildlife Leaflet 12, p. 5.

71. Ibid., 4; write Publications Unit, USFWS, #148 Matomic Bldg., Washington, D.C. 20240 or National Technical Technical Information Service (NTIS) for copies.

10
The Power of the "Pork Barrel"

Congress passed its first legislative act to promote conservation of wildlife, fish, and game in 1934.[1] In 1946 it passed the more stringent Fish and Wildlife Coordination Act.[2] Section 1 of that Act provides:

> For the purpose of recognizing the vital contribution of our wildlife resources to the Nation, the increasing public interest and significance thereof due to expansion of our national economy and other factors, and to provide that wildlife conservation shall receive equal consideration and be coordinated with other features of water-resource development programs through the effectual and harmonious planning, development, maintenance, and coordination of wildlife conservation and rehabilitation...the Secretary of the Interior is authorized (1) to provide assistance to, and cooperate with, Federal, State, and public or private agencies and organizations in the development, protection, rearing, and stocking of all species of wildlife, resources thereof, and their habitat....[3] [Emphasis added.]

Section 2(a) covers all federal and federally licensed water impoundments, diversions, or other modifications, except those involving less than ten acres, and requires water agencies such as the Bureau of Reclamation and the Corps of Engineers to consult first with the Fish and Wildlife Service. Section 2(b) requires them to submit to Congress, along with their own engineering surveys and project specifications, the reports and recommendations of federal and state resource agencies. Other sections of the Act deal with other aspects of its purpose and intent.[4]

In 1981, Oliver Houck, visiting professor of law at Tulane University, pointed out why the Fish and Wildlife Coordination Act of 1946, as subsequently amended, was falling far short of its stated intent. Construction bureaus had failed to consult with fish and wildlife bureaus; fish and wildlife bureaus had failed to prepare mitigation reports; Congress "had simply looked the other way" and courts of law, when "faced with bald violations of the Act..., commonly found compliance with its provisions judicially unenforceable."[5] Houck, an authority on environmental law, cited numerous points and authorities to substantiate his charges.

Fish and Wildlife officials are inclined to bow to Bureau desires because the Bureau is the project leader in designing and constructing reclamation projects encompassing fish and wildlife amenities such as reservoir recreation facilities and wetlands. These officials usually are not boat rockers, nor are the state and local officials who, by the provisions of the Act, would seem to have considerable authority to act in the best interests of fish and wildlife survival in areas under their jurisdiction.

There is interesting and challenging work to be had in the Fish and Wildlife Service, but on the administrative level it tends to be as political as the Bureau. It has, however, attracted extraordinarily competent and dedicated scientists; it is frustrating to them to find that the language in the Fish and Wildlife Coordination Act is viewed as weak and little more than unenforceable. Part of the unenforceability lies with the lack of legal expertise on the part of attorneys bringing suit, as Houck makes clear. Another part lies with Interior Department solicitors who, because of their role as interpreters of reclamation law, are viewed as purveyors of decisions favorable to the Bureau rather than to FWS. The National Environmental Policy Act of 1969, although it strengthened the position of FWS to protect fish and wildlife refuges from the Bureau and the Corps, appears to require much more aggressive leadership by FWS administrators than has been evident.

The Comptroller General (General Accounting Office) is on call to investigate noncompliance with legislation passed by Congress. March 16, 1972, Congressman John Dingell, chairman of the Subcommittee on Fisheries and Wildlife Conservation, wrote the Comptroller General regarding noncompliance by the Bureau and other federal construction agencies with sections 2 and 3 of the Fish and Wildlife Coordination Act of 1958. Section two requires construction agencies to consult first with the Fish and Wildlife Service, and then "with the head of the agency exercising administration over the wildlife resources of the particular State wherein the impoundment, diversion, or other control facility is to be constructed, with a view to the conservation of wildlife resources by preventing loss of and damage to such resources as well as providing for the development and improvement thereof in connection with such water-resource development...."

Section 3 of the Act emphasizes the intent to improve and protect wildlife habitats on the land and in the water, and spells it out:

> ...The use of such waters, land, or interests therein for wildlife conservation purposes shall be in accordance with the general plans approved jointly (1) by the head of the particular department or agency exercising primary administration in each instance, (2) by the Secretary of the Interior, and (3) by the head of the agency exercising the administration of the wildlife resources of the particular State wherein the waters and areas lie....[6] [Emphasis added.]

As Professor Houck has pointed out, federal and state departments of fish and wildlife tend to be remiss in preparing mitigation reports and recommendations.[7] The GAO in its 1974 report recommends "Improved federal efforts...to equally consider wildlife conservation with other features of water resource developments," to make it easier for fish and wildlife administrators to implement the laws Congress passed to protect these natural resources. Failure to enforce the fish and wildlife coordination acts may lead to serious mistakes. For example, the GAO investigators found that the Bureau had been cautioned by Service personnel during the early stages of construction of Teton Dam about the need for a storage pool large enough to protect the reservoir's fish population. The Bureau agreed to design the pool to the requested specifications; then, without further dialog with Service personnel, it altered the plans--reducing the reservoir pool level by 23 percent. Bureau officials could not account for their failure to consult with Service personnel when they were interrogated by the investigators.[8] But the report is strangely silent about the circumstances, leading one to suspect that Service personnel were less than vigilant in following the progress of construction. In this instance it made little difference, for the cutthroat trout fishery which was to be protected by a properly designed reservoir pool was destroyed several years later when Teton Dam failed while the reservoir was filling.

Whether the dam will be rebuilt is up to Congress. To what extent the fishery will revive if the dam is not rebuilt is up to nature. In the interim the ignominy of the dam's failure rests heavily upon the Bureau. Shortly thereafter an independent committee of consulting engineers pinned the blame for the dam's failure on the Bureau's "unfortunate choice of design measures together with less than conventional precautions...."[9] Within the Interior Department a selected group of experts said "a safe dam could have been built at the site utilizing design concepts that were known at that time."[10] More recently the editor of Engineering News-Record said, in contemplating the Bureau's future: "The agency's technical credibility and managerial reputation suffered a major blow with the failure of Teton Dam...." After noting that the Bureau had spent years "trying to rebuild its image," by 1985 the administration was "making mincemeat" of its construction budget.[11]

The history of dam building in Idaho is one of private as well as public entrepreneurship. Even before the Carey Act of 1894, which helped to finance subsequent projects, significant strides in irrigating the land were being made. By the time the Bureau came on board some of those projects had failed. The Bureau took some of them over and enlarged them but mostly it built new projects. With appropriations for massive projects and excellent damsites to choose from it was entrepreneurship-without-risk for Bureau engineers. In time the Bureau achieved the reputation of having in its employ many of the best engineers in the country. Some of its most impressive projects are in Idaho.

Two years before the Reclamation Act was passed in 1902,

Idaho had 1,200,000 acres under irrigation.[12] In 1910, with completion of the first Bureau projects, that figure nearly doubled to 2,200,000.[13] By the mid-1920s there was so much land under irrigation with the consequent over production of basic foods that Idaho farmers were putting themselves out of business.[14] During the 1930s farmers throughout the nation were going bankrupt, especially in Idaho. Banks holding their mortages were in jeopardy and many of them failed. The beneficiaries were the investors who bought up land at drastically reduced prices: the advent of agribusiness was at hand. There still are small farms in Idaho, but once there were a great many--more than 45,000 in 1935; fewer than 11,500 in 1959. As they diminished in number they increased in size.[15]

Water impoundments constructed or taken over and completed by the Bureau in the early years are indicators of how quickly an abundant supply of irrigation water was made available to Idaho farmers. In 1909 Minidoka Dam was providing over 95,000 acre-feet of storage; in 1911 the three Deer Flat dams were providing 169,000; in 1915 Arrowrock Dam was providing 186,600; in 1927 American Falls Dam was providing 1,700,000.[16] With an abundant supply of water Idaho farmers raised bumper crops of potatoes and grains that were staples in the East and Middle West; when freight rates became favorable, Idaho's bumper crops jeopardized the economy of those Eastern and Middle Western states.

When Idahoans demanded more water, new projects were built and old projects enlarged. With completion of the Palisades Dam in 1959, acre-feet of storage in the Minidoka project reached 3,322,780. With six storage reservoirs, two power plants, diversion dams, and distribution systems, that project became the largest in the state. Anticipating future expansion, additions "as needed through the years" are provided for in the design.[17]

Idaho's 7.4 percent of the country's potato production in 1947, increased to 19.7 percent in 1963, or almost one-fifth of a crop that can be grown profitably in most of the states. Furthermore, nearly 60 percent of Idaho's potatoes were produced on lands getting Bureau of Reclamation water. By providing that cheap water the Bureau had "substantially reduced the incomes of nonreclamation potato farmers" in Idaho and other reclamation states.[18] This was the status of production when Congress passed the Lower Teton Division Act on

September 7, 1964,[19] to irrigate more potatoes. The Act provided for a dam and reservoir, a pumping plant and power plant, and canals and water distribution facilities to "assist in the irrigation of arid and semiarid lands in the upper Snake River Valley."[20] There was little in that Act to benefit farmers in the Teton River Valley and a good bit less when the dam failed in 1976. For many years those farmers had irrigated their crops with water stored behind small dams that had not interfered with the cutthroat trout habitat so dear to fishermen; such flooding as infrequently occurred was of more concern to farmers in the vicinity of the Snake River's Henrys Fork. It must have been an exercise in ingenuity for the Bureau to have come up with a benefit-cost ratio of 1.2 to 1.0 to justify a dam for which some of its personnel had little enthusiasm.

In Idaho and nearby states there was strong opposition to the dam, especially from fishermen and other environmentalists. The Idaho Environmental Council, viewing the Bureau's benefit-cost ratio as ridiculous, ran its own and came up with a ratio of 0.73 to 1.0.[21] But Mormon power got construction underway. Mormons have been pro-irrigation ever since they arrived in the West and saw irrigation in practice--albeit primitive--by their Indian neighbors. They learned what they could from observation and then improvised and modernized their own systems. In "The Lord's Beavers," a chapter in Rivers of Empire, Donald Worster credits the Mormons with being the first "Americans of northern European ancestry" to successfully practice irrigation on a large scale in the West.[22]

With failure of Teton Dam, Mormon irrigationists experienced criticism as well as sympathy, censure as well as charity. For the Bureau there was peer criticism and Congressional censure. Representative Leo Ryan of California grabbed the initiative and interrogated the culprits. Representative Gilbert Gude of Maryland assisted Ryan in eliciting information from the witnesses and in the preparation of a devastating report.[23] Senators Frank Church and James McClure of Idaho prepared reparations bill S.3542:

> Be it enacted by the Senate and House of Representatives of the United States of America in Congress assembled, That the Congress finds that without regard to the proximate cause of the failure of the Teton Dam, it is the purpose of the United States to fully

> compensate any and all parties which have been directly injured as the result of flooding following the failure of said dam. The purposes of this Act are (1) to provide just compensation for the personal injuries and deaths, and the loss and damage to property, including the destruction and damage to irrigation works, caused by the flooding following the failure on June 5, 1976, of the Teton Dam in the State of Idaho, and (2) to provide for the expeditious consideration and settlement of claims for such personal injuries, deaths, and property loss and damage.[24]

Other provisions in the bill spelled out in detail how the legislation should be implemented by the Secretary of the Interior. Idaho representatives George Hansen and Steve Simms introduced "like legislation" in the House. As if to further justify the legislation, Hansen remarked to Senator Church: "I would venture that I may have as many relatives in the area as possibly you and Senator McClure together might have."[25]

President Carter had responded immediately to the disaster with a request for $200 million. Church called that "just a start." Based on estimated damages he wanted about one billion.[26] Also available to the dispossessed were the various legislative acts such as the Federal Disaster Relief Act of 1974 and the Bureau's own funding authority for damages and injuries connected with failed projects. The deputy assistant attorney general was asked to elaborate on the latter.

> Mr. JAFFE. Yes, Senator. In Public Law 94-180, the appropriations bill for the Bureau of Reclamation, there is a provision which authorizes the payment of personal injury and property damage claims.
>
> The only difficulty with that is that it is reimbursable, not reimbursable from the person to whom it is paid but reimbursable in the sense that the Bureau must recoup it in order to replenish the funds. There is no separate appropriation. All the funds appropriated for the Bureau of Reclamation are available. That authority appears under the administrative

> provisions: All appropriations for the Bureau shall be available for "payment of claims for damages to or loss of property, personal injury or death arising out of the activities of the Bureau of Reclamation."
>
> ...However, further on in the bill it indicates that such expenditures must be reimbursable: "Sums appropriated herein which are expended in the performance of reimbursable functions of the Bureau of Reclamation shall be returnable to the extent and in the manner provided by law." That would be reimbursable.
>
> Senator CHURCH. Reimbursable from whom?
>
> Mr. JAFFE. The Bureau has fees and charges, for example, for its water and for other services that it renders. Fees and payments are made to it as though it was a utility. This would become a cost of operation and they would have to increase those fees and charges.
>
> Senator CHURCH. What you are really saying, then, is that under existing law, if compensation is paid, then the Bureau must recover whatever is paid out by imposing additional fees on the water users.
>
> Mr. JAFFE. That's correct, and it does not contemplate--reimbursement does not contemplate a disaster of this magnitude. However, the authority is there.[27]

The legislation prepared by Senator Church was passed and the public picked up the tab.

Historian F. Ross Peterson in "The Teton Dam Disaster: Tragedy or Triumph?"--an invited lecture delivered at Utah State University--described how the disbursal of the funds did and did not serve the immediate and future needs of the flood victims, "nearly 95 percent" of whom were Mormons.[28] Unlike the accounts of the journalists who covered the dam failure and its impact on the victims,

Peterson's is an insider's account told from the perspective of a historian who has written extensively on Idaho. He told of the over 40 thousand volunteers who lent their skills and performed much of the cleanup work; of the victims of whom there were some who questioned the "very foundation" of agriculture in the arid West--"irrigation and man-made dams"; of those victims who saw their dilemma as God-ordained to test their ability to survive--to triumph over adversity.

Within hours after the flood, disaster relief was on its way from the Federal Disaster Assistance Administration, the Red Cross, the Small Business Administration, the Bureau of Reclamation, the Soil Conservation Service, the Department of Housing and Urban Development, the Corps of Engineers, the National Guard, various state relief agencies, and churchs of many denominations. Ricks College, where the Red Cross established its headquarters, provided a haven for the homeless who were sheltered in dormitory rooms and adjacent apartments.[29] "The thousands of cheerful volunteers had a fantastic effect on the victims of the flood," said Peterson. "Work which would have taken weeks was completed in two days" and on one occasion a call for 150 electricians brought over 400.[30]

Housing and Urban Development (HUD) trailers were brought in to serve as offices where victims could file their claims. Bureau personnel from the Rexburg office were brought in to assist them. These government officials could approve the claims "completely" or they could negotiate them; or the victims could sue the government and some of them did. Later some of the claimants felt that they had settled for too little and that others had gotten too much, but there were very few "blatant cases of attempted fraud." The dissatisfaction some of them felt was mainly over the tight deadline in which to file--a process designed for their benefit to facilitate the release of funds and enable them to reestablish their homes and businesses as soon as possible.[31]

Peterson mentioned in his lecture that there are "many aspects" of the Teton disaster that remain unresolved, such as: will the dam be rebuilt and, if it is, will that once great potato land regain its productivity? Since then there has been pressure to rebuild the dam. The Mormons do not approve of welfare, but the use of federal funds for another Teton is in reality a form of welfare. The failed dam had a tremendous overrun, typical of federal water projects, and, if rebuilt, would far exceed the original cost. Furthermore, well over a billion dollars may have been paid out in reparations. Initially all claims were open to the public under the Freedom of Information Act, so ruled the Interior Department, but a suit was subsequently brought by a citizens' group to maintain privacy for the claimants and a federal judge has ruled in their favor.[32]

The Teton River, once known as Pierre's River, is less than 80 miles in length. Irrigated agriculture was first practiced in the lower basin. By the 1880s irrigated farms were prevalent in the upper basin, once known as Pierre's Hole, a fur-trapping area in the early 1800s.[33] Teton Dam was located several miles above the mouth of the river's 22-mile canyon. At the canyon's mouth is the town of Teton which the floodwaters narrowly missed. The nearby town of Wilford was washed away. The river enters Henrys Fork of the Snake several miles below Rexburg. That only six lives were lost by drowning and five by flood-connected accidents is due to the effective warnings transmitted at a time when residents could respond quickly. Had the dam failed at night, the loss of life would have been in the thousands.[34]

August 5, 1976, Congressman Leo Ryan described the course of the flood to his subcommittee:

> The huge reservoir covering 17 miles of the upstream river and holding 80 billion gallons of water burst through the collapsing wall and tore into Idaho countryside with an almost unbelievable force. It stripped top-soil from fields; it tore the pavement from roads; it twisted railroad tracks from their beds; it lifted houses and barns off their foundations; it uprooted trees; and it swept thousands of livestock along in its flood.
>
> In the end, 11 people were dead. Thousands were homeless. Whole towns were destroyed--literally ripped apart by the force of the water--then coated and littered with tons of mud and silt and debris.[35]

As Marc Reisner wrote in Cadillac Desert, the floodwater was "no longer liquid, but semisolid" when it hit Sugar City, a town of 8,000 people.[36] Spreading two miles in width in some places, the deluge rampaged down the Snake River Valley. Water was released at a furious pace at the Bureau's American Falls Dam. Had that dam failed, others below it were expected to fail and flood the rest of southern Idaho. A chain of large dams on a river can be a risky proposition when an upstream dam fails.

The failure of Teton Dam caused astronomical losses in five Idaho counties: Madison, Jefferson, Bonneville, Fremont, and Bingham. It caused the loss of 16,000 head of livestock, mainly in Madison County where 10,000 were lost. Five thousand farms and the buildings on them were destroyed in Bingham County; over a thousand were destroyed in Jefferson County and as many more in Fremont County. Almost 500 homes were destroyed in Madison County; another 300 in Jefferson County. Only Bonneville County escaped residential destruction though 38 homes sustained damages. Madison County reported over 2,000 damaged homes. All five counties sustained heavy damages to farmland: 45,000 damaged acres in Madison County; 17,500 in Jefferson County; 10,000 in Bonneville County; 14,000 in Fremont County; 10,000 in Bingham County.[37]

These are sobering statistics that Idaho politicians and irrigators may wish to forget. They had ordered a dam that was the undoing of many people who had little or nothing to gain from it. Therefore, should the liability provision in Public Law 94-180 have been bypassed because Senator Church and other Idaho legislators did not wish to impose "additional fees on the water users"?[38] Aside from the fact that Commissioner Floyd Dominy had a way with Congress, the wording of the Lower Teton Division Act shows that Congress, although it may not have known what was going on behind the scenes in Idaho, knew for whose benefit the Act was intended. One of the reports that followed the dam failure documented the local political machinations.

This 1977 report of the Senate Subcommittee on Energy Research and Development reviews the circumstances that led to the authorization and funding of Teton Dam: 1961 had been a drought year and irrigators had run short of water during the late summer months; 1962 was a wet year. Flooding had been severe in the lower Teton basin and on the Snake River plain. Henrys Fork, tributary to the Snake, was responsible for some of that flooding on the plain. Dominy, who knew he had the backing of the Fremont-Madison Irrigation District for a dam on the Teton because it would also serve irrigators in the Henrys Fork area, informed Secretary Udall on March 25, 1963, that the "plan proposed for the lower Teton division would alleviate both the drought and [the] flood problems...."[39] Presumably this information is what justified passage of the Act in 1964.

Long before Dominy had become commissioner in 1959 he had pushed the Bureau to do his will. It would not have occurred to him to investigate conditions that caused Idaho irrigators to run short of water, such as putting ten acre-feet per acre on potatoes annually. Some areas of Idaho do have porous soil, but the tendency to over-irrigate was general throughout the state and had been particularly noticeable during the ten-year period preceding the 1961 drought.[40] Furthermore, there was evidence that the drought had not interfered with potato production; production in Fremont and Madison counties during 1961 had gone up.[41]

Although the 1961 drought and the 1962 flood were publicized as the reason for Teton Dam, the Idaho state legislature had petitioned Congress and the President for this project on January 24, 1961, months before the drought occurred. That petition was sent at the behest of the Fremont-Madison Irrigation District and appears to have been urged by the rich farmers on the Rexburg Bench, the local Chamber of Commerce, and other special interests. It sought "the development of facilities to provide additional irrigation water and flood control along the lower Henrys Fork and Teton Rivers."[42] However, "flood control" is not mentioned in the enabling legislation signed into law on September 7, 1964, and neither is Henrys Fork.[43] Flood control was not needed by the Rexburg Bench farms, nor were they flooded when Teton Dam broke.[44] What appears on the face of the legislation and the Bureau's Definite Plan Report which followed in 1969 has the makings of a cozy deal for the irrigators in Henrys Fork Valley and on the Rexburg Bench.[45] When the dam failed what few benefits Teton Valley residents expected to enjoy were washed away with their possessions and a few lives while the irrigators on the Rexburg Bench remained high and dry.

During one of the congressional investigations which followed the disaster, Idaho Environmental Council president Russell Brown testified that "although environmental destruction provided the motivation [for opposing the dam], the most compelling arguments against the project were legal. The economic justification presented to Congress was, as seems to be standard practice in Bureau projects, fraudulent." Regarding the active faults at the damsite which Bureau personnel ignored, Brown said: "The fact that the dam did not fail for seismic reasons should not be comforting to apologists for the dam-building agency. If the hazard existed, it should have been considered in the public forum. The fact that a failure occurred because of the even more dangerous incompetence of the Bureau does not mitigate the long-term seismic problems."[46] What disturbed Congressman Ryan and his subcommittee most was that the Bureau failed to consider warnings that the damsite was faulty, especially the warnings of Geological Survey geologists. The subcommittee's criticism appears in the report under the caption, "Construction Momentum Overrides Safety Considerations."

A seismic hazard did exist, for the dam site was in a Zone 3 earthquake zone. Survey geologists were concerned about that hazard, and they prepared a report which their superiors held up for six months before sending a watered-down version to the Bureau during July 1973.[47] The Survey's official version of what transpired can be read in correspondence between the Director and Senator Henry M. Jackson, Chairman, Committee on Interior and Insular Affairs.[48] An environmental impact statement had been prepared by the Bureau's environmental specialist, a scientist highly respected for his expertise and integrity. What was missing to mitigate or stop this flawed project? NEPA then was relatively effective; a number of court cases bear this out. But it appears to have had no effect on construction of Teton Dam, for the momentum of the Bureau to build was strong and safety considerations voiced by geologists were not considered; neither were the concerns of the public.

To be fair to the Bureau its critics need to widen their investigations. Proposed dams and other public works requiring federal funds tend to sail through Congress with little opposition. What our legislators succumb to on the floor of Congress is everybody's business. Robert Gottlieb in A Life of Its Own: The Politics and Power of Water has described "pork barrel" politics and "logrolling" in operation.[49] It is not wise to attack a colleague's pet project on the floor. The practice of congressional leaders in the early 1960s of seeing to it that each district had a go at the pork barrel was especially prevalent.[50]

Congressional hearings in the areas of opposition to a project as well as those held in Washington, D.C., for the purpose of deliberating the pros and cons of proposed bills could serve a useful purpose. Local hearings merit and get good coverage in the local press and can stimulate support for the congressional representatives who are motivated to serve the country as well as their constituents. When John Dingell, who is now in his 18th term of office, asked the General Accounting Office to provide information on federal construction agency practices in 1972,[51] he was serving the needs of Congress for information upon which to legislate corrective measures to mitigate environmental damage caused by these agencies.

Another example of how a legislator serves the public interest is the public use he or she makes of a GAO report. A recent investigation of the Bureau's Central Utah Project by the GAO turned up accounting irregularites that indicated the Treasury Department would "lose at least $100 million" and that a great deal more would be lost through the Bureau's practice of extending generous repayment schedules and interest-free loans. According to the Washington Post, Senator Howard M. Metzenbaum said the GAO reports "offer convincing evidence that the Bureau of Reclamation is more interested in making cozy deals with local interests than protecting all Americans from unjustified, budget-busting subsidies."[52]

The deal that attracted the most attention provided a Utah town with a $450,000 six-lane bowling alley for which the Bureau contributed $375,000, ostensibly because the town had lost a movie theater, three churches, and four bars due to Central Utah Project construction. David Goeller for the Associated Press put it this way: "Municipal and federal officials say the [bowling alley] will bring much-needed recreation to the 1,730 residents, but a congressional critic says the bureau has rolled a gutter ball."[53] The Bureau backed off as soon as Congress got wind of the deal: beneficiaries of the Central Utah Project may be required to repay $281,150 through "water charges." Moaned Utah's Congressman Howard Nielson, "I would not have supported it had I known the money was going to have to be repaid."[54]

It is this attitude of legislators who specialize in serving the special interests of powerful constituents that is detrimental to the image of Congress and often to that of the Bureau. Such constituents have demanded of the more susceptible members of Congress many ill-advised projects and other concessions. Congress would do well to constrain those in its midst who seek success at the polls by serving the special interests of self-centered constituents.

NOTES

1. Act of March 10, 1934, ch. 55, 48 Stat. 401.
2. Act of August 14, 1946, ch. 965, 60 Stat. 1080.
3. Ibid.
4. Ibid.
5. Oliver A. Houck, "Judicial Review Under the Fish and Wildlife Coordination Act: A Plaintiff's Guide to Litigation," Environmental Law Reporter, July 1981, 50043.
6. Act of August 12, 1958, 72 Stat. 563, amending the Act of March 10, 1934, 16 U.S.C., secs. 661-664.
7. Houck, supra, 50043.
8. U. S. Comptroller General. Improved federal efforts needed to equally consider wildlife conservation with other features of water resource developments (Washington, D.C.: U. S. Government Accounting Office, 1974), 23. When GAO investigated the matter in 1972 it interrogated personnel formerly in the Bureau of Sports Fisheries and Wildlife, a branch within the Fish and Wildlife Service. To avoid confusion, Fish and Wildlife Service is used as an umbrella designation. For the origin of the BSFW see Jeanne Clarke and Daniel McCool, Staking Out the Terrain/ Power Differentials Among Natural Resource Management Agencies (Albany: State University of New York, 1985), 83. The BSFW and the Bureau of Commercial Fisheries were Interior Department bureaus from 1956 to 1970. They were administered by what the authors call "a kind of phantom agency"--the U. S. Fish and Wildlife Service. An Assistant Secretary for Fish and Wildlife was in charge. That position has since been expanded to Assistant Secretary for Fish and Wildlife and Parks. For the origin of the Fish and Wildlife Service, established in 1871, see p. 77, ff.
9. U. S. Department of the Interior and State of Idaho.

Independent Panel to Review Cause of Teton Dam Failure. Wallace L. Chadwick (chairman), et al. *Report to U.S.D.I. and State of Idaho on Failure of Teton Dam* (Washington, D.C.: USGPO, 1977, x.

10. U. S. Department of the Interior. Teton Dam Failure Review Group, F. William Eikenberry, chairman. *Failure of Teton Dam*. Final Report (Washington: USGPO, 1980), 7-1.

11. ENR Cover Story, "BuRec searching for a new role after 83 years," *Engineering News-Record*, October 1, 1985, 29.

12. Federal Writers' Project. *The Idaho Encyclopedia*, 120. In 1880 irrigated acreage was about 200,000 and in 1890, when the population was about 160,000, irrigated acreage was about 800,000. By 1900 irrigated acreage was about 1,200,000.

13. *Ibid*.

14. F. Ross Peterson. *Idaho/A Bicentennial History* (New York: Norton and Company, 1976), 139-141. Peterson questions the opening of new farmland at a time when there was an over-production of potatoes. Idaho was especially hard hit by the nationwide depression of the early 1920s. Potatoes selling at $1.51 a bushel in 1919 dropped to $0.30 a bushel within the next three years.

15. Idaho Department of Commerce and Development. *The Idaho Almanac* (Boise, Idaho, ca. 1963), 373.

16. *Ibid*., 402.

17. *Ibid*., 399-400, 402.

18. Charles W. Howe and K. William Easter. *Interbasin Transfers of Water* (Baltimore and London: Johns Hopkins Press, 1971), 156.

19. *Ibid*., 154.

20. Public Law 88-583, 78 Stat. 925, section 1.

21. Reisner, *supra*, 402. Full citation, 3, note 28.

22. Donald Worster. *Rivers of Empire/Water, Aridity, and the Growth of the American West* (New York: Pantheon Books, 1985), 74.

23. U. S. Congress. *Teton Dam Disaster*. Hearings before a Subcommittee of the Committee on Government Operations, House of Representatives, 94th Cong., 2d sess., August 5, 6, and 31, 1976.

24. U. S. Congress. *Teton Dam*. Hearing before the Subcommittee on Energy Research and Water Resources of the Committee on Interior and Insular Affairs, U. S. Senate, 94th Cong.,

2d sess., on S.3542, a bill to authorize the Secretary of the Interior to make compensation for damages arising out of the failure of Teton Dam, a feature of the Teton Basin Federal Reclamation Project in Idaho, and for other purposes. S.B.3542, dated June 9, 1976, appears on p. 3-4.

25. Ibid., 33.

26. Ibid., 18.

27. Ibid., 29-30.

28. F. Ross Peterson, "The Teton Dam Disaster: Tragedy or Triumph?" (66th Faculty Honor Lecture at Utah State University, Logan, printed as a pamphlet in 1982), p. 2.

29. Ibid., 18-19.

30. Ibid., 21.

31. Ibid., 22.

32. Ibid., 28, fn. 36.

33. Edith Haroldsen Lovell. Captain Bonneville's County (Idaho Falls, Idaho: The Eastern Idaho Farmer, 1963), 15, 33, and map inside hardback cover.

34. Reisner, supra, 442.

35. U. S. Congress. Teton Dam Disaster, supra, 9.

36. Reisner, supra, 420.

37. U. S. Congress. Teton Dam, supra, 18.

38. Ibid., 30.

39. U. S. Congress. Teton Dam Disaster. Prepared at the request of Frank Church for the Subcommittee on Energy Research and Development of the Committee on Energy and Natural Resources, Publication No. 95-34 (Washington, D.C.: USGPO, 1977), 7.

40. Howe and Easter, supra, 114.

41. Reisner, supra, 400.

42. U. S. Congress. Teton Dam Disaster... (1977), supra, 7.

43. Public Law 88-583, supra.

44. Reisner, supra, 423.

45. Public Law 88-583, supra, section 2; U. S. Congress, Teton Dam Disaster...(1977), supra, 8.

46. Teton Dam Disaster, Ibid., 60.

47. U. S. Congress. Teton Dam Disaster. House Report No. 94-1667, 94th Cong., 2d sess. Thirtieth Report by the Committee on

Government Operations, September 23, 1976 (Washington, D.C.: USGPO, 1976), 14-23; Teton Dam Disaster hearings of August 1976, supra, 548-49.

48. V. E. McKelvey to Hon. Henry M. Jackson, letter of June 11, 1976.

49. Gottlieb, supra, 48. Full citation, 6, note 53.

50. Ibid.

51. U. S. Comptroller General, supra, cited in note 8.

52. Cass Peterson, "Accounting Questioned At Utah Water Project," Washington Post, October 9, 1985, A17.

53. David Goeller, "Dam Project Spills Into Bowling Alley," Washington Post, September 18, 1985.

54. Ibid.

11
The Changing Scene: Indian Rights, Reclamation Reform, and Water Marketing

During Senate Committee on Small Business hearings in 1975 and 1976 the following question was addressed: "Will the family farm survive in America?" It soon became clear from the testimony of witnesses that the Reclamation Act of 1902, as amended, had not fulfilled its initial mandate in the regions of its jurisdiction--the arid but arable regions of the Western states. "The fact of the matter is," said Interior secretary Stewart Udall, "as I look back over my service in Washington 20 years ago, we paid lip service to the family farm, but we really worshiped at the altar of agribusiness."[1]

What especially distressed Udall was the information that construction of the San Luis Unit of the Central Valley Project in California had not increased farm ownerships from 1,050 to an anticipated 6,100 as its congressional proponents had promised; instead the 1,050 ownerships in 1960 had been reduced to 214.[2] What had happened in the interim was the accumulation of more acres per farm by the landowners who earlier had prevailed upon the Bureau of Reclamation to build the San Luis Unit. The landowners had not been satisfied to irrigate only the lands shown on the San Luis Service Area map presented to Congress when it was deliberating the proposed legislation; instead they waited until 1962 to pressure the Bureau into expanding the service area to include marginal lands that when drained brought on the Kesterson disaster--a dilemma worse than the failure of Teton Dam for selenium is causing problems where irrigation drain water from the Bureau's numerous projects throughout the West is entering and contaminating fish and wildlife refuges.

Emerging now to further confound the Bureau are demands from Indian tribes for some of that water behind Bureau dams and dams constructed by the Corps of Engineers that serve some of the Bureau's projects. Because Reservation Indians, for a variety of reasons, have not made much use of their waters does not materially jeopardize their rights to them; they are not affected by the first-in-time, first-in-right concept embodied in Western water law.[3] Known as "Winters rights" in legal circles, the phrase is derived from the 1908 Supreme Court decision in Winters v. United States. Their rights are further strengthened by the 1963 Supreme Court decision in Arizona v. California.[4] To some extent Indian tribes have been beneficiaries of Bureau projects. More often their waters have been captured to serve non-Indian irrigators. The authors of Water Policies for the Future have described that sorry chapter in American history:

> Following Winters, more than 50 years elapsed before the Supreme Court again discussed significant aspects of Indian water rights. During most of the 50-year period, the United States was pursuing a policy of encouraging the settlement of the West and the creation of family-sized farms on its arid lands. In retrospect, it can be seen that this policy was pursued with little or no regard for Indian water rights and the Winters doctrine. With the encouragement, or at least the cooperation, of the Secretary of the Interior--the very office entrusted with protection of all Indian rights--many large irrigation projects were constructed on streams that flowed through or bordered Indian Reservations, sometimes above and more often below the Reservations. With few exceptions the projects were planned and built by the Federal Government without any attempt to define, let alone protect, prior rights that Indian tribes might have had in the waters used for the projects....[5]

Just how the Bureau will respond to present Indian demands for irrigation projects should be apparent soon. With a huge deficit to cope with, Congress is not in a mood for new federally-subsidized water projects but it has been quite generous with funds for completing and updating existing projects. Conceivably some of those projects could include diversion canals to nearby Reservation lands. However, under the reservation system most of the tribes were given marginal lands where selenium and other toxic elements have since been discovered: to irrigate them will mobilize those toxics, especially selenium. Furthermore, The Reclamation Act does not meet the needs of Indians who do not wish to become farmers. Water marketing, if available to them, could offer a more flexible solution to their economic woes with less consumptive use of the resource. If water to which they have rights is not obtainable for marketing purposes they will have to obtain it by increasing the scope of their farming operations. Indian tribes have made it clear: they want back what is theirs.

The Bureau of Indian Affairs is not likely to be of any more use to the Indians in claiming their water rights than the Bureau of Reclamation has been to small-scale family farmers, having failed the latter by giving agribusiness a competitive advantage. Reservation Indians are belatedly making some progress when they assert their rights to water, minerals, and other natural resources. Unlike family farmers, they have more congressional support; also, reservation lands have a trust status that courts tend to observe. Under the Reclamation Reform Act of 1982, family farmers are not likely to fare any better than they have in the past. One reason for the Act was to accommodate agribusiness in return for which it was to cease flouting reclamation law. Now Congress is confronted with the spectacle of Interior secretaries undoing the intent of the new law by emasculating the hammer clause at the behest of agribusiness. For family farmers competing with agribusiness it is a no-win situation.

The Reclamation Reform Act had been in the making since the late 1970s when the Carter administration was in power. Volumes of government hearing reports found their way to library shelves before the 1982 Act emerged with a provision that required irrigators to renegotiate their contracts by April 12, 1987, to reflect a more realistic charge for subsidized water and to bring leased land under the acreage limitation. If they preferred, they could stay with the low rate on owned land until contracts expired but must "pay full cost on all <u>leased</u> land in excess of 160 acres."[6] That requirement, known as the "hammer clause," prompted the large landowners to devise a system by which they could get around the new 960-acre limitation in the Act as they had previously done with the 160-acre limitation in the 1902 Act.[7]

It appears that while giving lip service to the intent of the hammer clause the Bureau permitted its agribusiness clients to believe they could get around the provision by creating a new brand of paper farmers. Whenever the Bureau involves itself in questionable tactics, it is wise to look behind the scene. Even before Secretary Hodel's appearance in Reagan's cabinet, regional director David Houston was asked by a California journalist, "Do you think the Interior Department will take a lead in opposing this provision?" Houston replied, "I guess I would say I think that we will."[8] That the remark was made late in 1983--three years before the rules and regulations implementing the hammer clause were published in the Federal Register, November 7, 1986--reflects as much the Department's desires as it does the Bureau's.

During that three-year period, Congress was asked to repeal the hammer clause but it did not do so either before November 1986, or after the public comment period expired on February 5, 1987. It appearing by January 1987 that Congress was not going to cave in to Department desires, a contingent of water district executives and their attorneys flew to Washington. (Money flows to the seat of power and heavily subsidized irrigators have a lot to spare.)

Newspaper coverage indicates that Commissioner C. Dale Duvall was "shunted aside in favor of regional subordinates in Sacramento" and "the rules were rewritten by a small group of Interior lawyers headed by Solicitor Ralph W. Tarr, a Californian with ties to some of the most powerful growers in the state, and pushed through the Office of Management and Budget by Secretary Donald Hodel."[9] In on the deal was the Western Coalition of Senators who had invited Hodel to breakfast on January 23, and then had commenced to pressure him to order the rules and regulations for the hammer clause rewritten to make room for the new brand of paper farmers.[10]

Actually the Coalition did very little for Western agribusiness, except in California where Westlands became the principal beneficiary.[11] Houston and Tarr participated in writing the revisions. (Previously Tarr had the dubious honor of being ordered by Hodel to write the opinion giving Westlands Water District the millions in past and future water subsidies to which it was not entitled under the Krulitz opinion.)[12] Such maneuvers emanating in the Interior secretary's office and serving primarily California leave the impression that they were prompted by Bureau personnel in the Sacramento office to serve a favored client. Each such instance deserves careful scrutiny, for agribusiness in California (and elsewhere) has Congressmen and state legislators at its beck and call.

The Bureau has endured some difficult years of its own making with such colossal failures as Teton Dam and Kesterson Reservoir and partly because of them it came close to losing its identity in 1984 when David Stockman decided the expense of keeping it in business did not justify its separate and largely autonomous existence. But he was rebuffed when Interior secretary William Clark was authorized to ask Edwin Meese (then White House counselor) and Caspar Weinberger (then Secretary of Defense) to "deep-six the proposal" of the Office of Management and Budget to merge the Bureau with the Corps of Engineers.[13] Under the guise of cutting some of the costs of government the Reagan administration initially supported the merger and various other devices to reduce the cost of water projects such as cost-sharing which had been urged by the Carter administration. Reagan, finding his stand on these sensitive issues unpopular with Western water and irrigation districts and their friends in Washington, often backed down.

Confronting Reagan when he took office were the three billion dollars in farm and crop subsidies, exclusive of water, which were slated to be slashed to reduce deficit spending. Instead, to his discredit, he permitted the $3 billion to become $30 billion by 1986, an estimated cost to "each non-farm family [of] about $700 a year."[14] Who benefited most? Not the family farmers who were going bankrupt in the West and elsewhere in the nation, but agribusiness which managed to grab the lion's share.[15]

Obtaining huge subsidies requires the able assistance of well-connected attorneys, among whom are some who learned the game when they were employed as government attorneys. In California their offices are primarily in Sacramento and Fresno. Their connections in Washington include other law firms, lobbyists, congressmen, Interior and Department of Agriculture attorneys, et cetera. Now that burgeoning ware-houses of surplus foods and fibers--the consequence of over production--have become an embarrassment to Congress along with the immediate need to reduce the national deficit, the Bureau's overly generous water-subsidy program is likely to be curtailed.[16]

If the Bureau would sell more of its water to municipalities and less to agribusiness irrigators, it could wipe out some of its clients' indebtedness to the government. (Southern California cities, for example, are presently paying about $250 an acre-foot for water from the State Water Project.) Economists are considering various options for reallocating and pricing water. Agricultural economist Kenneth Frederick thinks that limiting the profits on water the districts might sell directly to such M&I customers would "stifle incentives to conserve water and restrict opportunities to transfer water to higher-value uses." He believes that limits should instead be "placed on the subsidies provided irrigators, not on the farmers' profits."[17] Congress has some prickly problems ahead in devising water marketing systems that serve urban users and also protect the small-scale farmers whom taxpayers thought they were serving by subsidizing their water.

In California, irrigators are demanding more water despite the deterioration of much of their crop land where selenium, salts (especially boron), arsenic, and other toxics are present. Inasmuch as good land down gradient from the marginal land can remain productive if irrigation of toxic soils is terminated, the desire for more water now may indicate an intention to sell water to the highest M&I bidders when water marketing becomes more acceptable there.

With a view to alleviating the distress of the Merced County ranch owners whose lands were ruined as a result of water-logging caused by the Bureau's hydraulic disaster and to opening up economic solutions to farmers with salt- and selenium-damaged lands that should be abandoned, Congressman George Miller presented to the Interior and Insular Affairs Committee in 1986, H. R. 4905 incorporating the concept of water marketing. Under the bill's California Water Exchange provision the Interior secretary was authorized to approve the sale of irrigation water to cities that wished to augment their supply. Westlands would then have a market for water to compensate it for abandoning its toxic land areas and the ranchers damaged by Kesterson would be paid fair compensation for the lands which had been water-logged and polluted with salts and selenium.

Although one Washington lobbyist predicted that Westlands would "suck this up as fast as a milkshake,"[18] it opposed the bill for fear passage might somehow interfere with its agreement for additional water then pending in the Interior secretary's office.[19] Miller's aide Dan Beard sized up the situation with the remark, "It doesn't take a genius to figure out that nothing moves in the valley unless Westlands says OK or is in support of it."[20] Westlands' manager Jerald Butchert explained that "his district's private reservations were passed on to Rep. Tony Coelho, D-Merced, and that the bill never got out of committee."[21]

In describing H.R. 4905, a bill that Congress would do well to dust off and revise for arid states with salt and selenium-damaged land, Miller said: "This legislation establishes the framework we need to resolve the drainage problems which threaten the future of irrigated agriculture in California."[22]

A Western Water Management Study, initiated by the National Research Council's Water Science and Technology Board, is expected to address water marketing and related problems.[23] The NRC, organized in 1916, functions as a research arm of the National Academy of Sciences, founded in 1863 as a private organization. The National Academy is looked to by the federal government for scientific expertise. Its recommendations to Congress in 1879 played a significant role in setting up the Geological Survey. The NRC directs the activities of the Water Science and Technology Board and other boards with specific specialties. In 1987, NRC's WSTB and the Board on Agriculture drafted "A Proposal to Assess the Reallocation of Western Irrigation Water Supplies on Economic Growth and Environmental Quality."[24] Earlier, WSTB had noted in its Newsletter that 80 to 90 percent of Western water supplies are devoted to agriculture and that the NRC "could play a vital role in clarifying legal, institutional, and environmental roadblocks currently limiting the development of water markets...."[25] The November 1988 Newsletter stated that the study was expected to get underway early in 1989.[26]

The effectiveness of NRC committees depends largely on how they are received by government personnel with whom committee members will be working to resolve the issues for which their expertise is sought. After the Kesterson issue had virtually destroyed the credibility of the Bureau in California, NRC was prevailed upon to establish what became the Committee on Irrigation-Induced Water Quality Problems. From the outset of the committee's interaction with the Bureau it was apparent to some observers that Region II's David Houston had his own ideas on how to proceed with the committee's recommendations and consequently compliance by the Bureau was delayed for almost a year.[27]

It was also apparent to some observers that the makeup of WSTB's Committee was not as balanced as it might have been; with fewer agricultural engineers and professors of agriculture committed to irrigating marginal land there could have been more emphasis on hydrology, economics, public health, and the natural environment of San Joaquin Valley. Urging, as the committee did, the so-called wet-flex method, supposedly capable of containing selenium, brought on criticism from scientists who were more familiar with hydrogeological conditions at the reservoir.[28] When it became evident after the expenditure of millions of dollars that Lawrence Berkeley Laboratory could not contain the selenium in the Kesterson ponds with its method, and notwithstanding recently publicized data that groundwater contaminated by the selenium was moving down-gradient toward the river at the rate of up to 1000 feet a year,[29] the committee, in a letter to Houston, urged that the experiment be permitted to continue:

> ...This letter contains comments from committee members on the proposed flooding option [the wet-flex method] and the opportunities as we see them, presented by the circumstances at Kesterson....
>
> ...Keeping the ponds at Kesterson Reservoir flooded would allow an opportunity to fully evaluate the environmental impact of this management approach. We believe that an assessment of this management option is important to future concerns in the San Joaquin Valley and, perhaps, elsewhere....[30]

What was not generally known when this September 1986 letter was written was that during that year the chairman had addressed an irrigation conference where he downplayed the seriousness of selenium as a factor in completing the San Luis Drain, stating that the concentrations of selenium and other "elemental toxics" would have been "low enough to avoid detection or concern."[31] When asked by this author in October 1987 for supporting data to justify extending the drain to the Delta, the chairman said he didn't have any but neither did the other side have data proving that the drainwater would damage the Delta and the Bay. Such a remark is reminiscent of the Bureau's tendency to construct the project first and take care of the problems later.

The chairman's position on the drain has brought his committee into disfavor in circles where to mention the San Luis Drain is anathema. To their distress the drain issue has again been raised--this time by the California regional water quality control board that was responsible for letting the Bureau use the Kesterson ponds for Westlands' drainwater without first obtaining a permit.

The Committee is planning to issue a report soon. It is expected to reflect also the expertise of new members on the committee. The Department of the Interior having asked it to address selenium problems in other Western states, it has since 1986 been participating in Interior's National Irrigation Drainage Program as well as in the San Joaquin Valley Drainage Program.[32] Therefore the report carries the promise of a wider view of the selenium problem.

Expecting, as Senator Cranston and others did, that the Bureau's credibility could be restored by calling in a prestigious scientific organization seems a bit naive. The Bureau found it convenient to use the Academy committee as a foil and so did officials in the Interior secretary's office. When the latter were faulted by the press for the shortcomings of Interior's reports dealing with selenium, the committee was cited as the reviewer. In 1988, when the reconnaissance studies were released, they were severely criticized for not having addressed public health aspects of contamination at the various refuges receiving selenium-tainted water because of the danger to families eating what hunters and fishermen may be bringing home. Congress had asked Interior in 1985 to ascertain "whether the contamination has been, is, or might pose a threat to public health." When under attack in December 1988, Interior's Jonathan Deason defended his department by saying: "The work has been reviewed by the National Academy."[33]

Members of NRC's WSTB committees are reimbursed for lodging, food, and travel expenses; their expertise is donated. They can be of value to Congress when properly utilized and they can chart new courses of action for bureaucrats who get stuck in a rut. The Bureau is now attempting to move out of a rut as outlined in brochures released to the press in October 1987.[34] Titled "Assessment '87" and "Implementation Plan," they were developed soon after a federal interagency symposium in August 1986 at which a featured speaker and consultant to the Bureau and other government agencies put the Bureau's current problems and mode of operation in perspective:

> During the more than 15 years I've been consulting with the Bureau of Reclamation I've seen it undergo considerable change. But over the past 2 years I've been involved with four projects for the Bureau which have convinced me that the Bureau has about 5 to 10 years to make some very fundamental changes or it won't exist as the entity it is now. It is a standard rule of thumb that when a bureaucracy begins to realize that it is in danger, it is almost too late already. The Bureau is beginning now to openly address the need for change, and while that is a promising sign, it is also a sign that the change had better happen quickly....[35]

In agreement with this candid statement are career men in the Bureau with many years of experience, at least one of whom had been urging the change for more than a decade. Whether the change happens quickly will depend on Congress. In facilitating that change scholarly studies, such as an NRC committee addressing Western water management could do, should be useful to Congress.

If the brochures featuring the Bureau's new direction mean what they say, the Bureau is headed for water resources management. Topping its list of priorities are "Water quality-environmental restoration and enhancement" and "Operations and Maintenance." A press conference to announce the Bureau's new direction which mentioned environmental restoration and water quality enhancement was held in Washington on October 1, 1987. Spokesman for the Interior Department was James Ziglar, then Interior's assistant secretary for water and science, who said that the Bureau would be changed "from being a construction company to being a resource management agency."[36] Although Bureau personnel with whom this author spoke were amenable to taking on restoration projects, they did not see them as having a very high priority unless state governments and the general public put up most of the money.

At a National Conference on Hydraulic Engineering of the American Society of Civil Engineers, August 8, 1988, two top officials in the Denver office of the Bureau gave talks on "The Bureau of Reclamation in Transition" and "Making the New Bureau of Reclamation Work-Reorienting"[37] that were so uninformative that attendees were asking each other, "What did they say?" The most memorable remark from one of the speakers, deputy commissioner and chief operating officer Joe D. Hall, was: "We are going to win."[38]

In Interior's 1987 new-look brochures the Bureau is presented as an agency in a leadership role: a leader in water quality restoration, in groundwater management, in EPA's Superfund program. "Implementation Plan" posits that it "is in a unique position of having the technical expertise to assume a major role" in Superfund cleanups.[39] In querying scientists as to whether this is true the author was told that it could serve a useful purpose in overseeing the work of private-sector contractors doing toxic waste disposal for EPA--such agreements are being negotiated--but that it will need to attract highly qualified and experienced scientists to assume a "major role." This is also true in the groundwater management field where neither the Bureau nor EPA have nearly the expertise of the Geological Survey. The Survey, however, prefers its ivory tower research role to being a leader in water resources management.

A leadership role the Bureau could assume is in the area in which the Secretary's office has little interest--water quality restoration in streams and rivers impacted by the Bureau's projects. Such projects can be initiated in regional offices, and in Sacramento there is some interest in small-stream restoration which can be undertaken with less cash outlay, especially when a state, such as California, already has a stream improvement program, albiet an urban one. Unless owners of lands on streams impacted by Bureau projects participate in the restoration, what the Bureau may do to improve water quality and fisheries may fall short of expectations. Examples of stream degradation abound. Dr. Peter B. Moyle and his team of investigators found shocking conditions in California:

> ...Most of these small streams are continuously being altered. These changes are occasionally caused by construction of large dams and diversions but more often more subtle factors are to blame: continuous overgrazing of watersheds, trampling of banks by livestock, small diversions for irrigation, small channelization projects associated with road or bridge construction, rip-rapping to protect houses built too close to the streams, organic pollution from leaky septic tanks or small sewage treatment plants, small oil and pesticide spills, use of streambeds by offroad vehicles, introduction of nonnative fish species, and many other localized insults to the integrity of the streams. Individually, these small actions may have little effect on a stream; collectively over a period of years, they can turn a clear stream into a muddy ditch.[40]

If the Bureau, during the current transition period, can keep its diverse staff of planners, biologists, sociologists, and other professionals it will have the personnel to deal with its irrigators in obtaining their cooperation in restoring areas along streams damaged by careless irrigation practices. Further cooperation can be anticipated when fishermen, hunters, environmentalists, and conservationists see the Bureau involving its personnel in stream restoration. Not many know that California Trout and Trout Unlimited for years have been creating wild trout habitats, cleaning up streambeds, reporting septic tank leakage, and using their collective brawn as well as their brains to get the job done. Should the Bureau undertake a leadership role in water quality "restoration and enhancement,"[41] it will need to get acquainted with the organizations that have been doing this all along.

At present a high priority with Interior is shedding the Bureau's projects, not in mitigating the damage they have done. Particularly serious is its failure to provide the customary environmental impact statement where water reallocation is an issue. The Implementation Plan states that the Bureau has had a "long-standing policy of transferring facilities to local water user organizations for operation and maintenance" and that 361 have been transferred to date. Of those remaining only 51 are "candidates for transfer"[42] and some of them may be turned over to states. Among the 109 facilities that may be retained are several involving international treaties, and others for which "no known entity exists that will accept" them.[43] Of the 51 candidates for transfer, there are 40 listed in Assessment '87 with an introductory paragraph:

> Opportunities for Transfer. A Region-by-Region list of the projects which are candidates for transfer is shown below. Some may require legal, policy, or other clarification prior to completing the transfer. Efforts to transfer should be started immediately. The multiple-use status of a project is not necessarily justification for retention by the Bureau. Some of these candidates for transfer are in the construction stage and others already are in operation.
>
> Southwest Region: McGee Creek, Closed Basin, [and] Platoro Dam and Reservoir
>
> Lower Colorado Region: Boulder City Water System
>
> Upper Colorado Region: Animas-LaPlata and Dallas Creek
>
> Missouri Basin Region: Fresno Dam, Lake Sherburne Dam, Anchor Dam, Pactola Dam, Dickinson Dam, Tiber Dam and Dike, Calmus Dam, Deerfield Dam, [and] Colorado-Big Thompson
>
> Mid-Pacific Region: Delta Cross Channel, Delta-Mendota Canal, O'Neill Pumping Plant, Tracy Fish Collecting Facilities, Corning Canal System, Funks Dam, Tehama-Colusa Canal, Pacheco System, [and] San Luis Drain
>
> Pacific Northwest Region: Prosser Diversion Dam, Roza Diversion Dam, Grassy Lake Dam, Island Park Dam, North Dam, Dry Falls Dam, O'Sullivan Dam, Pinto Dam, Tieton [sic] Dam, Keechelus Dam, Anderson Ranch Dam, Kachess Dam, Arrowrock Dam, Bumping Lake Dam, Cle Elum Dam, [and] Clear Creek Dam.

These projects are listed under six regions. Recently the Southwest Region was merged with the Missouri Basin Region to become the Plains Region.[44]

Among the projects presently being transferred to the private sector are the Central Valley Project's Friant-Kern and Madera canals which serve the east side of San Joaquin Valley as far as Bakersfield, a distance of about 180 miles. The 152-mile Friant unit delivers 1.68 million acre-feet of water annually to the 23 irrigation districts whose contracts are beginning to come up for renewal. Pending are state water board decisions to reallocate some of the state's waters to other beneficial uses after the current three-year hearing period is over. Therefore, an environmental impact statement is considered imperative.

As of late October 1988 the Bureau was still on record as complying with the EIS requirements of the National Environmental Policy Act preliminary to negotiating with its clients who demand the same quantity of water as the expiring contracts provided. But Region II director David Houston stonewalled the EIS and relieved the irrigators of the need to practice conservation. His action has not the clear support of the Bureau nor even the complete support of the solicitor's office, but it does have the support of San Joaquin Valley congressmen Tony Coelho, Charles Pashayan, William Thomas, and Richard Lehman. Characteristic of how the Bureau has operated since 1902, government attorneys--in this instance Solicitor Ralph Tarr who wrote the opinion desired by the Friant irrigators and the San Joaquin Valley congressmen--are brought in to write an interpretation of law that has the effect of law. Even Dale Duvall disapproved, saying to Houston, "We do not necessarily agree with your conclusion that contractors are entitled to renew their water-service contracts for the same quantities of water."[45]

What transpires during project transfers and the rationale for them are of general interest. Apropos the transfer of the Friant unit in 1986, Acting Region II Director Neil W. Schild wrote the author that it was premised on an Office of Management and Budget policy decision, known as Circular A-76, which mandates that executive and defense department agencies shall not "carry on any activity to provide a commercial product or service if the product or service can be procured more economically from the private sector."[46] In August 1986 a ten-year 37-page contract was negotiated by the Bureau and the newly formed Friant Water Users Authority, the latter representing the irrigation districts served by the Friant-Kern Canal. To ease the shock and help those irrigation districts over the rough realities of private entrepreneurship, the newly established Authority was promised $3.12 million in federal funds, the Bureau's field office, its heavy equipment such as trucks and bulldozers, and whatever else had been acquired for the project's management.[47]

Circular A-76 does not preclude an environmental impact statement, nor does the Act of July 2, 1956[48] which Solicitor Tarr cited as conclusive. A suit naming Houston who has since resigned, Hodel who has been succeeded by the former New Mexico congressman, Manuel Lujan, and Friant Water Users Authority was filed in 1988 by 15 fish, water quality, and conservation organizations demanding that the Bureau produce an EIS as required by law.[49] Subsequently California's attorney general, John Van de Kamp, filed an amicus curiae brief in support of plaintiffs' suit.[50] Since then, while the Council on Environmental Quality was reviewing the case at EPA's request and the suit was before the court, Secretary Luhan succumbed to pressure from the governor and "San Joaquin Valley's entire congressional delegation" and approved a 40-year contract renewal for the first of the Friant contracts, thus setting a precedent for the rest.[51] Although the renewals increase the price from $3.50 to $14.84 per acre-foot--the $0.84 is to be applied on current indebtedness--the $14.00 rate does not begin to cover the cost to the government of delivering the water.

Bureau employees with whom this author spoke were not happy with the outcome of either Houston's meddling or with Interior's action. The last resort now is the State Water Resources Control Board's authority to reallocate water if and when it becomes imperative to do so: delivery of water under the Friant contracts could be cut back or terminated during the 40-year period of their duration, but under a development-oriented governor this is unlikely to happen. The pending court action can compel the Bureau to issue an EIS, which it was in the process of completing when Houston nixed it.

Reagan's move toward privatization early in his first term has caused abrupt changes in Bureau operations that are disturbing to employees and contribute to low morale. Not only is this evident in the Bureau, but in the Fish and Wildlife Service and the Geological

Survey, both of which have scientists qualified to do the research and write the kind of reports that have been contracted out to private sector consultants at great expense to the government. The Kesterson disaster brought personnel in the three Interior bureaus into a close working relationship but that did not generate an atmosphere in which scientists could assist the Bureau in coping with the toxics in the ponds and reducing the impact of irrigation drainwater on San Joaquin Valley. Like the National Academy committee they were instead used as a foil. Such research as those scientists were asked to do was scrutinized with a scalpel in the Secretary's office before their reports were made available for distribution to the public, so sensitive had the selenium issue become. An obvious advantage of having private-sector consultants is that their reports need fall only into the hands of the few. Perhaps that is what the Reagan administration had in mind.

The Bureau's operating priorities for 1988-1998 are in Interior's Implementation Plan and Assessment '87 brochures which are available to the general public as well as state and local decision makers. They are quite frank about divesting the Bureau of 51 of its projects. A few of those projects may go to states, the rest to irrigators who set up water user authorities.[52] The brochures also are quite frank about the future of personnel who do not fit into the privatization goal inherent in those projected transfers.[53] The redistribution or dismissal of personnel in 1988 caused considerable concern, especially when the Bureau's Acreage Limitation Branch, based in Denver, was cut to half of its normal size and its director, who had fought for stronger enforcement of the 1982 Reclamation Reform Act, was transferred to a position for which he had neither experience nor the specialized expertise it required.[54] By June 1988 Congress had become "leery" of the shuffle,[55] but has since done nothing to protect the Bureau from further dismantling by Interior Department secretaries.

NOTES

1. U. S. Senate Committee on Small Business. Will the Family Farm Survive in America?: Federal Reclamation Policy. 95th Cong., 2d sess., Report No. 95-702 (1978), 12.

2. Ibid., 4.

3. Winters v. United States, 207 U. S. Reports 564. Arizona v. California, 373 U.S.Reports 546.

4. Arizona v. California, supra. For an analysis of Indian water rights see Richard B. Collins, "Indian Reservation Water Rights," Journal AWWA, October 1986, 48-54. For a definitive study of Indian rights in general see Charles F. Wilkinson, American Indians, Time, and the Law (New Haven and London: Yale University Press, 1987).

5. National Water Commission. Water Policies for the Future (Washington, D.C., June 1973), 474-75.

6. Don Villarejo and Judith Redmond. Missed Opportunities -- Squandered Resources (Davis, CA: California Institute for Rural Studies, 1988) 11; Federal Register, April 13, 1987 (Vol. 52, No. 70), 11938.

7. Villarejo and Redmond, supra, 19-55.

8. Rita Schmidt Sudman, "Cost Share Examples," Western Water, November/December 1983, 11.

9. Cass Peterson, "California's King-Sized Farms Keep Their Subsidies/Interior waters down its water rules after farm lobbyists turn on the pressure," Washington Post National Weekly Edition, May 25, 1987, 31. This full-page article quotes a number of participants in the rewriting of the rules and regulations, including one of the landowners' principal lobbyists.

10. Ibid. Senators Dennis DeConcini (Arizona) and Pete V. Domenici (New Mexico) cochaired the Western Coalition that produced the January 30 letter to Hodel. The letter was signed by senators from Arizona, Nevada, New Mexico, Idaho, Utah and Wyoming, "as well as Democrats Quentin N. Burdick of North Dakota, Timothy E. Wirth of Colorado and Thomas A. Daschle of South Dakota." The letter was not signed by California senators Alan Cranston and Pete Wilson, ostensibly to avoid "the sticky problem of Westlands..."

11. Ibid. See The Water Reporter, May 1987, 49, 51-54, for an explanation of how the new rules benefit Westlands in particular and Central Valley Project irrigators in general. On page 53 an official is quoted as saying, "As it stands now we have provided four criteria for showing how to avoid paying full cost, or even O&M, rather than

trying to protect the intent of the Congress and the interests of the taxpayer. We are not stopping the subsidy to the large operations...."

12. Editor, The Water Reporter, August 28, 1986, 173-74, 182. To compare Solicitor Tarr's Memorandum of June 17, 1986 with the preceding opinion see Solicitor Krulitz Opinion M-36901 of June 1, 1978.

13. Lou Cannon and Dale Russakoff, "Reagan aides help stop water-agencies merger/Stockman wanted system streamlined," Washington Post, December 18, 1984. Dale Russakoff and Howard Kurtz, "Stockman's Thirst for a Water Agency," Washington Post National Weekly Edition, January 7, 1985, 33.

14. Anon., "This money does grow on trees," Oakland Tribune, January 8, 1987, B6.

15. Ibid. Stored in government warehouses was wheat enough to feed the nation for a year; 5.8 billion bushels of corn (90% of total annual production); cheese and other products. Also see Sonja Hilldren, "Farm law seen 'embarrassing' by economists as costs soar," Fresno Bee, July 27, 1986.

16. H. R. 1443, introduced by the Hon. Sam Gejdenson of Connecticut on March 5, 1987, would amend the Reclamation Projects Act of 1939 "to require the Secretary of the Interior to charge full cost for water delivered to any reclamation or irrigation project for the production of any surplus crop of an agricultural commodity." For Gejdenson's introductory remarks see Congressional Record, March 5, 1987, E782.

17. Kenneth D. Frederick, "Comment and Discussion" on Chapter 3, "Irrigated Agriculture and Mineralized Water" by Robert A. Young and Gerald L. Horner, in Agriculture and the Environment edited by Tim T. Phipps, Pierre R. Crosson, and Kent A. Price (Washington, D.C.: Resources for the Future, Inc., 1986), 77-121, at p. 119. For the point of view of law professor Harrison C. Dunning, see Water Allocation in California: Legal Rights and Reform Needs, Institute of Governmental Studies, Univ. of California, Berkeley, 1982.

18. Anon., "Miller bill offers solutions for Valley's water problems," San Francisco Examiner, May 23, 1986, B10.

19. Lloyd G. Carter, "Westlands killed bill to aid owners of land, aide says," Fresno Bee, January 13, 1987.

20. Ibid.

21. Ibid.

22. Anon., "Miller bill offers solutions for Valley's water problems," supra.

23. Sheila D. David (ed.), "Western Water Management Study," WSTB Newsletter, Vol. 5, No. 4 (July 1988) 6.

24. National Academy of Sciences/National Academy of Engineering/National Research Council, "A Proposal to Assess the Reallocation of Western Irrigation Water Supplies on Economic Growth and Environmental Quality," a Joint Project Proposal of the Board on Agriculture and the Water Science and Technology Board. Draft, n.d., ca. 1987, 1.

25. Water Science and Technology Board, Annual Report/ 1986, National Research Council, 1987, 17-18.

26. David (ed.), WSTB Newsletter, vol. 5, no. 6, 7.

27. W. H. Allaway to David G. Houston, letter report of October 10, 1985; Lloyd G. Carter, "Council critical of Interior plans," Fresno Bee, November 19, 1985, B4.

28. David R. Dawdy, "Comments on Ground Water Movement from Kesterson Reservoir" March 25, 1985; "Further Comments on Kesterson Ground Water Movement" April 1, 1985; "Effect on Permeability of Removal of Borrow Material" May 19,1985; "A Simple Minded Mass Balance" May 21, 1985; for additional references see Proceedings of the Third Selenium Symposium, March 15, 1986, and Fourth Selenium Symposium, March 21, 1987, edited by Alice Q. Howard (in press), (Sausalito: The Bay Institute of San Francisco, 1989); testimony before the State Water Resources Control Board, January 26, 1987, addressing "Kesterson and Its Impact Under the Wet-Flex Plan," and supplemental statement dated January 28.

29. CH2M Hill and Jones & Stokes Associates, Kesterson Program Preliminary Draft Environmental Impact Statement, February 1986, 4D3-4D4.

30. Jan van Schilfgaarde to David G. Houston, Letter report of September 5, 1986.

31. "Agriculture, Irrigation and Water Quality," in Proceedings/1986 Meetings, U. S. Committee on Irrigation Drainage Toxic Substances in Agricultural Supply and Drainage/Defining the Problems (Denver: U. S. Committee on Irrigation and Drainage,

1986) 174, 179.

32. National Research Council. Water Science and Technology Board Annual Report 1987, 12.

33. Tom Harris, "Congress calls hearings on selenium studies," Fresno Bee, Dec. 18, 1988, D1.

34. U. S. Department of the Interior/U. S. Bureau of Reclamation, "Assessment '87/A New Direction for the Bureau of Reclamation," an Executive Summary issued September 10, 1987, and "Implementation Plan/A New Direction for the Bureau of Reclamation," issued on the same day.

35. James L. Creighton, "If There Were a New Bureau of Reclamation, What Role Would Social and Institutional Factors Play?" Invited address delivered August 27, 1986, Salt Lake City, Utah, at a Federal Interagency Symposium on Social Analysis and Natural Resource Agencies.

36. Cass Peterson, "Dam Builders Throwing in The Trowel," Washington Post, October 1, 1987.

37. American Society of Civil Engineers, "National Conference on Hydraulic Engineering and International Symposium on Model-Prototype Correlations," Colorado Springs, Colo., August 8-12, 1988.

38. From notes taken by the author.

39. USDOI/USBR, "Implementation Plan...," supra, 4.

40. Peter B. Moyle, Larry Brown, Bruce Herbold, and Georgina Satol, "Evaluating the Condition of California's Streams Using Indices of Biotic Integrity: Evidence for Continuing Decline," Technical Completion Report W-659: Water Resources Center, Univ. California, Davis, June 1986, 2.

41. USDOI/USBR, "Implementation Plan...," supra, 3.

42. Ibid, 4; "Implementation Plan: Update '89," 21.

43. Ibid; "Assessment '87," supra, 8.

44. "Assessment '87," supra, 9; "Implementation Plan," supra, 15; the formation of the Plains Region was scheduled for completion in January 1989.

45. Michael Doyle and Jeanie Borba, "Water contract fought/Renewal wanted for 40-year pact," Fresno Bee, December 11, 1988, B1, B4. In an October 22 article for the Bee, Borba reported that the Bureau "maintained that the environmental reports are required by the National Environmental Protection Act to detail how

much water is needed, how it would be used and how it would affect the environment."

46. Neil W. Schild, Assistant Regional Director, letter to the author of October 2, 1986.

47. Mary Pitman, "Canal management switch planned," Fresno Bee, August 21, 1986, C1, C2.

48. 43 U.S.C. sec. 485h. For Tarr's point of view see Memorandum (M-36961) of November 10, 1988, to the assistant secretary of water and science.

49. Natural Resources Defense Council, et al. v. David G. Houston, Donald P. Hodel and Friant Water Users Authority, Civ. No. S 88-1658 LKK, U. S. District Court, Eastern District of California; Jim Mayer, "Water lawsuit filed/ Friant contracts are challenged," Fresno Bee, December 22, 1988, B1, B4; Michael Doyle and Jeanie Borba, "Director leaves void at reclamation bureau," Fresno Bee, December 26, 1988, A1, stating that "Houston pushed hard to allow the contract renewals without environmental review...." (effective January 9, 1989, Houston resigned to join the firm of Drexel Burnham Lambert, Inc.

50. John K. Van de Kamp to Dinah Bear, General Counsel for CEQ, 4-page undated letter transmitting brief.

51. Michael Doyle, "Lujan OKs first Friant water pact/ Valley legislators' pressure won renewal," Fresno Bee April 12, 1989; Mike Connolly and Lynn Ludlow (from staff and wire reports), "Renewal of water pacts set," San Francisco Examiner, April 12, 1989, A1, 18.

52. USDOI/USBR, "Assessment '87," supra, 8-9; "Implementation Plan," supra, 15.

53. "Implementation Plan," Ibid., 11; Michael Doyle, "Upheaval starts at Bureau of Reclamation," Fresno Bee, June 21, 1988.

54. Cass Peterson, "Interior Department Dismantling Irrigation-Law Monitor," Washington Post June 10, 1988.

55. Michael Doyle, "Lawmakers leery of reclamation shuffle," Fresno Bee, June 13, 1988; Doyle, "Reclamation bureau's painful evolution," Fresno Bee, December 25, 1988, A1, A8.

Selected Bibliography

Government Publications

Alexander, Lt. Col. B. S., Maj. George H. Mendell, and Prof. George Davidson. Irrigation of the San Joaquin, Tulare, and Sacramento Valleys, California. U. S. Govt. Printing Off., 1874.

Anderson, M. S., H. W. Lakin, K. C. Beeson, Floyd F. Smith, and Edward Thacker. Selenium in Agriculture. Agricultural Handbook No. 200. Agricultural Research Service, U. S. Dept. of Agric., in Cooperation with the Geological Survey, U. S. Dept. of the Interior, Washington, D. C., August 1961. A review of 212 articles on selenium.

Bertoldi, Gilbert L. Chemical Quality of Ground Water in the Dos Palos-Kettleman City Area, San Joaquin Valley, California. Geological Survey Water Resources Division, Dept. of the Interior, March 11, 1971.

Byers, Horace G. Selenium Occurrence in Certain Soils in the United States with a Discussion of Related Topics. Technical Bulletin No. 482. U. S. Dept. of Agric., Washington, D.C., August 1935.

Chittenden, Captain Hiram. Examination of Reservoir Sites in Wyoming and Colorado. House Document No. 141, 55 Cong., 2d sess. [Serial 3666.]

Crist, Marvin A. *Selenium in Waters in and Adjacent to Kendrick Project, Natrona County, Wyoming.* Geological Survey Water-Supply Paper 1360-G. U. S. Govt. Printing Off., 1974.

Davis, G. H., and J. F. Poland. *Ground-Water Conditions in the Mendota-Huron Area, Fresno and Kings Counties, California.* Geological Survey Water-Supply Paper 1360-G. U. S. Govt. Printing Off., 1957.

Eaton, Frank M. *Boron in Soils and Irrigation Waters and Its Effects on Plants with Particular Reference to the San Joaquin Valley of California.* U. S. Dept. of Agric., 1935.

Federal Water Pollution Control Administration Proceedings. *Conference in the Matter of Pollution of the South Platte River Basin in the State of Colorado.* 3 vols. U. S. Dept. of the Interior, 1966.

Follansbee, Robert. *Upper Colorado River and Its Utilization.* Geological Survey Water-Supply Paper 617. U.S. Govt. Printing Off., 1929.

Gates, Paul W. (with chap. by Robert W. Swenson). *History of Public Land Law Development.* U. S. Govt. Printing Off., 1968.

Holmes, Beatrice H. *A History of Federal Water Resource Programs, 1800-1960.* USDA Economic Research Service, Misc. pub. no. 1223. U. S. Dept. of Agric., 1972.

______. *History of Federal Water Resource Programs and Policies, 1961-1970.* USDA Economic Research Service, Misc. pub. no. 1379. U. S. Dept. of Agric., 1979.

Horwitz, Elinor Lander. *Our Nation's Wetlands/An Interagency Task Force Report.* U. S. Govt. Printing Off., 1978.

Hutchins, Wells A. *Irrigation Districts/Their Organization, Operation and Financing.* Technical Bulletin No. 254. U. S. Dept. of Agric., June 1931.

Lakin, H. W., and H. G. Byers. *Selenium Occurrence in Certain Soils in the United States with a Discussion of Related Topics.* Sixth Report. Technical Bulletin No. 783. U. S. Dept. of Agric., 1941.

______, and D. F. Davidson. *Selenium.* Geological Survey Professional Paper 820. U. S. Govt. Printing Off., 1973.

LaRue, E. C. *Colorado River and Its Utilization.* Geological Survey Water-Supply Paper 395. U. S. Govt. Printing Off., 1916.

______. Water Power and Flood Control of Colorado River Below Green River, Utah. Geological Survey Water Supply Paper 556. U. S. Govt. Printing Off., 1925.

Montgomery, Mary, and Marion Clawson. History of Legislation and Policy Formation of the Central Valley Project. U. S. Dept. Agric., Bureau of Agric. Econ., Berkeley, CA, Mar 1946.

National Water Commission. Water Policies for the Future. Final Report to the Congress of the United States by the National Water Commission. U. S. Govt. Printing Off., 1973.

Newell, F. H. (comp.). Proceedings. Second Conference of Engineers of the Reclamation Service. Water Supply and Irrigation Paper No. 146. U. S. Govt. Printing Off., 1905.

Powell, John Wesley. Report on the Lands of the Arid Region of the United States with a More Detailed Account of the Lands of Utah. 2nd ed. U. S. Govt. Printing Off., 1879.

Presser, Theresa S., and Ivan Barnes. Dissolved Constituents Including Selenium in Waters in the Vicinity of Kesterson National Wildlife Refuge and the West Grassland, Fresno and Merced Counties, California. U. S. Geological Survey Water Resources Investigations Report 85-4220. Menlo Park, CA, August 1985.

______. Selenium Concentrations in Waters Tributary to and in the Vicinity of the Kesterson National Wildlife Refuge, Fresno and Merced Counties, California. U. S. Geological Survey Water Resources Investigations Report 84-4122. Menlo Park, CA, May 1984.

Shacklette, Hansford, Josephine G. Boerngen, and John R. Keith. Selenium, Flourine, and Arsenic in Surficial Materials of the Conterminous United States. Geological Survey Circular 692. Washington, 1974.

Shacklette, H. T., and J. G. Boerngen. Element Concentrations in Soils and Other Surficial Materials of the Conterminous United States. Geological Survey Prof. Paper 1270. Washington, 1984.

U. S. Commission on Organization of the Executive Branch of the Government. Reorganization of the Department of the Interior. A Report to the Congress by the Commission on Organization of the Executive Branch of the Government, Appendices K and L. Washington, 1949.

______. Water Resources and Power. A Report to the Congress by the Commission on Organization of the Executive Branch of the Government, vol. 1. Washington, 1955.

U. S. Comptroller General. Changes in Federal Water Project Repayment Policies Can Reduce Costs. U.S.General Accounting Office, Washington, 1981.

______. Congressional Guidance Needed on Federal Cost Share of Water Resources Projects when Project Benefits Are Not Widespread. U. S. General Acct. Office, Washington 1980.

______. Federal Charges for Irrigation Projects Reviewed Do Not Cover Costs. U. S. General Acct. Office, Washington, 1981.

______. Improved Federal Efforts Needed to Equally Consider Wildlife Conservation with Other Features of Water Resource Developments. U. S. Gen. Acct. Office, Washington, 1974.

______. Improvements Needed in Making Benefit-Cost Analyses for Federal Water Resources Projects. U. S. General Acct. Office, Washington, 1974.

______. Negotiation of Contracts For Water From The Central Valley Project. B-125045, Bureau of Reclamation, Dept. of the Interior, 1968.

______. Reforming Interest Provisions In Federal Water Laws Could Save Millions. U. S. Gen.Acct. Office, Washington, 1981.

U. S. Congress/Congressional Budget Office. Procedures For Estimating the Subsidies Associated with Bureau of Reclamation Irrigation Projects. Washington, 1988.

U. S. Congress. Reclamation Reform Act of 1982, Title II, Public Law 97-293; 96 Stat. 1263.

U. S. Dept. of Agric.. Proposed Rules for Enforcement of the Reclamation Act of 1902: An Economic Analysis. USDA, January 1978.

U. S. Dept. of the Interior. Teton Dam Failure Review Group Report. U. S. Govt. Print. Off., 1977.

U. S. Dept. of the Interior/Bureau of Reclamation. Assessment '87/A New Direction for the Bureau of Reclamation and Implementation Plan/A New Direction for the Bureau of Reclamation, September 10, 1987.

U. S. Dept. of the Interior/Bureau of Reclamation. Implementation Plan: Update '89, Nov. 22, 1988. Appendix A contains "Charter for the Permanent Management Committee of the Bureau of Reclamation," signed by Sec. Hodel, Oct. 6, 1988, p. 25-27.

U. S. Dept. of the Interior. Federal Reclamation and Related Laws Annotated. 3 vols. U. S. Govt. Printing Off., 1972.

Articles

Biggar, James W., Dennis E. Rolston, and Donald R. Nielsen, "Transport of salts by water," California Agriculture, Oct. 1984.

Blum, Deborah, "US official threatens irrigation water cutoff," Sacramento Bee, Nov.17, 1984.

Carter, Lloyd, "Huge land buyout could clean up Kesterson," Fresno Bee, Nov. 16, 1984.

Collins, Richard B., "Indian Reservation Water Rights," Jour. AWWA, v.78, no.10 Oct.1986, 48-54.

Davis, E. H., "Oregon -- First in 'Portable' Irrigation," Oregon Historical Quarterly, December 1977.

Doyle, Michael, "Cover-up in reclamation agency?" Fresno Bee, Sept. 27, 1988.

Dunning, Harrison C., "The 'Physical' Solution in Western Water Law," Colorado Law Review, vol. 57, Spring 1986.

_______. "Reflections on the Transfer of Water Rights," Journal of Contemporary Law, vol. 4, Winter 1977.

Gressley, Gene M. "Arthur Powell Davis, Reclamation and the West," Agricultural History, vol. 42, 1968.

Howe, Charles W., "Project Benefits and Costs from National and Regional Viewpoints: Methodological Issues and Case Study of the Colorado-Big Thompson Project," Natural Resources Journal, vol. 27, Winter 1987.

Johnson, Ralph W., "Public Trust Protection for Instream Flows and Lake Levels," Univ. Calif., Davis, Law Review, vol. 14, no. 2, 1980.

Kelley, Amy K., "Staging a Comeback--Section 8 of the Reclamation Act," Univ. Calif., Davis, Law Review, vol. 18, no. 1, 1984.

Kelley, Robert L., and Ronald L. Nye, "Historical perspective on salinity and drainage problems in California," California Agriculture, October 1984.

Kubota, J., W. H. Allaway, D. L. Carter, E. E. Cary, and V. A.

Lazar, "Selenium in Crops in United States in Relation to Selenium-Responsive Diseases of Animals," Journal of Agricultural and Food Chemistry, vol. 15, May-June 1967.

Lemly, A. Dennis, "Toxicology of Selenium in a Freshwater Reservoir: Implications for Environmental Hazard Evaluation and Safety," Ecotoxicology and Environmental Safety, vol. 10, 1985, 314-38.

LeVeen, E. Phillip, "A Political Economic Analysis of the 1982 Reclamation Act," Western Journal of Agricultural Economics, vol. 8, no. 2 (December 1983), 255-66.

MacDonnell, Lawrence J. and Charles W.Howe, "Area-of-Origin Protection in Transbasin Water Diversions: An Evaluation of Alternative Approaches," University of Colorado Law Review, vol. 57, no. 3 (Spring 1986), 527-48.

Ohlendorf, Harry M., David J. Hoffman, Michael K. Saiki, and Thomas W. Aldrich, "Embryonic Mortality and Abnormalities of Aquatic Birds: Apparent Impacts of Selenium from Irrigation Drainwater," Science of the Total Environment, v.52(1986),49-63.

Presser, Theresa S., and Harry M. Ohlendorf, "Biogeochemical Cycling of Selenium in the San Joaquin Valley, California, USA," Environmental Management, v.11,no.6(Nov.1977), 805-21.

Saliba, Bonnie Colby, "Do Water Markets 'Work'?/Market Transfers and Trade-Offs in the Southwestern States," Water Resources Research, v. 3, no. 7 (July 1987), 1113-122.

Sax, Joseph L, "The Public Trust Doctrine in Natural Resources Law: Effective Judicial Intervention," Michigan Law Review, v. 68, no. 3 (1970), 471.

Shupe, Steven J., "Water Management in Indian Country," Journal AWWA, v. 78, no. 10 (Oct. 1986), 55-62.

Swain, Donald C., "The Bureau of Reclamation and the New Deal, 1933-1940," Pacific Northwest Quarterly, July 1970, 137-47.

Sylvester, Marc A., "Water Quality Issues Associated With Agricultural Drainage in Semiarid Regions," EOS, vol. 68, no. 30 (July 28, 1987) 652-53.

Weatherford, Gary D., and Steven J. Shupe, "Reallocating Water in the West," Journal AWWA, vol. 78, no. 10 (Oct.1986), 63-71.

Wilkinson, Charles F., "Western Water Law in Transition," Journal AWWA, vol. 78, no. 10 (Oct.1986) 34-47.

Books

Anderson, Terry L. (ed). *Water Rights: Scarce Resource Allocation, Bureaucracy, and the Environment*. San Francisco, 1983.

Dupree, A. Hunter. *Science in the Federal Government: A History of Policies and Activities to 1940*. Cambridge, 1957.

Engelbert, Ernest A. (ed), with Ann Foley Scheuring. *Water Scarcity: Impacts on Western Agriculture*. Berkeley, 1984.

Fenno, Richard F., Jr. *Congressmen in Committees*. Boston, 1973.

Frederick, Kenneth D. (ed), with the assistance of Diana C. Gibbons. *Scarce Water and Institutional Change*. Washington, D.C., 1986.

Golze, Alfred R. *Reclamation in the United States*. New York, 1952.

Haimes, Yacov Y. (ed). *Scientific, Technological and Institutional Aspects of Water Resource Policy*. Boulder, 1980.

Hart, Henry C. *The Dark Missouri*. Madison, 1957.

Hartman, L. M., and D. Seastone. *Water Transfers: Economic Efficiency and Alternative Institutions*. Baltimore and London, 1970.

Hirshleifer, Jack, James C. DeHaven, and Jerome W. Millman. *Water Supply: Economics, Technology, and Policy*. Chicago, 1960.

Howe, Charles W. *Natural Resource Economics: Issues, Analysis, and Policy*. New York, 1979.

Howe, Charles W., and K. William Easter. *Interbasin Transfers of Water: Economic Issues and Impacts*. Baltimore and London, 1971.

James, L. Douglas (ed). *Man & Water*. Lexington, 1974.

______, and Robert R. Lee. *Economics of Water Resources Planning*. New York, 1971.

Lampen, Dorothy. *Economic and Social Aspects of Federal Reclamation*. Baltimore, 1930; New York, 1979.

Lee, Lawrence Bacon. *Reclaiming the American West: An Historiography and Guide*. Santa Barbara and Oxford, 1980.

McCool, Daniel. *Command of the Waters/Iron Triangles, Federal Water Development, and Indian Water*. Berkeley, Los Angeles, and London, 1987.

Maass, Arthur, and Raymond L. Anderson. *...And the Desert Shall Rejoice: Conflict, Growth, and Justice in Arid Environments*. Cambridge and London, 1978.

Meyers, Charles J., and A. Dan Tarlock. Water Resources Management/A Coursebook in Law and Public Policy. New York, 1971. Revised edition indexed under Tarlock.

Phipps, Tim T., Pierre R. Crosson, and Kent A. Price (eds). Agriculture and the Environment. Washington, D.C., 1986.

Pisani, Donald J. From the Family Farm to Agribusiness: The Irrigation Crusade in California and the West, 1850-1931. Berkeley, 1984.

Reisner, Marc. Cadillac Desert. New York, 1986.

Ridgeway, Marion E. The Missouri Basin's Pick-Sloan Plan: A Case Study in Congressional Policy Determination. Urbana, 1955.

Robinson, Michael C. Water for the West: The Bureau of Reclamation 1902-1977. Chicago, 1979.

Rosenfeld, Irene, and Orville A. Beath. Selenium: Geobotany, Biochemistry, Toxicity, and Nutrition. New York and London, 1964.

Tarlock, A. Dan. Law of Water Rights and Resources. New York, 1988.

Warne, William E. The Bureau of Reclamation. New York, 1973.

Weatherford, Gary D. (ed), in association with Lee Brown, Helen Ingram, and Dean Mann. Water and Agriculture in the Western U.S.: Conservation, Reallocation, and Markets. Boulder, 1982.

Worster, Donald. Rivers of Empire: Water, Aridity, and the Growth of the American West. New York, 1985.

Monographs, Pamphlets, Papers, and Proceedings

American Indian Lawyer Training Program/American Indian Resources Institute. "Tribal Water Management Handbook." Oakland, 1987.

Angelides, Sotirios, and Eugene Bardach. "Water Banking: How to Stop Wasting Agricultural Water." Institute of Contemporary Studies, San Francisco, 1978.

Dunning, Harrison C. "Instream Flows, the Public Trust, and the Future of the West," Natural Resources Law Center Conference, University of Colorado, March 31, 1988.

Easter, K. William. "Interbasin Water Transfers--Economic Issues and Impacts" in Proceedings Series No. 6, AWRA 4th American Water Resources Conference.

Folk-Williams, John A., with research assistance of Lucy Hilgendorf. "Water in the West/What Indian Water Means to the West." Vol. 1. Santa Fe, 1982.

Foster, Charles H. W., and Peter P. Rogers. "Federal Water Policy: Toward an Agenda for Action." John F. Kennedy School of Government, Harvard University, 1988.

Howard, Alice Q. (ed). "Selenium and Agricultural Drainage: Implications for San Francisco Bay and the California Environment." Proceedings of the Second Selenium Symposium, Berkeley, 1985, published in 1986 by the Bay Institute of San Francisco, Sausalito; Proceedings of Selenium Symposium III and IV are in press.

James, L. Douglas. "Irrigation Water Management for Sustained Agricultural Productivity," in "Proceedings of The Philadelphia Society for Promoting Agriculture 1986-1987," Phil., 1988.

Martin, William E., and Helen M. Ingram. "Planning for Growth in the Southwest." National Planning Association, Washington, D.C., 1985.

Ohlendorf, Harry M., and Joseph P. Skorupa. "Selenium in Relation to Wildlife and Agricultural Drainage Water," Fourth International Symposium on Uses of Selenium and Tellurium, May 7-10, 1989, Banff, Alberta.

Schneider, Anne J. "Legal Aspects of Instream Water Uses in California/Background and Issues." Staff Paper No. 6, Governor's Commission to Review California Water Rights Law, 1978.

Wahl, Richard W., "Federal Water Pricing, Agricultural Land Values, and Kesterson Reservoir," 1985 Conference of the Western Economic Association.

Oral Histories

Bancroft Library Regional Oral History Office, University of California, Berkeley. "California Water Issues, 1950-1966." Interviews conducted in 1979 and 1980 by Malca Chall with Edmund G. Brown, Sr., Ralph M. Brody, B. Abbott Goldberg, and William E. Warne.

Appendix A
Exemptions, Modifications, Waivers, and Special Provisions Applicable to Land Limitation Provisions of Federal Reclamation Laws

A. Exemptions from acreage limitations:

1. Act of June 16, 1938 (52 Stat. 764), Colorado-Big Thompson Project - Colorado;

2. Act of November 29, 1940 (54 Stat. 1219), Truckee River Storage Project, Nevada-California, Humboldt Project, Nevada;

3. Act of August 28, 1954 (68 Stat. 890), Owl Creek Unit, Pick-Sloan Missouri Basin Program, Wyoming;

4. Act of September 3, 1954 (68 Stat. 1190), Santa Maria Project, California;

5. Act of July 24, 1957 (71 Stat. 309-310), East Bench Unit, Pick-Sloan Missouri Basin Program, Montana; (Beaverhead Valley lands only. See also C 1 hereinafter.)

6. Act of August 27, 1967 (81 Stat. 173), San Felipe Division (Central Valley Project), California; (North and South Santa Clara subareas only);

7. Act of August 28, 1970 (84 Stat. 830), Narrows Unit Pick-Sloan Missouri Basin Program, Colorado;

B. Modified size of nonexcess holding:

1. Act of August 11, 1939, as amended by the Act of October 14, 1940 (54 Stat. 1119), Water Conservation and Utilization Projects; (Size of farm unit as determined necessary by Secretary for support of family without other limitation.)

2. Act of June 27, 1952 (66 Stat. 282) San Luis Valley Project, Colorado; (Nonexcess holding established at 480 acres);

3. Act of July 30, 1947 (61 Stat. 628) Gila Project (Area disposed of as settlement lands, shall, so far as practicable, not exceed 160 acres, i.e., rule of approximation.)

4. Act of October 1, 1962 (76 Stat. 679), amendatory to the Act of March 10, 1943 (57 Stat. 14), Columbia Basin Project, Washington; (Authorizes nominal 1/4-section when in excess of 160 acres and platted prior to date of act. Also establishes 640 acre State agricultural school tract.)

C. Application of Class 1 Equivalency:

1. Act of July 24, 1957 (71 Stat. 309-310), East Bench Unit, Pick-Sloan Missouri Basin Program, Montana; (Bench lands only - Land equivalent to 130 acres of Class 1 land).

2. Act of August 28, 1958 (72 Stat. 963), Seedskadee Project, Colorado River Storage Project, Wyoming; (Equivalent to 160 acres of Class 1 land).

3. Act of September 27, 1962 (76 Stat. 634), Baker Project, Upper Division, Oregon; (Upper Division lands only - Equivalent to 120 acres of Class 1 land).

4. Act of September 2, 1964 (78 Stat. 852), Savory-Pot Hook Project (Colorado River Storage Project), Colorado-Wyoming, Bostwick Park Project (Colorado River Storage Project), Colorado, Fruitland Mesa Project (Colorado River Storage Project), Colorado; (Equally applicable to the three projects - Equivalency established on basis of 160 acres Class 1 land on Bostwick Park Project).

5. Act of September 25, 1970 (84 Stat. 861), Riverton Extension Unit, Pick-Sloan Missouri Basin Program, Wyoming; (Equivalent to 160 acres of Class 1 land).

6. Act of September 30, 1968 (82 Stat. 885-896); Animas-LaPlata Project (Colorado River Storage Project), Colorado-New Mexico, Dolores Project (Colorado River Storage Project), Colorado, Dallas Creek (Colorado River Storage Project), Colorado, San Miguel Project (Colorado River Storage Project), Colorado, West Divide Project (Colorado River Storage Project), Colorado, Seedskadee (Colorado River Storage Project), Wyoming. (Equivalent to 160 acres of Class 1 land for all projects listed.)

7. Act of March 11, 1976, (90 Stat. 205), Polecat Bench, P-SMBP, Wyoming, Pollock-Herreid Unit, P-SMBP, South Dakota. (Equivalent to 160 acres of Class 1 land for both projects.)

D. Use of interest payment on excess lands:

1. Act of August 1, 1956 (70 Stat. 775), Washoe Project, Nevada-California;

2. Act of August 6, 1956 (70 Stat. 1044), as amended, Small Reclamation Projects;

3. Act of April 7, 1958 (72 Stat. 82) Lower Rio Grande Rehabilitation Project, Mercedes Division, Texas;

4. Act of September 22, 1959 (73 Stat. 641), Lower Rio Grande Rehabilitation Project, La Feria Division, Texas;

E. Delivery of project water to certain categories of excess lands:

1. Act of July 11, 1956 (70 Stat. 524), Applicable to lands which become excess when acquired for foreclosure or other process of law, by conveyance in satisfaction of mortgages, by inheritance, or by devise; and

2. Act of September 2, 1960 (74 Stat. 732), Applicable to lands which become excess when held by a surviving spouse;

3. Act of July 7, 1970 (84 Stat. 411), Reclamation project lands owned by States or political subdivisions and agencies thereof;

F. Acts of Congress authorizing execution of specific contracts which incorporate modified excess land payout provisions, all negotiated pursuant to section 7 of the Reclamation Project Act of August 14, 1939 (53 Stat. 1187), as hereafter listed:

1. Act of May 6, 1949 (63 Stat. 62), Kittitas Reclamation District, Yakima Project, Washington;

2. Act of October 27, 1949 (63 Stat. 941), Vale Oregon Irrigation District, Vale Project, Oregon; Prosser Irrigation District, Yakima Project, Washington;

3. Act of June 23, 1952 (66 Stat. 151), Frenchtown Irrigation District, Frenchtown Project, Montana; Owyhee Irrigation District,

Gem Irrigation District, Ridgeview Irrigation District, Ontario-Nyssa Irrigation District, Advancement Irrigation District, Payette-Oregon Slope Irrigation District, Crystal Irrigation District, Bench Irrigation District, and Slide Irrigation District, Owyhee Project, Idaho-Oregon;

4. Act of July 17, 1952 (66 Stat. 741), Gering-Ft. Laramie Irrigation District, Goshen Irrigation District, and Pathfinder Irrigation District, all on North Platte Project, Nebraska-Wyoming;

5. Act of June 18, 1954 (68 Stat. 254), Hermiston Irrigation District, Umatilla Project, Oregon;

6. Act of June 30, 1954 (68 Stat. 359) Roza Irrigation District, Yakima Project, Washington;

7. Act of August 10, 1954 (62 Stat. 679), North Unit Irrigation District, Deschutes Project, Oregon;

8. Act of August 21, 1954 (68 Stat. 762), American Falls Reservoir District No. 2, Minidoka Project, Idaho;

9. Act of August 24, 1954 (68 Stat. 794), Black Canyon Irrigation District, Boise Project, Idaho;

10. Act of August 1, 1956 (70 Stat. 799), Tulelake Irrigation District, Klamath Project, California-Oregon.

G. Leasing restrictions:

1. Act of August 10, 1972 (86 Stat. 530) (Westlands Water District-Lemoore Naval Air Station lands to be leased as nearly as practicable in 160 acre tracts. One tract per lessee.) (See also State Lands Act of July 7, 1970, under E. 3.) (Leased and fee held lands of lessee not to exceed 160 acre total.)

Appendix B
Procedures for Estimating the Subsidies Associated with Bureau of Reclamation Irrigation Projects

At the request of the Subcommittee on General Oversight and Investigations of the House Committee on Interior and Insular Affairs, the Congressional Budget Office (CBO) reviewed the procedures that various institutions used to calculate the level of subsidization of Bureau of Reclamation (Bu Rec) Irrigation projects. The Subcommittee asked CBO to evaluate the various methods used in the calculations and provide an opinion regarding the validity of the estimates produced.

SUMMARY OF FINDINGS

CBO reached the following conclusions:

- o The "subsidy" measures that the Department of the Interior (DOI) and BuRec have provided are designed to measure the cumulative costs to the government of providing water to irrigation users;
- o The cumulative cost estimates by DOI ($9.8 billion) and the Denver office of BuRec ($24.4 billion) are likely to understate the government's costs;
- o Using BuRec data but adjusting its procedures results in estimates of the cost of providing the irrigation subsidy ranging from $33.7 billion to $70.3 billion; and
- o The most appropriate estimate of the subsidy depends on how the subsidy is defined.

Important policy issues exist that can be addressed using the cumulative government cost measure. For example, it would be useful to know the cost to the economy (as opposed to the government's cost) of providing these subsidies or the price that the government would have to charge irrigators to ensure the long-term funding of these projects without federal subsidies. Currently available data do not permit estimation of these alternative subsidy measures.

BACKGROUND

The costs and benefits of western water projects have long been subjects of heated debate. Proponents have argued that the projects were important in the development of the arid lands west of the Mississippi River and that they continue to provide economic stimuli to this region. Others argue that the projects benefit an economically advantaged class of people, distort the allocation of valuable resources, and add to the cost of other federal programs such as agricultural commodity programs.

In May of 1987, the House Interior Subcommittee on Water and Power Resources asked the Department of the Interior to estimate the cumulative and annual subsidies the government provided to BuRec irrigation water users. The Subcommittee did not provide a precise definition of the subsidy. In their responses, DOI and BuRec defined the subsidy as the present value (in 1986) of the difference between capital expenditures allocated to irrigation projects and repayments from users. The period of time considered in their estimates extends from the inception of a project to the end of existing contracts. BuRec and DOI then used different estimation procedures and arrived at significantly different answers.

A DESCRIPTION OF BUREAU OF RECLAMATION IRRIGATION WATER SUBSIDIES

Users of BuRec irrigation systems may benefit from at least four types of subsidies:

- Interest rate subsidies;
- Cross-use or cross-project subsidies, where funds from the sale of water to municipal and industrial users and from hydroelectric power are used to offset irrigation costs;
- Subsidization of operation and maintenance costs; and
- Subsidized prices for irrigators using power generated by the projects.

A review of BuRec's treatment of capital expenditures and repayments helps explain why these subsidies arise.

Bureau of Reclamation Procedures for Allocating Capital Expenditures

A dam may provide flood control, hydroelectric power, drinking water for nearby towns, recreational facilities, and irrigation. No clear way exists for determining what percentage of the dam's capital expenditures should be allocated to each of these uses. The method BuRec uses to allocate fixed costs is known as the separable costs/remaining benefits (SCRB) method.

The SCRB method employs several steps. The first step is to estimate the cost that each purpose would incur if it were provided separately. The separate cost for a purpose is compared with the benefits projected to be generated by that purpose, and the smaller of the two is defined as the justifiable expenditure. Next, the costs that could be avoided if a given purpose were dropped from the project--a measure called the separable cost--are calculated. The separable cost of each purpose is subtracted from its justifiable expenditure, and the differences are added to derive the remaining justifiable expenditure for the project. Finally, the joint costs of the project are calculated as the difference between total project cost and the sum of separable costs. Joint costs are allocated to each purpose according to the proportion each contributed to the remaining justifiable expenditure. Thus, total capital expenditures allocated to a given purpose are composed of the separable cost plus its calculated share of the joint costs. However, the total amount of capital expenditures allocated to a given use cannot exceed its justifiable expenditure.

Procedures Regarding Repayments

Different users are subject to different rules regarding repayment of BuRec water project costs. BuRec regulations require hydroelectric as well as municipal and industrial users to repay, with interest, the portion of the project's capital expenditures that the SCRB method described above allocated to them. In contrast, irrigators repay allocated capital expenditures without interest (hence the interest rate subsidy), and flood control beneficiaries repay nothing. The different rules of repayment may provide planners an incenative to allocate as much of the capital expenditures as possible to nonreimbursable uses to justify a project.

Besides avoiding interest costs, irrigators are charged for water based on their ability to pay. If for example, an irrigation district is judged unable to pay the full amount of capital expenditures allocated to the irrigation component of a project, the district is charged a lower rate. The portion of irrigation costs not covered by irrigators is recouped from other sources, principally hydroelectric power users. Payments from other users can come from within the same project or from other projects (the cross-use or cross-project subsidy).

Operating and maintenance (O&M) costs are supposed to be paid in their entirety by irrigation users and are included in the fixed-price contracts signed by BuRec and the irrigation districts. To the extent that these costs are not covered, they are supposed to be included in the capital costs of the project. Once included in capital costs, O&M costs can be refinanced over long periods of time and will benefit from the interest rate and cross-use or cross-project subsidies discussed above (the O&M subsidy).

Finally, irrigators also benefit from a subsidized rate for the power they use to pump water (the power subsidy). The rate they pay for power is supposed to cover the cost of operation, maintenance, and repairs, but not capital replacement. Other hydroelectric power users pay the difference between the full cost of power and the rate charged irrigators.

SUBSIDY ESTIMATING PROCEDURES USED BY THE BUREAU OF RECLAMATION AND DEPARTMENT OF INTERIOR

Both DOI and BuRec analyses attempt to estimate the cumulative historical cost to the government of providing subsidies to irrigation water users. Both use the same data, though at different levels of aggregation, and estimate the subsidy over the same time period. Beyond these similarities, the two approaches are significantly different.

The Bureau of Reclamation Approach

In its estimate, the BuRec considered the government's cost for the interest rate and cross-use or cross-project subsidies. BuRec used data for capital expenditures and repayments in each of 106 western water projects. For each year from the initiation of each project through 1986, BuRec estimated the net expenses to the government (capital expenditures less repayments). BuRec assumed that government borrowing financed net expenses. BuRec then added interest on this debt (calculated using an adjusted corporate bond rate before 1957 and the BuRec Small Reclamation Project Act rate from 1957 to 1986) to the next year's capital expenses. In this way, interest expenses were compounded through 1986. For years after 1986, BuRec included no capital costs, but considered only the present value (as of 1986) of repayments stipulated in existing water contracts. The repayment stream included only the repayments from irrigators. Because BuRec assumed that irrigators pay O&M costs in full, these costs were ignored; including O&M costs would increase capital expenses and repayments by equal amounts, thereby canceling one another out.

The DOI Approach

The DOI approached the cost-to-government calculation at a more aggregate level, using the net expenses (capital expenditures less repayments) for each year across all projects as the basis for their analysis. However, DOI apparently included not only repayments from irrigators, but also repayments credited to the irrigation account that nonirrigators actually paid. DOI used these net expense figures to calculate the interest expense associated with capital shortfalls. The interest rate DOI used was an estimate of the government's cost of borrowing during the pre-1957 period and the Small Reclamation Project Act rate after 1957. DOI did not compound these interest expenses. Like BuRec, DOI did not include O&M expenses in its estimate.

General Problems Faced in Estimating Irrigation Subsidies

The two issues underlying estimates of the cost of irrigation subsidies are the quality of the data and the choice of an interest rate for the analysis.

Data Issues. The Subcommittee provided CBO with the cost and benefit data that the BuRec used. CBO, while unable to verify the quality of the data, has several concerns about them. First, in many cases the initial construction costs for a project were simply allocated equally across the years of construction. The Boise project in the Pacific Northwest, for example, lists $704,000 as the irrigation capital expenditures in each year from 1906 until 1956. Clearly, these equal expenditures are a simplifying assumption and not actual data on irrigation expenditures. If more of these expenditures occurred in the early years of a project, the estimated subsidy would be significantly greater because the carrying costs associated with the subsidy would be increased.

Second, as noted, both BuRec and DOI exclude O&M costs from their calculations. Many critics question the validity of the assumption that the districts fully cover O&M costs.[1] These critics note that as O&M costs increase over time (because of inflation or obsolescence), the fixed price contracts often fail to cover O&M expenses. When irrigation districts fail to meet O&M expenses, the Bureau is supposed to increase the water district's outstanding capital obligations by enough to cover the shortfall. It is not clear whether or not the data BuRec and DOI used include accumulated O&M deficits in outstanding capital balances.

Finally, in constructing the estimates, both the DOI and BuRec calculate the government's costs relative to the capital expenditures assigned to the irrigation component of the individual water projects. The major underlying issue is the conceptually difficult problem of allocating fixed costs among different uses in multiproduct projects such as dams. The SCRB method that BuRec used is a systematic though somewhat arbitrary means of allocating the fixed costs associated with a project among different outputs.[2] Considering the nature of water projects, joint costs that must be allocated using the SCRB method are probably large relative to total costs. As a result, the validity and meaning of any estimate that depends on such a capital expenditure allocation is open to debate.

Choice of the Appropriate Interest Rate. Finally, DOI and OMB debated about the appropriate interest rate to use in calculating the subsidy level. As noted, DOI and BuRec are trying to measure the government's cost of providing the irrigation subsidy. The DOI suggests using the interest rate calculated for the Small Reclamation Project Act because that rate is used for "the repayment for all interest-bearing reimbursable functions under the Act." This rate is calculated using a formula based on Treasury borrowing rates. Since irrigation is not an interest-bearing reimbursable function, why this rate is appropriate is unclear. Using a Treasury borrowing rate (for example, a short-term Treasury bill rate) to determine the government's cost for providing the subsidy might be more appropriate.

The Office of Management and Budget, commenting on the DOI estimation procedure, advocates an approach designed to reflect the cost of funds for a comparable private sector borrower. Use of a private sector borrowing rate is an attempt to capture the value of opportunities forgone by the private sector as a result of the irrigation investment. This definition of the subsidy is somewhat different from the one BuRec and DOI have chosen. Neither the private cost approach favored by OMB nor the government cost approach that DOI and BuRec have chosen is inherently superior; they are measuring subsidies that are conceptually different.

Problems Specific to the DOI or Bureau of Reclamation Estimates

Several questions exist concerning the specific procedures used in the DOI and BuRec estimates. The basic procedural issues are what is included in the repayment stream, the treatment of interest on outstanding debt, and the composition of future capital expenditures and repayment streams.

Composition of Repayments. As noted, the irrigation repayment data DOI used apparently included funds that hydroelectric and municipal and industrial users paid, while BuRec did not. No apparent justification exists for DOI to include repayments received from hydroelectric or municipal and industrial groups in estimating the cost to the government of subsidies provided to irrigators. When undertaking a project, BuRec is required to show that the project as a whole is economically viable, but does not have to prove that each component is economically justifiable. Thus, in the context of project justification, inclusion of hydroelectric repayments in a stream of benefits ostensibly from irrigation is reasonable. However, an estimate of the degree of subsidization that one component of a water project enjoys should not consider repayments from other components of the project.

Interest Costs. A second important procedural issue concerns the treatment of interest costs. Specifically, the question involves whether to compound interest costs (paying interest on interest). Table 1 illustrates the approaches that DOI and BuRec have taken. Suppose that the outstanding balance for a water project is $100,000, the government's interest rate is 8 percent, and the irrigators pay $5,000 at the end of each year for their water. During Period 1, DOI assumes that the government incurs costs of $8,000 (.08 X $100,000) and that the unpaid balance is reduced to $95,000. In Period 2, assuming the interest and repayment rates remain unchanged, DOI would argue that costs of $7,600 (.08 X $95,000) are incurred and the unpaid balance is reduced to $90,000.

Because DOI does not compound interest costs over the life of the project, its method understates the true cost to the government. BuRec treats interest costs correctly. Returning to the example in the preceding paragraph, BuRec assumes that at the end of the first year the government would have to issue bonds in the amount of $8,000 to cover the interest due on the original $100,000. The irrigators would pay the government $5,000, enabling it to retire a portion of its outstanding debt. Thus, as the second year begins, using the BuRec approach, the government would have $103,000 in outstanding debt, not the $95,000 calculated using the DOI method. At the end of the second year, the government would pay interest on the $103,000 ($8,240) and would once again receive $5,000 from the irrigators, leaving the outstanding balance at $106,240.

The DOI rejects the BuRec method of estimating the interest

subsidy as "absurd" because this approach produces a subsidy estimate that "will increase indefinitely." If repayments are less than the interest due on outstanding balances, DOI is correct in saying that the subsidy would increase indefinitely. However, labeling this an absurd conclusion is not correct. For example, suppose a homeowner is unable to pay his or her mortgage. With an understanding banker, the homeowner may be able to refinance the house but either the new unpaid principal will include all accumulated interest owed to the lender or the lender will be forced to reduce its own capital by the amount forgiven.

Future Expenditures and Repayments. Both the DOI and the BuRec subsidy estimates include the present value of expected future payments from irrigators through the end of existing irrigation contracts. Neither of them includes any future expenses; capital expenditures and interest on unpaid balances are both assumed to be zero in future periods. Even if future capital expenditures are unknown, the interest expenses associated with outstanding capital balances can be estimated. An estimate of the irrigation subsidy should include projected interest expenses since they represent payments made by the government on behalf of water users.

REVISED ESTIMATES OF BUREAU OF RECLAMATION IRRIGATION SUBSIDIES

Using capital expenditure and repayment data for each of 106 BuRec projects and a variety of interest rates, the government's cost for the irrigation subsidy was recalculated using two slightly different procedures. The first procedure is the original BuRec approach. Specifically, net subsidies from a project's inception through 1986 were expressed in 1986 present-value terms by adding the interest expenses on the previous period's outstanding balance to current-year net expenditures. This procedure assumes that the outstanding balance is refinanced at the new interest rate in each year through 1986. In future periods, only the discounted value of repayments was considered. The calculation did not include subsidies associated with O&M expenses and power charges. Table 2 includes these estimates under the title "Original BuRec Approach." As these figures illustrate, selection of the interest rate series is a critical variable in determining the estimated size of the irrigation subsidy. Thus, the estimated cumulative subsidy cost may be as little as $18.1 billion or as much as $37.8 billion. Note that the original BuRec estimate of $24.3 billion is reproduced when the BuRec interest rate series is used.

The second approach, entitled the "Modified BuRec Approach" in Table 2, followed the first approach for the historical period but included projected interest costs associated with unpaid balances in future periods. The estimates did not include the power subsidy and the O&M subsidy. Including future interest expenses almost doubles the size of the estimated subsidy; estimates range from $33.7 billion to $70.3 billion, depending on the interest series chosen.

As Table 2 shows, the size of the estimated subsidy is positively related to the interest rate. Thus, as the rate of interest increases from Treasury rates to the prime rate, the cost of the estimated historical subsidy also increases. The estimate using the Treasury rate or perhaps the municipal bond rate would be appropriate in determining the cost of the subsidy to the government. An estimate more in keeping with OMB's suggestion would use the corporate bond rate or the prime rate.

CONCLUSIONS

The second column in Table 2 provides estimates of the cumulative opportunity cost of transfers from taxpayers to BuRec water users. This cost arises because irrigators are not required to pay interest on the costs allocated to them and because payments from other BuRec water users cover part of their costs. As noted above, numerous factors limit the accuracy of these estimates: the quality and inclusiveness of the data, the capital expenditure allocation system, and uncertainty about O&M expenditures.

Alternative Measures of the Bureau of Reclamation Study

A more fundamental concern is the usefulness of a historical measure of the cost to the government of providing the subsidy. The economic relevance of the estimate would be enhanced by examining the cost to the economy of providing the subsidy, measuring the subsidy relative to full replacement costs, or calculating the subsidy relative to the long-run marginal cost of providing an additional unit of irrigation water.

Costs to the Economy of the Bureau of Reclamation Irrigation Subsidy. Measuring the cumulative economic cost of the subsidy requires a broader definition of costs and benefits than the one used to measure government costs. One way to estimate the cost to the economy is to ask how much the private market would have charged the recipient for the good or service the government provided. Estimates of the direct benefits (increased crop production) and indirect benefits (complimentary investments farmers make to enhance productivity) would be needed to determine the total economic returns from the project. The impact of the project on regional development is another factor to consider in such an evaluation.

Opting for a measure of the private benefit of a subsidy means that the interest rate used in the calculation should reflect private borrowing costs. Private borrowers cannot provide absolute assurance that they will be able to repay money lent to them; they must, therefore, pay a risk premium. Any number of private rates (for example, the prime rate or corporate bond rate) could be used. This historical measure, like the government cost estimates discussed above, has limited economic relevance because past subsidies probably are not recoverable.

Full Replacement Cost Pricing. If past transfers are not of greatest immediate economic relevance, the focus could be shifted to determining how much would have to be charged to maintain, in perpetuity, a given level of services. The difference between the current amount charged and this full replacement cost would be a measure of the subsidy.

The expected cost of replacing current irrigation water supplies and the operating and maintenance costs of such systems would be the basis for such a calculation. The distinction between private versus government costs also applies to the full replacement cost approach. For example, to determine the price required to amortize a future investment, either a private or a government interest rate could be appropriate, depending on the question asked. Because the data concerning future replacement costs were not available, this analysis could not provide estimates of the full replacement cost subsidy.

The DOI did provide the Subcommittee with estimates of the full-cost rate on a per-acre basis for most of the projects. The DOI estimates, reproduced as Table 3 in this report, include only capital repayment because DOI assumes that O&M costs are fully covered by the irrigation districts. The DOI documents do not indicate whether or not the capital costs considered are historical or whether they represent the replacement costs of these facilities. In addition, the reservations regarding the capital cost allocation procedure, the assumption about O&M expenses, and exclusion of the power subsidy discussed above are germane to this discussion.

<u>Pricing Based on the Long-Run Marginal Cost of Water</u>. An approach related to full replacement cost pricing is to price water based on the cost of providing an additional unit of water. The price charged should at least equal the cost of providing the additional unit. This approach must use the long-run marginal cost so that the calculation includes the cost of long-lived assets such as dams. This approach would be particularly relevant for new projects or extensions of existing projects.

Estimating the long-run marginal cost of irrigation water requires data on the expected life of the project, capital costs of the additional capacity, and the O&M expenses over the life of the project. Further, if the calculation includes the power subsidy, estimates of the full cost of power and the amount to be used would be required.

The major difference between marginal-cost pricing and the full-cost pricing approach is akin to the distinction between stocks and flows. The full replacement cost pricing approach is an estimate of the cost of maintaining the level of services that already exist (a focus on the stock of services). In contrast, marginal-cost pricing focuses on the cost of adding to existing capacity (a flow orientation).

All the alternative estimating procedures discussed have formidable estimating obstacles and data requirements. However, if they provide information that is useful to the policy process, the added difficulties and expenses involved might be worthwhile. The full-cost pricing estimates currently available from DOI are a step in the right direction.

---

1. See, for example, E. Phillip LeVeen and Laura B. King, Turning Off the Tap on Federal Water Subsidies (San Francisco: Natural Resources Defense Council Inc., 1985); National Wildlife Federation, "Shortchanging the Treasury: The Failure of the Department of the Interior to Comply with the Inspector General's Audit Recommendations to Recover the Costs of Federal Water Projects" (Washington, D.C.: NWF, 1984); or U. S. Department of the Interior, Bureau of Reclamation, Summary Statistics Volume II, Finances and Physical Features (Washington, D.C.: 1983).

2. The discussion about allocation of fixed costs is long and unresolved. See, for example, Jon R. Miller, "The Political Economy of Western Water Finance: Cost Allocation and the Bonneville Unit of the Central Utah Project," American Journal of Agricultural Economics, vol. 69 (May 1987), pp 303-310. Miller quotes Ciriacy-Wantrup as writing, "The problems of cost allocation have been discussed in numerous committees and commissions. There is a voluminous literature on the subject written by engineers, lawyers, accountants, and economists. After lengthy arguments, sometimes reminiscent of medieval dialectics on ecclesiastical dogma, the conclusion is invariably reached that cost allocation must be more or less arbitrary."

TABLE 1. CUMULATIVE SUBSIDY COMPARISONS (In dollars)

Period	Principal Outstanding	Interest Cost	Repayments
	Department of Interior		
1	100,000	8,000	5,000
2	95,000	7,600	5,000
3	90,000		
	Bureau of Reclamation		
1	100,000	8,000	5,000
2	103,000	8,240	5,000
3	106,240		

SOURCE: Congressional Budget Office.

TABLE 2. ALTERNATIVE ESTIMATES OF COST OF THE CUMULATIVE BUREAU OF RECLAMATION WATER SUBSIDY (In billions of dollars)

Interest Rates Used	Original BuRec Approach	Modified BuRec Approach
Treasury	18.1	33.7
Municipal Bond	21.0	39.1
BuRec Series	24.3	45.1
Corporate Bond	34.7	64.4
Prime	37.8	70.3

SOURCE: Congressional Budget Office.

TABLE 3. DEPARTMENT OF INTERIOR ESTIMATES OF FULL-COST PRICING OF BUREAU OF RECLAMATION IRRIGATION WATER

Pacific Northwest Region	Subsidized Rate/Acre	Full-Cost Rate/Acre
Arnold, OR	1.14	1.74
Baker, OR	1.17	20.95
Boise, ID-OR	0.64	6.40
Columbia Basin, WA	2.63	63.18
Crescent Lake Dam, OR	0.85	1.58
Crooked River, OR	3.27	22.24
Deschutes, OR	2.73	11.76
Frenchtown, MT	1.40	1.83
Little Wood River, ID	2.04	5.10
Mann Creek, ID	3.99	60.52
Michaud Flats, ID	5.16	30.15
Minidoka-Palisades, ID-OR	2.77	9.15
Owyhee, ID-OR	1.61	7.47
Rathdrum Prairie, ID	4.33	102.38
Rogue River Basin, OR	4.80	39.29
Spokane Valley, WA	7.42	54.78
Umatilla, OR	0.35	2.45
Vale, OR	2.53	8.40
Wapinitia, OR	5.82	16.59
Yakima, WA	3.44	10.85
Mid-Pacific Region		
Cachuma, CA*	8.81	114.98
Central Valley Project, CA **		
Humboldt, NV		b/
Klamath, CA-OR	1.00	b/
Newlands, NV	0.14	b/
Orland, CA*	1.96	2.07
Santa Maria, CA	6.76	a/
Solano, CA (Solano ID)*	2.32	21.77

Upper Colorado Region	Subsidized Rate/Acre	Full-Cost Rate/Acre
Bostwick Park, CO	3.32	94.70
Central Utah, UT		
Bonneville Unit	17.84	306.40
Jensen Unit	3.68	204.60
Vernal Unit	2.04	51.40
Colbran, CO	.98	21.50
Eden, WY	1.30	49.10
Emery County, UT	3.43	54.10
Florida, CO	1.96	39.00
Hammond, NM	2.73	146.50
Hyrum, UT	3.12	2.20
Lyman, WY	1.14	24.10
Mancos, CO	1.10	2.90
Newton, UT	3.43	8.30
Ogden River, UT	3.07	16.10
Paonia, CO	2.22	35.60
Preston Beach, ID	1.26	4.10
Provo River, CO	1.77	6.20
Silt, CO	2.71	73.60
Smith Fork, CO	2.16	33.80
Uncompahgre, CO	2.07	3.40
Weber Basin, UT	2.27	80.60
Southwest Region		
Middle Rio Grande, NM	4.15	21.05
Tucumcari, NM	1.97	10.56
Vermejo, NM	5.28	20.99
W. C. Austin, OK	1.10	1.90
Lower Colorado Region		
Boulder Canyon, AZ-CA-NV	11.95	18.50
Gila, AZ	8.35	31.37
Yuma Auxiliary, AZ	9.42	12.70

Missouri Basin Region	Subsidized Rate/Acre	Full-Cost Rate/Acre
Colorado-Big Thompson, CO	0	a/
Fryingpan-Arkansas, CO*	46.19	150.68
Huntley, MT	1.17	2.79
Milk River, MT	1.11	3.04
North Platte, WY-NE	0.22	8.18
Pick-Sloan Missouri Basin Program		
Ainsworth Unit, NE	2.43	57.79
Angostura Unit, SD	3.25	106.28
Belle Fourche, SD	0.77	3.04
Boysen Unit, WY	1.30	9.90
Crow Creek Pump Unit, MT	0.78	53.31
East Bench Unit, MT	2.25	58.63
Farwell Unit, NE	6.35	52.35
Fort Clark Unit, ND	0.83	55.72
Frenchman-Cambridge ID, NE	7.71	97.18
Frenchman Valley ID, NE	0.64	22.79
Glendo Unit, NE-WY*	2.80	7.27
H&RW ID, NE	3.26	86.54
Hanover-Bluff Unit, ND	2.51	90.83
Heart Butte Unit, ND	2.30	25.15
Helena Valley Unit, MT	1.60	90.61
Kansas-Bostwick ID, KS	9.45	80.95
Keyhole Unit, WY	2.20	b/
Lower Marias Unit, MT	2.00	6.35
Nebraska-Bostwick ID, NE	6.43	68.56d
Owl Creek Unit, WY	0	b/
Rapid Valley Unit, SD	0.65	25.43
Riverton Unit, WY	1.23	74.63
Sargent Unit, NE	2.71	10.03
Savage Unit, MT	3.55	39.66
Shadehill Unit, SD	2.25	45.84
Shoshone, MT-WY	1.55	8.36
Sun River, MT	.90	5.88
Trinidad, CO	4.66	b/

SOURCE: Department of the Interior.

NOTES:

a. Excluding paidout project, Water Conservation and Utilization Act Projects, and projects which are exclusively funded under the Small Reclamation Projects Act or Rehabilitation and Betterment Act.

b. Full cost has not been calculated because the project is exempt or there is no land exceeding acreage limitation.

---

* These projects are on a per acre-foot basis, rather than per acre.

** Table 3 does not include a breakdown for the Central Valley Project. However, in 1987 the Mid-Pacific Region published "Irrigation Ratesetting Policy/Public Review Document/Central Valley Project/California," which contains related information.

Index